THERE IS *a* REASON

THERE IS a REASON

Amanda's Journey, Half Way Home

Lori A. Proctor

XULON ELITE

Xulon Press Elite
555 Winderley Pl, Suite 225
Maitland, FL 32751
407.339.4217
www.xulonpress.com

© 2024 by Lori A. Proctor

All rights reserved solely by the author. The author guarantees all contents are original and do not infringe upon the legal rights of any other person or work. No part of this book may be reproduced in any form without the permission of the author.

Due to the changing nature of the Internet, if there are any web addresses, links, or URLs included in this manuscript, these may have been altered and may no longer be accessible. The views and opinions shared in this book belong solely to the author and do not necessarily reflect those of the publisher. The publisher therefore disclaims responsibility for the views or opinions expressed within the work.

Unless otherwise indicated, Scripture quotations taken from the Holy Bible, New Living Translation (NLT). Copyright ©1996, 2004, 2007 by Tyndale House Foundation. Used by permission of Tyndale House Publishers, Inc.

Paperback ISBN-13: 978-1-66289-810-5
Ebook ISBN-13: 978-1-66289-811-2

Dedication

To my loving God and Father, You are my Everything. You alone know that among all the choices I have made in my life, there is none that filled my heart and soul more than You. The choice I made to follow You forever changed me. Am I perfect? No. But You are and You saved me. May I offer this book and the words written on the pages first and foremost to You.

Thanks

To my wonderful husband Mike, your encouragement helped make this dream a possibility. Thank you for your help with this book and thank you for always being there for me.

Special thanks to my daughter Mindy, Holly and Jade James, for proof reading and editing my work before printing and giving it a thumbs up.

In addition, a huge "Thank you" to my many friends who encouraged me to keep going.

I also give a huge shout out and thank you to the Pastors at my church, The Bridge Christian Church, for your leadership and guidance through your amazing teachings. Thank you.

Plus a "Thank you" to Xulon Publishing and the very awesome team of people that worked so hard for me on their end to publish this book.

Last but not least, to the readers of this book; I pray that you will see God's truth, love and forgiveness through just ordinary and sometimes broken lives. May God's beautiful words be written in your heart. Thank you for reading this story.

I now take Your hand God, and begin the words. Please guide my hand as I write and help me climb into the awe of Your Word as I live in the here and now, with random thoughts of past and future too. All mixed together and held together by You.

My story began in what I thought was the end; but now I am able to see that it wasn't the end at all, but perhaps a plan and a hope for a future. As the writer of this story, I now see through Your eyes, the new beginning. There is a reason. Thank you again my Father, my God, my Love. You are my Everything.

Lori A. Proctor

Disclaimer

This book is a work of fiction, except for all the parts about God, Jesus and the Bible. All the verses are from the Tyndale NLT. Some of the moods, events, people and places may resemble some familiarity, but rest assured they are fictional and from my imagination and over exaggeration. Please enjoy.

Please note

My book does briefly mention 'suicide'. I want to make sure that my readers know that it is never the answer to life's struggles. If you or someone you know is struggling and needs help, please see a doctor and/or please call this National Suicide Prevention Lifeline. It's number is 988. It offers free and confidential emotional support. These counselors are highly trained to assist people.

God Bless You.

Table of Contents

Dedication vii
Disclaimer. ix
Prologue xv

1 Summer 2027, Amanda 1
2 July 13 2027, Carrie 7
3 Summer 2027, Amanda 13
4 July 13 2027, Carrie 20
5 A Report of Amanda's Week 22
6 July 13 2027, Carrie 36
7 June 2027, Amanda and The Ladies 39
8 July 13 2027, Carrie 55
9 Roxie 57
10 July 13 2027, Carrie 66
11 The Day Before Continued 69
12 July 13 2027, Carrie 77
13 Nell. 82
14 July 13 2027, Carrie 91
15 The Day Before Continues, Amanda 94
16 July 13 2027, Carrie 109
17 Friday Night Continues 111
18 July 13 2027, Carrie 113
19 The World and The Church 121

20 July 13 2027, Carrie	131
21 Silvia and Ruth	136
22 July 13 2027, Carrie	140
23 Amanda and Mary Jane	142
24 July 13 2027, Carrie	148
25 A Cliff is in Sight.	151
26 July 13 2027, Carrie	155
27 Roxie	176
28 July 13 2027, Carrie	183
29 Nell and Valerie	187
30 July 13 2027, Carrie	203
31 Amanda	205
32 July 13 2027, Carrie	210
33 Mary Jane and Susie	214
34 Silvia, Ruth and Susie	221
35 July 13 2027, Carrie	227
36 A Look Back, March 2027	229
37 July 13 2027, Carrie	237
38 Late June 2027	240
39 July 13 2027, Carrie	247
40 Nell	250
41 Mary Jane	257
42 July 13 2027, Carrie	266
43 Late June 2027	268
44 July 13 2027, Carrie	279
45 The CHIPS to LINCS	281
46 July 13 2027, Carrie	289
47 Late June 2027, Ruth	294
48 July 13 2027, Carrie	303
49 Amanda and Debbie	305
50 July 13 2027, Carrie	317

51 Mid July, Today is the Day ... 325
52 July 13 2027, Carrie ... 336
53 Early July, The Funeral ... 340
54 July 13 2027, Carrie ... 349
55 Today is the Day Continued ... 351
56 July 13 2027, Carrie ... 360
57 The Meeting ... 364
58 There is a Reason ... 367
59 July 13 2027, Carrie ... 374
60 The Meeting Continued, The Plan ... 377

Final Chapter Half Way Home ... 389

Sneak Peek into Book 2.....The Ranch, Next Generation ... 398

About the Author ... 403

Prologue

The notes kept appearing from the brain of the machine. Over that short time, they gave much wisdom and insight. They were written words that filled the voids. The notes held many answers and solutions they all looked for. They gave guidance for us. There was a reason to take the words seriously. But would we find the way, even when the words only pointed in one direction?

Debbie

Debbie had saved the printouts over the last few months. She brought them home secretly where they would be safe. She laminated them to protect them, to be given at the proper time. But when will that time come? The more she does the less she feels secure. They all needed the notes and honestly, they needed them now, but she couldn't risk it, not yet.

Carrie

Carrie smiled as she read. The words sounded just like her mom. Exactly the way she talks. She felt a little guilty, like she was reading her mom's secret diary and that really excited her.

She had let herself in with her key and was alone in her parent's home waiting, and decided it was ok to read these secret writings of her mom's. After all, if it were reversed, her mom would probably read *her* diary, if she had the chance. She chuckled at the thought and made herself comfortable as she continued flipping through the pages randomly.

Behind the Scenes

Dr. Prong was angry as he spoke to Joe his assistant, "Why isn't this working, you need to change it up, get it to work….this is on you, not me….understand….?"

"Actually, this is on you….*you're* the one that's rushing this…. besides, I can't change it up….if I do anymore, this experiment will pass…..*YOU* understand?" Joe barked back.

Chapter One

Summer 2027, Amanda

*L*ife is a mystery for most. It is suspenseful and ever changing from day to day. Kinda like this story. Pieces begin to fit in when we least expect. There are good days and there are bad days for all of us. We all deal with stuff, sometimes the same stuff but in different ways, and sometimes we can be quite different in our approach to living a spectacular life. Freewill is given to all of us. Do we choose to live the way God created us to live or do we go our own way? There is always a reason to do one or the other. No matter which way we go, there is no riding the fence. It is one way or the other. There is no middle ground.

Most of the women have been coming to this class for years now. We meet year round, once a month and always on the first Saturday. Today was different. It was still Saturday and still the first Saturday of the month, but everything was backwards. We started our women's Bible study with prayer requests, something we always do at the end of class. At first it was exciting to change things up a bit. But as one person after another started talking and explaining the specifics of their most important prayers, full of details and moving around from one person to the next, it became clear that we were all either exaggerating the facts, telling half truths, dramatizing or even border line gossiping. Or could it be, we were just afraid of exposing our deepest fears, thoughts and secrets. Secrets locked in the rooms of our minds.

I myself had secrets, ones I was willing to share when the time was right, but not until then. Most of the souls in that room were either struggling or pretending to be fine. Most were in pain. Some were in mental, emotional, or physical pain, and others definitely suffered spiritual pain. It was like we all were just surviving, needing each other for encouragement and accountability. All of us wanted to be heard.

I sometimes wonder if we were walking to the light or away from it in our efforts. How do we pray? How do we ask for what we need most? Are we just going through the motions or emotions of life? Are we keeping it real?

I have no doubt we would all protect each other, pray and be there for one another. Yet, did we really trust the ones that sat here in the circle around us? Each person here had secrets, whether they were from the past or in the here and now. The one thing that was for sure, our futures all depended on and needed the prayers of the others. All of us were walking in the valley of uncertainty, seeking forgiveness and wanting a life with meaning and value here on earth. We were all searching for some purpose and reason for life. What was our real purpose? Was there really a reason?

Somehow, we all fit together in this life, like pieces of a puzzle. So how do we finish with all the pieces intact? Will the voids in our hearts be filled?

Summer 2027, Amanda

I must add this particular day was unusual. Each person had a story to tell, but left out the main part, the real reason for the prayer in the first place; the part that they themselves played. How did I know this? I am sure you are wondering, how I can even know any of this as truth. We will get to that soon enough.

The outside temperature today was already 92 degrees with the forecast of a high 107 degrees for the day. Yet, we sat there freezing every time the AC clicked on. It was a typical summer day. The room felt either too hot or too cold depending on the snap of the AC. It was like that no matter where you were in the beautiful sunshine state of Arizona.

The room where we meet is small, and has a warm color of light beige. It has an appearance of peace and warmth, decorated in sunflowers and mirrors to make it appear larger. It stands out with a sunshine like glow. It is a peaceful room and I love it.

I love meeting here every month for Bible study, it clearly is my favorite room. I think that most of the women feel the same. It is an all-purpose room at our church used for many activities. The room is comforting and it holds a perfect awe about it.

Today however it felt different. It even had a different smell about it. Almost like an all-purpose cleaner mixed with something.

"Squirrel." Now that was a random thought. But that smell? These squirrel-random moments came often in my brain and I will try not to bore you with them.

Today as the women spoke of their various situations and tried to put them into a prayer requests, my mind tried not to jump to conclusions or be judgmental of anyone. *Yet* somehow I knew things. How did I know what they were not saying to the others? It is not like me to interfere or to be pushy about other people's lives. However today something was somehow different. I wanted to blurt out what I knew but I could not, not now, probably not ever. Like I said, something felt different.

The things I knew needed a more one on one discussion with each lady but I never did like confrontations so I guess I probably will remain silent with all the information. Although my mind scrambled to make sense of what was really being said. What was true and what *really* was being left out? Maybe, I will just write to each of them. Writing is what I like to do.

The Bible says when Christ comes; He will bring our deepest secrets to light and reveal our motives. Mine included. Only He can see into the heart, into the very soul of the person. So then how could I know more of what they were not saying? The sadness, the grief, the gloom, the guilt, the indifference, the coldness, the shame and the remorse, I knew these things yet *how* did I know them? I told you, wait….we will get to the answer soon enough.

My own story; which was to be *the end* was actually the beginning and now, *at* the end, it was the beginning. I know, it sounds crazy but it is true.

As months go by, they seem to linger. We never did get to the lesson this particular day. However, we all needed another lesson and another.

The notes from my lesson kept appearing in my thoughts as I sat there listening. If we could just get to the lesson, we would see that the lesson would help us in our life's journey, and give key insights to our joy and happiness. The lesson could give purpose to our lives as it gave verses and direction for each of us. If only we could focus on the Word, the Word of God.

As each lady shared their stories, I mean prayers, with coffee in one hand and a pen in the other taking notes; I couldn't help but wander off in my own thoughts about where

I had come from, and how I got here, in this room, with these ladies today. I had answers and opinions to add, things that would help them all. If only we could get to the lesson.

I wanted to shout, "It's NOT a journey TO Jesus it's meant to be a journey WITH Jesus, our life has purpose because He is the reason." It was today's lesson and I was ready to get it started, present the information, the verses and notes to support my findings.

But I didn't get a chance, as like many other meetings lately, I didn't even have a chance to voice my own prayer requests, my own stories of struggles, because time ran out and before I knew it, the ladies had shared and then needed to leave. So again, this month as with the many before, we needed to say the quick ending prayer so that the meeting could end. Maybe we should not have started with prayer requests today.

I did have to remind myself that one of the reasons we meet every month is for the prayers that we pray for each other. We all needed God to hear our prayers. We all needed each other to pray them. And I do know that God hears them. He hears them and they will be answered, that alone is the reason we pray them. This I totally know.

***

The night before our meeting, I couldn't sleep. I paced the house with so much on my mind. My fears and my anxiety were at an elevated limit for reasons unknown.

"Oh Father, please calm my anxious thoughts, please help me think straight. My mind is so mixed up, feeling like I'm not awake and feeling like I cannot rest, not sure where I am and not sure where I'm supposed to be. Please help my mental and emotional thoughts along with my spiritual and physical needs as well, thank you, Amen." I cried out in an uneasy and uncertain voice.

At around two in the morning, I concluded that it would be a good idea to switch things around. Mostly for myself I must admit, because I desperately needed to voice my struggles, even if I really did not know what to say. I needed to get some encouragement. I then decided to take another sleeping pill to fall back to sleep. I popped it in my mouth, and grabbed the water.

Hi, my name is Amanda and I am a writer. A writer of this story and oh how I love to write. But as I sit and look back at all my writings, poems and stories I feel as if some days, it seems as if only my paper and pen in hand knew what was written and what I had to say. Just like with the lesson, the chapters go unread. I cannot rewrite any of the pages and at times I wish I could. To keep the hidden secrets lost in my mind seems worth the unnoticed attempts to expose them. Timing is important. It's worth its weight in gold, so they say. I laugh as I ask, "Who is 'they'?"

My story, well it began many sunrises ago. There is a reason, to get up at the dawn of the day, to fight the fight. The battle we don't always see.

1 Corinthians 4:5 (NLT) So don't make judgments about anyone ahead of time—before the Lord returns. For he will bring our darkest secrets to light and will reveal our private motives. Then God will give to each one whatever praise is due.

Chapter Two

July 13 2027, Carrie

After letting herself into her parent's home, Carrie picked up the big, heavy, purple, four-inch binder full of her mom's writings. It was sitting on the coffee table in the living room. It was titled 'IT WAS ALL ABOUT ME, NOW IT'S NOT'. She flipped to one of the poems written a few years ago. She wondered about the title and began to read:

A cry of defeat
A cry of defeat…..an unhealed wound
They fight against me…..they fight against You
Ones that are loyal…..are feeling alone
Those that were along for the kill…..
have turned and left the fight
Those that we try to reach…..are now no longer in sight
Where is my drive…..where is the sting
Do I continue on……. continue the fight
Is my light in hiding…..or is it snuffed out……..
can it be ignited…..can it shine again
Do they even care…..will we win some…..or even one

There Is A Reason

The sorrow is too hard to bare…..the pain too deep for words
Is it worth it….where is the reason
Where do I turn….or do I go straight
I reach up….. I am received
You hold my head high…..You walk along with me
Forward we go…..into the battle we see
The battle may be lost…..but the war will be won
Some will be standing…..others will fall
The light shines brightly…..on which way to go
I can't do it alone…..you're not alone You say
You lead me down Your narrow path…..
and that is where I stay
Those who follow……will not be lost
I need You now ……as I needed You then
So I choose to carry on….. You lift me high so I can see
I thank you Lord…..with my life…..so on to victory…..
You and me

Carrie smiled as she read. The words sounded just like her mom. Exactly the way she talked. She felt a little guilty, like she was reading her mom's secret diary and that really excited her.

She had let herself in with her key, was alone in her parent's home waiting, and decided it was ok to read these secret writings of her mom's. After all, if it were reversed, her mom would probably read *her* diary, if she had the chance. She chuckled at the thought and made herself comfortable as she continued flipping through the pages randomly.

Carrie had taken the day off from work to spend time with her parents, but this alone time was actually exactly what she needed at this moment. It was still very early in the morning, at least for most. Her mom has always said the early mornings were the best time of day. She had to agree.

Reading has always comforted Carrie. She thought about her own home and how she had walls of bookshelves, completely filled with books. It was amazing that her floors hadn't fallen through her small manufactured home with the weight of them. She could easily start her own library.

Carrie had moved into her own place a year after finishing high school. Her friends that helped her move were equally surprised at how many boxes of books she had. The weight of each box was extremely heavy. The boxes all needed to be lifted and set into the back spare bedroom where she planned to make three of the walls, from floor to ceiling into bookshelves. The forth wall would have her desk and office supplies along with her filing cabinet and the large tall safe her dad had bought for her. Having her own personal library and office excited her the most when she moved into her own place.

Her mind went to the day her mom prayed with her about all her random books.

"Ya know Carrie, we better pray about all these books and ask God to strengthen your floor." Her mom laughed in her 'you better listen to me' tone.

The crazy thing is, a week after moving in she had a huge leak. The pipe under the sink in her kitchen caused the floors to be flooded with water. It destroyed her lower kitchen cabinets and most of the vinyl flooring in the kitchen and living room. As luck had it, her foundational subfloors were ok, but it was recommended that she do some reinforcing. Everything had to be removed and replaced.

Thankfully, she had saved up an emergency fund of money before moving out for those unexpected situations. She just did not plan to use it so quick.

Carrie pulled up the old vinyl flooring with some help from her friends and put down some DUROCK cement board throughout the whole home and then had ceramic tile installed. The change in the flooring felt so much stronger and even though it cost her, the whole amount she had saved it was a Godsend, as it could have been much worse.

Her mom's response was; "See how awesome prayer is?" She was always trying to find the silver lining in every disaster and as she puts it, '*all* good comes from God.'

Carrie knew her mom was right about prayer. Prayer changes things. God hears the prayers of His kids. He hears them every time. The prayers may not be answered as quickly as a microwave, but they will be heard when they are prayed. He is coming with protection, love, comfort and peace. Carrie knows this and trusts this with her whole heart. She believes and trusts in God and in the Bible.

Carrie loves that in the book of Daniel, when Daniel prayed in chapter 10 verses 12-14 that God said; He heard Daniel the first time he prayed. She loves that God sent His messenger to Daniel right away. The verses help her to get a glimpse at the spiritual warfare that is happening. God sent the messenger right away but he had been detained for three weeks, because he was challenged by the evil forces and had to fight them. God heard the prayer and immediately sent help, and Daniel, he kept praying and trusting God the whole time.

Carrie bowed her head, with her eyes open staring at the words her mom wrote many years before. 'I thank you Lord..... with my life.....so on to victory.....You and me.'

July 13 2027, Carrie

"Thank you God for today. I know You are here with me and I know You know what's best and You comfort me and give me peace as I wait. Thank you, Amen."

Carrie really did not want to think about the spiritual warfare that was going on that very moment. She just prayed, knowing that her prayer was heard and it will change things.

Most people do not think about the real fight, the one that is behind the scenes; the powerful one that is being fought every day. Her mom has always told her that most people want to just think about the good and only focus on that, her included. But the truth is, there is a real enemy fighting against us. It is not a fantasy, satan is very real.

Carrie knows that she should never give satan (with a little 's' as her mom puts it, little 's' man) any foothold in her life. She stays connected to God and He blesses her and protects her.

However, it does not change the fact that these powerful armies, in the spiritual realms, have a goal to destroy God, His church and His people. The cool thing is; victory is already won and is already ours, because Jesus has defeated death. If we are His kids then we have the power of the Holy Spirit, we can prevail, and our prayers will be heard. Prayer is so powerful and it really does change things.

Behind the Scenes

Debbie had saved the printouts over the last few months. She brought them home secretly where they would be safe. She laminated them to protect them, to be given at the proper time. But when will that time come? The more she does the less she feels secure. They all needed the notes and honestly, they needed them now, but she could not risk it, not yet.

James 1:17 (NLT) Whatever is good and perfect comes down to us from God our Father, who created all the lights in the heavens. He never changes or casts a shifting shadow.

Ephesians 6:10-12 (NLT) A final word: Be strong in the Lord and in his mighty power. Put on all of God's armor so that you will be able to stand firm against all strategies of the devil. For we are not fighting against flesh-and-blood enemies, but against evil rulers and authorities of the unseen world, against mighty powers in this dark world, and against evil spirits in the heavenly places.

Chapter Three

Summer 2027, Amanda

A quote I had read once traveled through my mind....... 'Didn't anyone know the quietness of my voice was actually a scream?' I needed and wanted to voice my prayers to the prayer warriors of this group. But like I said, I didn't get a chance. As 11:10 am hit the women were ready to wrap it up, without even looking at the lesson. I needed to share the lesson. I needed to give the information to these women in hopes that they would bestow the blessing back to each other as well as to me. I spent all month preparing it, laying out all the details that Jesus wanted me to offer.

Today my mind felt at odds. My body felt overheated and I could not think straight. I felt as if my mind was in a fog that had lasted for months. I was not dealing well with the fibromyalgia that often attacked my body and that I tried to ignore. Plus the three sleeping pills I took probably were not helping me one little bit, as I just wanted to sleep. Let the zzzz's happen soon. Oh, this easily could be a random squirrel moment, but I do not dare think about sleeping right now.

Truthfully, I have been so extremely tired. I can honestly say for months now. I know I'm no different from most people. We are all tired and I really try *not* to complain about it. But right now, yes again, I am inserting a "squirrel" moment and I am complaining.

"I'm extremely tired and I can't concentrate, darn those sleeping pills."

There I said it. Ok, ok I did not say it out-loud, just in my head. What is with the attitude I have today?

"Father, I know that my strength right now comes from You. Please help me to focus, help me to pay attention….thanks. Amen." I prayed a quick popcorn prayer, not out-loud, but in silence as I redirected my brain to open up because all it wanted to do was yawn.

I pulled up a Bible verse from my memory bank that I learned many years ago, Philippians 2:14 says, do everything without grumbling or complaining.

"Really God, *everything*? Even now?" I laughed to myself, as it was clear that I was complaining about *not* complaining. I know that God was probably laughing with me, as He knows that it is an area I try to work on. I am sure His answer was a clear, "Yes Amanda….everything."

As a rule, I try to start the lesson right away or at least by 9:15 am. Then afterwards, the stories, I mean the prayer requests.

Again, I chuckled to myself. I know, I should not laugh, but sometime those prayer requests, can easily turn into life stories. As I said, today my mind felt at odds, a little anxious, a little sad, and a little grumpy for some reason. I just wanted to scream and laugh at the same time, just to stay awake.

As I thought back to the prayers from the months before, I realized they were almost the same. Had any of them been heard? Had any of them been rectified? Had any of them been turned into praise? Had anyone actually prayed for the things that we listed? I know I do not need to question this. Of course, they are heard and of course, they were prayed.

As the months go by, and the time flies quickly into the past, the things of the world seem to stay the same. Are we stuck in the quicksand of life afraid to move? Or are we fighting so hard that we are actually sinking, waiting to go under? I myself at times felt like I was drowning under the sand.

In the stillness of prayer to our Heavenly Father, outstretched before Him in the quietness of our soul is the only way to be heard. I know how hard it is to fight, but sometimes I am lost on what it is I am fighting. I do however know *whom* it is that I'm fighting and I know *how* to fight this little 's' man, but it is easy to get distracted and off course.

Listening to the ladies in this Bible group I see that we are all searching, we are all looking for purpose and an unconditional love that only the Father can give to each of us. Only He can fill the voids in our heart and in our lives.

We all want to give advice and opinions to each other's personal situations, while sharing our own. It is like we can problem solve for each other but not for ourselves. Or could it be, we just want someone to give us the okay in our situation and tell us what we want to hear? Yet we all know, we need honesty and sometimes even brutal truth if needed, not kisses and agreements if we are the one in the wrong.

It can take an hour to get through the prayer requests, even though we have a KISS rule, Keep It Simple Sister. Don't get me wrong, the prayer requests are not only for our own situations. Many of the women ask for prayers for others as well. Most of them will stay and hear all the prayer requests. Some stay longer than the closing prayer because they just want the fellowship and will even stay until the actual church service, which starts at three in the afternoon not wanting to go home.

I normally enjoy the prayer time. I enjoy being able to encourage the women in the group. The prayer requests I write down encourages myself in some ways too. We all have things going on. Some small, some big, some we exaggerate, some that need to be let go from our past. None of us are alone in this. We all go through the same things, in different ways. We all need each other to pray for us as we pray for them. We all know this and we all need this time. We are definitely stronger together. There is a reason we always meet monthly.

Our women's Bible study group consists of about six women, seven including me that are consistent every month and a few that come occasionally. Today there were only a few of the regulars, which probably is why the ones that were there, were even *more* chattier than normal.

Old lady Nell, which is what she asked us to call her, was one of the women that did not make it this particular day. She had called me the night before. Yet it seemed so far in the past, almost like a dream from long ago.

"Focus Amanda focus!!" I yelled to myself.

"Amanda, oh sweet Amanda, I am so sorry, but I won't be able to make it to your class tomorrow." Nell was trying to sound like she was okay. Even though she is sixty-two and a bit older than I am, by almost twelve years, I never did like calling her 'Old lady' Nell, even if she did insist.

Summer 2027, Amanda

"Nell, are you okay?" A slight pause and no answer so I spoke again, a little louder this time "Nell is there anything you need?" I found myself saying, even though I needed to get outside to my husband, who was hopefully waiting patiently for me in his truck to go out for dinner.

My mind was drifting and thinking about all I had to do when I got back home, to get things ready for our class the next morning. My day had been challenging to say the least. Feeling a little bit guilty, I secretly hoped she did not need my help. I had so many of my own mixed up thoughts going on already in my own mind, and like I said, my own day was not going as planned. My whole week, my whole month had not been going smooth. Months of downward spirals were happening to me. I just could not take on anything more. There has got to be a reason for all the setbacks right? I know that God does not cause them, and His Word says that all things work together for the good of those who love Him.

I know who it is to blame, and I try very hard not to look in his direction.

Nell's words were sweet this evening, not her usual bitter and negative tone that she has shown over the last couple of years. She never has really warmed up to any of us. Although I have noticed that she has become a little bit kinder over the last year, since Ruth started coming. I have even noticed a little softness in her, and a kind distant smile that she gives to Ruth the seventeen-year-old girl with cancer, every time she comes to Bible study with her mom, Silvia. As a matter-of-fact, Ruth was missing today too.

I did however, hold out hope that Ruth would come and be here to read the Bible. She loved to do that especially lately, and I really enjoyed listening to her voice, as she read God's Word.

There was a short pause and then she said, "No, no I just don't feel like coming. I have decisions to make." Then another short pause and with her usual bitter tone, the one I am more used to hearing, she said "......and well, I just don't want the ladies to try and solve them." She seemed hesitant in a way, almost like she wanted to share but refused herself to do so. She had my attention and I couldn't understand her reasoning but told her to call me if she did want to talk or even come in the morning, if she changed her mind.

"Oh darling Amanda, I doubt I'll change my mind." It was all she said as she hung up the phone.

Well, that's Old lady Nell, the bittersweet old lady. As far as I know she had remained single her whole life, she has never talked about family or kids or a real home.

Sometimes I wonder if she is even paying attention when she comes for the lessons. Or does she? She always has a distant look in her eyes as if she is in a far off secluded lonely place deep in her mind, except, like I said, when the younger girls are around. They seem to spark a flicker of light in her and a smile that is almost unnoticeable on her face.

The only real thing I know about Nell is that she loves to knit. She is always knitting little pink and blue beanie baby hats for the hospital maternity ward. She will sit in class and on most Sundays during the service, and knit right there in the middle of all that is going on around her, yet always with that distant look on her face.

Summer 2027, Amanda

    I have never asked her if she has gotten right with God, but lately I have been feeling like it is my job as her small group leader, to make sure she has made that decision in her life. She never has given any indication that she has. She doesn't usually contribute much in class and she declines to read or look up verses in the Bible, which I believe is why she brings all her knitting stuff and keeps her hands busy. She usually can finish three beanies in the two hours of class time. It is pretty amazing how fast she is.
    Nell is there for most of the monthly Bible study classes yet like I said, really not mentally there so it seems. As a matter-of-fact, I have only seen her around once lately.
    I decided that if she does show up today, to this meeting, I will try to ask her if she has gotten right with God. As I focus on this and put the words together in my brain, so that it does not feel threatening but does sound urgent, I notice she is not the only one missing. So far, she was a no show, along with Ruth, Debbie and Roxie.

Proverbs 15:29 (NLT) The LORD is far from the wicked, but he hears the prayers of the righteous.

Proverbs 27:6 (NLT) Wounds from a sincere friend are better than many kisses from an enemy.

Chapter Four
July 13 2027, Carrie

Carrie flipped a few more pages then decided to go to the back of the binder, a page not yet punched and inserted fell to the ground. It was not dated and was titled …..Unfinished Things:

Too many unfinished things……..I cannot leave
Tired of pretending….barely making it by
God please listen to my cries…….please hear my prayers
I seek You day and night…..yet I feel alone at times
I feel overwhelmed…..my heart, my soul
My mind is so confused….please renew my strength
Please hurry….for the lights will go out
The darkness will fall upon me
I don't belong….I don't fit in
My life is a mess….but I have so much
What I want is Your presence
You said if I seek You….I will find You
Have I not looked hard enough?
The peace I have is from You….so why can't I live
I cannot live….and I cannot die

July 13 2027, Carrie

I have no more fight……I will drown
Why do I feel so empty…..where do I belong
I'm not as together as I think I am
I'm doing my best……I cannot yet see
It's taken a lifetime….. so I must continue
Please hurry God…..and rescue me

Tears began to moisten Carries eyes as she sighed, "Oh mom." Carrie looked around the room for a better place to sit with more light, so she could read better through her tears. She spotted her dad's big recliner with the light overhead in the corner of the room and went over and turned it on and made herself comfortable with the extra pillows and flipped a few more pages and began to read some more.

Behind the Scenes

Months of printouts had been collected, all with direction from God's Word. Debbie knows that each of the women from the Bible study would benefit from them. Some were in desperate need as far as she could tell. She herself had over heard some of the conversations.

The brain of the machine only printed when she was there. But how did it know? And when can she tell the others? She struggled with her choices. Had she made the right ones so far? It was not like her to keep secrets and she has never taken matters into her own hands. She shrugged and shoved the notes into her pocket.

Psalm 32:8 (NLT) The LORD says, "I will guide you along the best pathway for your life. I will advise you and watch over you.

Chapter Five
A Report of Amanda's Week

It was a busy week for Amanda. Normally she had the lesson done a week before class. She had been so distracted lately and was having a hard time concentrating.

Over the years, she has been able to hide her anxiety, her depression and her fears. It has always been so easy. She knows the only reason is because she stays absorbed and engaged in God's Word. It is only in Him that she is able to move forward each and every day, especially on those hard days. He has always been with her. Although, she sometimes wonders if these times of anxiety are her own fault. Has she wandered off on a detour path of her own making and that is when satan, with the little 's' tries to attack her? Has she wondered into little 's' mans space? She knows she must cling to Jesus twenty-four seven, because if she doesn't, little 's' is ready to attack.

Amanda knows we all live in a broken world. And there are many things that can push a person over the edge of a cliff, and one of those things is pain. Physical pain is hard to deal with and pushing through it day by day is exhausting. Then there is mental and emotional pain that seems to creep in as well.

It seems as if when pain is in control, you are not. You cannot control the pain. Yeah, that is nothing new under the sun, and she knows she is not the only one who deals with it.

Her fibromyalgia pain is excruciating, intense, agonizing and any other word you can use for uncontrollable pain throughout your body. It seems to attacks when it wants and lingers when it is being nice. She has dealt with its harassment for years. The pain often disrupts her sleep. Which is why she started taking the sleeping pills but they too seem to fight against her and make her increasingly sleepier for days. She just cannot win. The fogginess in her brain called 'fibro fog' is what she hates the most. It impairs her ability to focus, to pay attention and to concentrate all at the same time. It is a fight, one she frequently loses to.

She often thinks about Paul in the Bible. His pain didn't control him to a point that he couldn't serve God, and his strength all came from God. She must endure.

The news on TV this week has been horrifying to say the least. It is 2027 and the world has been going crazy for decades now. But in all history, this last decade seems to be the worst. She has spent much of her time watching the events on TV unfold over-and-over. The worldly fear inside of her has been so overwhelming; she feels she has almost reached the point of collapse.

This month's lesson is titled 'It's not a journey TO Jesus; it's a journey WITH Jesus, because of Jesus'. It is all about faith and trust as we live in a relationship with God. Taking a stand and not compromising our beliefs in an out of control world and walking as Christ walked consistently every day, one day at a time, with Jesus and His guidance.

She knows it is not a perfect walk, no one is perfect. Only Jesus was perfect and He was the perfect sacrifice for every one of us. He chose to be. He could have walked away but He didn't because He loves us that much. Everyone of us. Everyone of us matters to Him.

Sometimes she wonders if her own journey was WITH Jesus or was it still traveling TO Jesus, seeking more? Would she stand or would she actually crumble in fear? The expression 'Faith over Fear' is easier said than done, some days. She does trust Jesus with her life, but is she walking with Him day-to-day like she should be? What about her fears? How does she control them, so they don't control her? She knows full well that God does not want her to fear and the Bible has 365 verses that say, "Do not fear" and "Don't be afraid." Yet as she watched the TV even though she knows God's Word is what gives us all direction and strength, the fear of the world none-the-less still frightens her.

Amanda knows full well that spending good quality time with God daily is the answer, because He does comfort her with His Words. She loves to read her Bible but sometimes she has so much to do that she puts it off. She knows it's not a good idea because it is God's Word that keeps her grounded in her relationship with Him. Listening to His direction in His discipleship class is really the highlight of her life. She does not like to miss her time with Him.

Amanda thinks about when she first started her journey with Jesus back before Carrie or Christopher was born. It had not been easy. Her and her husband Chris decided to try the church stuff because the world was a mess and Amanda was just as bad of a mess and down about life. She had a huge void in her heart; one that she found out years later could only be filled with the love of God as she spent time in her relationship with Him.

It has been twenty-seven years ago when they first walked into the Christ Community Christian Church. The CCC church. 'Come and CCCCCCCC all about God, Jesus and the Bible' was the slogan they used. The commercials were entertaining so they decided to go and CCCCCCC what it was all about. Best decision they ever made in their life individually and as a couple. It has been a huge adventurous journey with Jesus, living their life for Him. They decided to get right with God a few weeks after they started going to the CCC church and are always so thrilled with what they get to learn each and every week and apply to their lives. God through the church has truly made a huge difference in each of them and as a couple.

The more she thought about it, the more she was convinced that yes her journey was with Jesus, in an intimate relationship. There was no way she would even be here if it hadn't been for Him and His leading her through the Holy Spirit, that she had received as a gift when she accepted Jesus as her Lord and Savior and was baptized that beautiful day in July, 2000. Twenty-seven years ago, on her birthday. She has learned so much and the time has flown by so quickly. Each sunrise brings new learning and insight.

Amanda

It wasn't until Thursday that I finally finished the lesson. It turned out great as I reread it out loud to God with a stronger strength I thought I had lost somewhere along the way lately.

I felt warmth in my mind and soul. "You are amazing. Thank you Lord."

I laid the lesson down and prayed again "Father, I need You, I need You so much. Please strengthen my body to complete the task-at-hand. I also pray for the ladies that come to class, may they be filled with Your spirit and learn exactly what You want them to know. Help me Lord not to focus on the worldly things, but focus on Your total protection around me, mentally, emotionally, physically and spiritually, thank you so much....Amen."

I finished praying as tears welled up in my eyes. It occurred to me that I have prayed these same prayers with almost the same words over-and-over the many years behind me. The words give me both comfort and strength, as I know God hears them. Protection all around is what I pray for every single day for my family, friends, my church and myself. I can easily look back over the years and see that God has answered my prayers. I pray wholeheartedly, even the small prayers that come up throughout my day. I call those, my popcorn prayers.

I love the quote that was given by my Pastor: "If your heart remains unbowed, it doesn't matter what your head is doing." Oh how those words speak to me. Prayers should always come from our heart and prayed wholeheartedly.

As I sat and thought about that, another quote I read days before, written in sharpie on the back of the bathroom door at the grocery store of all places said, 'The impossible journey is the one you never begin.' Oh, how true that felt at this moment in time. There is always a reason for our journey, always a reason to stay on course and to keep the finish line in sight. There is always a reason to fight the fight, begin and continue the journey. If not for our self, it is always for others.

It had been a challenging morning already with all the aches and pains of my fibromyalgia.

I tried to make copies of the lesson, but the paper in the printer kept getting jammed. After about what seemed to be an unsuccessful two hours I gave up. So far, I maybe had three full copies. I was frustrated and decided I was not going to finish and I would try again later after Chris got home, so he could fix the printer of its jam.

Crazy how things go when you wait until the last minute to finish something, procrastination has never been my friend. The peace I felt moments ago, with the finished lesson…..well, it was still there fighting with me to be calm.

I walked back out to the living room and began to watch the news. The headlines today were just as crazy as every other day; people out to destroy God. The last few years have gotten incredibly bad.

A doctor who was facing prison time because he told his patient and her husband, who had gone to him for an abortion, that their fetus was a human being. So the mom and dad were suing him. They were demanding that he perform it since he was their primary doctor. Their claim is that they pay him for a procedure, not his moral advice.

The laws were changing in many states, and a few years ago they said that all doctors were required to provide the procedure if the law for their state required it. There were very few doctors around who refused to do it, and because of the pressure, many did. This doctor was just trying to inform these parents that their baby was a human being.

"Really!?!?" I yelled at the TV. I sat wondering……doesn't this lady know, by the time her baby is 17 to 20 days old, the baby's heart beats. Most women do not even realize they are pregnant at this time. In addition, the arms and legs begin to form as well as the face, ears, nose and mouth. And at 42 days, that is only 6 weeks, brain waves are detected. At 52 days, the baby hiccups and yawns…..52 days! At 8 weeks ALL organs have formed. At 9 weeks, the baby has fingerprints, different from anyone else's. How cool is that!

It is incredibly sad that many states were pushing for a 15 week cut off for abortions. At 15 weeks which is almost four months, the baby is so far along in development and they want to tear it apart in the womb. It's so crazy, I don't even like to think about it.

With all the technology we now have, a baby is an amazing miracle. The physical life of the baby BEGINS at conception and logically nothing grows if it is not living. Period. That is science. The joining of the father's sperm and the mother's egg is when life begins. How can they not see this? I questioned God and yelled at the TV. "Unborn lives matter. IT. IS. A. HUMAN BEING!!" My blood pressure started to rise.

I started to think back to the lesson about how we are created by God in our mother's womb. A new, unique human individual forming and beginning his or her journey of life. I sat and recalled the research I did and how amazing every bit of genetic information is there for the baby's development.

It is so cool how God designed this. The sperm and egg officially merge into one single cell, called a zygote. The zygote typically has forty-six chromosomes, twenty-three from each parent. Chromosomes from the mother and the father are combining to decide the baby's gender….yup the gender. We are not assigned a gender after birth; we are created by God, male or female. Will this baby be a boy or a girl? It is already decided well before birth; as well as hair and eye color, the way God has created this precious human being to be. Even their awesome personality is forming! The baby starts to draw nourishment about 5-9 days after the father's sperm and mother's egg meet. So much is going on in such a short time. I always laugh when I picture the meeting of the fathers sperm and the mothers egg.....it's like; "Hey there beautiful, let's make a baby." "Squirrel", go ahead read that again, this time with a deep manly voice...."Hey there beautiful, let's make a baby." Ok, so I thought that was funny.

"Did these people not learn this in school?" I continued to ask the TV. I remember learning it and being fascinated at the miracle of a baby. We even watched a movie with just the girls present in middle school. I didn't know much about God at the time, and I didn't realize that God created us in our mother's womb until later in life, after I started reading my Bible.

Each week of the baby's journey of development is so amazing. I think it is time to redo the lesson with the women and invite the teen girls as well. Everyone should be encouraged to research the creation and development of a human being. Look around, there is a good reason for that.

Thinking about our crazy world and how easy it is to just decide you want to kill your baby in the womb, reminded me of how in the Bible there were Nations that killed their babies to the false gods as a sacrifice. God made it clear it was detestable, forbidden, and unthinkable. It actually was refreshing to see a doctor take a stand even if it does cost him his license and possibly some prison time.

"He is standing for what is right, please protect him God." I clicked the pause on the TV and said a prayer for this doctor and all the ones out there that they are trying to force to do things that are against their beliefs, and against God's direction, standards and morals.

As I un-paused the TV a small caption caught my attention about the CHIPS to LINCS. As of last week, people were still being fired from government jobs, just like in 2020. Back then, it was because of the jab. Now it's because of the CHIPS.

For the second time in my life, they were weeding out the good people from government positions. At least back then, many stood up to the masks and jab mandates and several of the larger businesses had to let go of some power over their workers or they would go under.

I truly believe it was only a test run for control of the people back then. Now only a few years later it has gotten even worse. It seems to be a strike on good, honest, Christian people that are well under open attack and destroy, since most of them are against the CHIPS. This time the CHIPS are being forced on people and with no exceptions.

The CHIPS to LINCS is a new way of keeping track of all people. Everything about you is programmed onto an actual computer Nano chip, shaped like a grain of rice and then injected into your body. This Nano chip is then capable of connecting to a national directory where it can be updated to, downloaded from, searched for and tracked. Soon everyone will need to get it if they want to bank, shop, vote, work, see a doctor, or even send a letter.....everything.

A Report of Amanda's Week

Computer Human Injected Pairing System (CHIPS) to (LINCS) Life Information Network Cataloging Storage. Crazy right?

My best friend Debbie is a nurse, and she told me that by the year 2029 every nurse, doctor and anyone now working in the medical field would have to agree to have it installed or quit. So far, they haven't been very pushy about it, but she says it is coming. However, in the meantime any new personnel needs to have it, which is why the staffing is so scarce.

Not only is the medical field affected, but also all NEW military personnel and first responders have to have it injected, again without exceptions. It became mandatory for them two years ago in 2025 and they have remained the test subjects for it. All new technology and updates to the CHIPS are given to them first. By the end of this year, 2027 all law enforcement of any kind will need to have the CHIPS injected in their hand or lose their job and all the fighting and court appeals will not stop it. The attack is coming from who knows where. A lot of speculation, but whoever is pulling the strings, they are ruthless and relentless.

The government has been saying that it is no big deal, but in my mind, it will be like taking the mark of the beast that Revelations refers to and warns us against. I decided I need to do more research on this one, but I actually have already decided that there was no way I was going to let them put any CHIPS in me. I stood my ground in 2020 against the jab and now this....NO WAY....this is worse.

Trying to force people to do this has been a real challenge for them as there are many who oppose and refuse it. The problem is that pressure is being put on most businesses, and they will lose their business license if they do not enforce it for all their employees with no exceptions. They are hoping that my generation passes quickly and the next one will just comply.

The news stations try to make it seem like everyone is doing it, but I know better. They're liars. I feel an uprising is coming all around. Almost everyone I know has already decided not to get the CHIPS. Plans are in the works and my husband Chris is very involved in them in order to protect our family when the time comes, even to go into hiding if necessary. I again push the pause on the TV to pray for our world.

The next headline was about the schools and how teachers are no longer allowed to say 'him' or 'her' when referring to a child. Even the parents are not allowed to be called mother or father any more. It's now changed to parent number one and parent number two. Gender neutral has become a thing in the last decade. God did not leave it up to us. He created us male or female in our mother's womb. You are either a boy or a girl, no matter what you want to say, do, or change to. So far, science has not come up with any other gender. But lies and brainwashing are being told to the next generation starting in preschool.

It is crazy, because if you research it, you would see that science has proven there are 6,500 genetic differences between a male and a female. That's right, genetic differences. Yet many still cannot or will not define what a woman or a man is. In case you are wondering, a woman is a female human being and a man is a male human being as determined by God when He created us in our mother's womb. It is pretty simple, common sense. Trying to change from one to the other, cutting off body parts or taking hormone drugs or dressing differently is not going to change who you are genetically. God did not leave that option open; believe it or not.

It is sad that this is being pushed on the young children who do not know the real facts. Moreover, from what I can see, many parents don't know or don't care themselves. Instead, they are allowing their children to be taught to hate everyone and to hate themselves. They are teaching them to hate who they were/are created to be. And if these children do not know they were created by a loving, caring God they will go through life confused, sad, broken and lost, with no purpose or hope. We cannot let this happen. The little 's' man cannot win this battle. We must speak up. We need to speak the truth in love no matter what. How will they know if we don't tell them? So far, our religious freedoms and right to speak are not totally gone, but the evil doers are working on that. They are working very hard behind the scenes to silence us and to silence the Word of God.

Most of the people I know are now homeschooling their children together in groups. They meet at different homes. One home teaches English, the next math, the next physical education, and another home teaches history and science and one even teaches survival skills including gardening. They have all the bases covered, for each grade level. If my daughter and son were still young I definitely would be homeschooling them with these groups of parents.

The next day, Friday, March 5, 2027 was not any better for me. Even though Chris had fixed the printer so that the paper would feed through, the printer did not like me. Copies were coming out this time, but barely readable. My frustration began first thing when I realized that I never did go down to the store and buy more ink last month when the printer kept stopping and saying, 'black ink is low'. I shook the ink cartridge but it was totally empty. Surprise, surprise.

Already exhausted and hungry I decided to make some breakfast and eat before getting ready to go out. As I turned to grab my now cold coffee, I ran right into the chair I had just pulled out a few minutes ago so I could sit and read a few verses from God's Word. Stubbing my big toe on the leg of the chair made me let out a scream of pain as it throbbed like a drum with my own heart beat rhythm. Limping to the couch and spilling my cold coffee all over the end table, was about all I could handle.

"Aaaawwwwww, really?" I questioned the air with almost a cry and a shout at the same time. I know you are wondering; do I always talk to myself? And out loud? Why yes, yes I do.

It was only 9:30 in the morning and I already needed a nap. I decided to lie down for a few minutes and then go back to the kitchen to read and make some toast. It was 10:30 when I woke to the loud noise of the garbage truck driving away from my home.

"No, no wait....my garbage!!!" I yelled as I jumped up off the couch and ran with a limp to the front door, threw it open and looked at my very full garbage can still up near the house. Between Chris and I, we missed the truck again this week.

"What else can go wrong today?" I yelled out-loud in total defeat and with anger at myself. "Please Lord, help me stay sane today and keep it together."

A Report of Amanda's Week

Psalm 139:13-15 (NLT) You made all the delicate, inner parts of my body and knit me together in my mother's womb. Thank you for making me so wonderfully complex! Your workmanship is marvelous—how well I know it. You watched me as I was being formed in utter seclusion, as I was woven together in the dark of the womb.

Chapter Six
July 13 2027, Carrie

Carrie found a section in her mom's binder titled Real Time Posts or RTP for short. Copies of her mom's social media posts were in their own section in the binder. She was amused and did not realize her mom was such a rebel and spoke out on social media. Carrie herself hardly ever used any of the social media that was out there. It drives her crazy to see pictures of people's dinners and game scores. In addition, she feels like so many hide behind their screen to say stuff they would not say face to face with people. She knew however, that her mom used the social media as a tool for God. She stopped at one dated a few years back: June 2022:

My prayers this morning are for our Nation.
I'm reading in Jeremiah chapter five and six. These two chapters kinda showed me where our Nation may be right now. America has been rejecting You as our Creator, as our Everything. Oh God, You are the one who establishes our government, our president and kings. They are in these positions because You have put them there. Just like with Jerusalem in

July 13 2027, Carrie

Jeremiahs day, we too, as a Nation are turning away from and rejecting You. Punishment is deserved. We have an evil king, evil president, evil regime in our land. You have placed them there in hopes to show us that we NEED You. We need to turn our Nation back to You. So many things in place that are so blatently against You, Your principles, Your standards and Your morals. Things where evil and wrong is good and where good and right is wrong. It is horrible to watch it play out. Help us Lord, please rescue us.

Jeremiah 5:1-2 (NLT) says…….. "Run up and down every street in Jerusalem," says the LORD. "Look high and low; search throughout the city! If you can find even one just and honest person, I will not destroy the city. But even when they are under oath, saying, 'As surely as the LORD lives,' they are still telling lies!"

May we, who are called by Your name, humble ourselves. May we be just and honest when You look to our Nation. And may You see many many, many, many of Your people crying out to You, LORD, You are searching for honesty.

You had struck Your people, but they paid no attention. You crushed them, but they refused to be corrected. They were foolish and they refused to repent. They brought it on themselves.

May we be people who REPENT!!! Every single one of us that confess You as our God, our Everything. May we be HONEST about Your truth. May we ALL rise up even when the leaders of our Nation reject You……. I know that the rebellion seems great and the sins are many all around us, and the world doesn't even blush at the evil things they do and support………. and even some of Your people do not blush at the evils of this world………. But we Your people ask that You begin to restore our land before it is totally gone and before our freedoms are no longer there to even pass on to the next generations. Little by little, they are being stripped away. May You give us strength to rise up and walk 24/7 in Your ways in our lives and give us courage to speak Your truths and hold steady to them. There is a reason.

So, my friends who are reading this, I will let you read the rest of chapter five and six yourself. May it speak to you as it did to me. What will you do when the end comes? Turn to God now, do not wait. We all need to unite together in prayer. Be Ready! God Bless You and God Bless America.

Carrie felt a renewing in her soul from her mom's RTP writings and she felt proud of her mom for speaking out, writing behind her screen and encouraging other people who may read her rant.

Behind the Scenes

Debbie quietly went in. She didn't want to wake the brain of the machine. The light turned on and the words printed out. How does it know she is in there? She quickly glances down at the Bible verses written in handwriting and then quickly tears them off and shoves them into her folder.

2 Chronicles 7:14 (NLT) Then if my people who are called by my name will humble themselves and pray and seek my face and turn from their wicked ways, I will hear from heaven and will forgive their sins and restore their land.

Chapter Seven
June 2027, Amanda and the Ladies

I tried to let out a sigh as I said another quick prayer to God in my head. "Father Lord, I pray for these ladies. Please give me the correct words to say to each one directly this month as we go over the lesson. May each lady hear what You want them to hear to add to their relationship with You as they travel the narrow road. Thank you God. Amen."

Mary Jane had the floor for almost the whole time the women were there; the others trying to also get their stories and prayer requests in when she took a breath of air. It was almost quite comical if I could laugh. I listened to each of them go about their business, their stories and their requests, but I had no solutions, no opinions and no advice to give today. I just sat there in my own thoughts, waiting for someone to notice I was even there. Maybe shake me awake, (yawn) or to ask if I had anything to say, share or add. Although today, I really had nothing. I only had a lesson in my mind that was not given and inward struggles of my own.

A small tear fell from the corner of my eye but it went unnoticed. I was a little lost in my thoughts when I finally focused on what Mary Jane was saying.

"Pray for Old lady Nell, she has stuff going on again this month and I think she feels like she needs forgiveness but she won't ask for it and she may not come back to class, so just pray for her ok?" She took a quick breath, "And if you haven't noticed she has missed a few weeks of church service too. And as I have said these last few months, it has something to do with the hospital and the fact that they don't want her little ol' hats anymore."

Mary Jane was bold and factual in her tone. A little rude actually, and almost gossipy I might add. Rudeness and sarcasm was her idea of strength. It put her in control. None of us was equipped to handle it, our hearts were too soft. We just ignored her when she directed the rudeness directly to us. Sometimes, I think she purposely annoys us and we are actually the crazy ones that take it.

So how did I get here in this place in my own mind, so disconnected? Why did I feel so closed off in this room, my favorite room? So closed off from the women, my friends.

Again as I sat there listening to my own thoughts deep in my mind another "squirrel" detour took me back to the smell, it seemed like it was a mixture of bleach and cigarettes, yeah, I think that's what it was. Why am I so focused on that? Snap out of it!! Pay attention girl.

Susie, the newest lady, interrupted Mary Jane and started talking about herself and her own request for prayers. She had stuff to say and wanted us all to know it.

Mary Jane who is sixty-five and a newly retired rancher had worked hard her whole life. And like I said, she is a controlling, strong woman, and she was talking again about how her family hated her and how she may end up without a home because they did not want to care for her.

"Ladies, I neeeeeeed your prayers, I may be homeless, I don't know why they hate me so much, but they do, especially my crazy daughter and she keeps............."

Right on cue as Mary Jane said the word "homeless" Susie started to talk over her in an even louder voice at first so she could be heard, "WELLLL....... I LIVED AS A HOMELESS PERSON MOST OF MY LIFE and being homeless is horrible, but not always. I was on the street and we lived under a bridge, well several different places around many towns and sometimes in the city."

She had every ones attention, even mine. She was sitting about eight feet directly across from me in the circle around me. As she spoke, I could smell cigarettes on her breathe. The smell lingered in the air.

Ha, that is where the smell of cigarettes is coming from, but what about the bleach? Oh how I love to clean. I love the smell of cleaning products. Everything fresh and clean…..aaawww there I go again with a squirrel moment, "Snap back." I quietly spoke to my brain.

Susie started to kinda mumble to herself for a few seconds. I couldn't make out what she had said so I really tried to tune in with my good left ear trying to pay attention. She continued in a softer voice but still very energetic and with an almost forceful whisper as she demanded the attention of the room. She was almost as forceful as Mary Jane.

"I ran away when I was fifteen from my adoptive parents. I just couldn't live there any more they were so cruel to me, so very mean, but not all the time, just sometimes. So living on the streets, it was the best thing for me, even though it was awful at times, and the people there were also cruel, but some were nice. Most of them stayed to themselves and some didn't, we had no money and sometimes we did, my boyfriend he tried." She said each word so we could understand them, almost practiced words, like she had said them before. Although the words seemed jumbled and confusing with most of them contradicting each other, she seemed composed and collected in her story.

"Do you *stilllll* live on the streets?" Mary Jane asked in one of her sarcastic, you interrupted me voices, as Silvia questioned, "How old are you?" and Valarie, who sat to her right, was shocked and kept saying, "Oh my, oh my, that's horrible, so sorry, oh so bad, oh my."

It was as if Susie could hear all the questions at once and continued to talk very fast. "I lived on the streets from fifteen years old, off and on, mostly on…… but…… under the bridges, here and there, all different states and cities, well until ten years ago when I married my husband Hal. He found us a mobile home on the outskirts of town, and we have been living there ever since. But I'm still on the streets. I go everyday to see the people. I'm forty-six years old and now…….." She nodded to Silvia and took a deep breath, coughed and continued. Aw, there's the cigarette smell again.

"I am helping the people on the streets, in their situations, the situation I was always in, the hard knocks of life. I go there every day to help them. I'm not afraid of them, well some of them I am. I understand them and I talk to them, all of them, some are mean and some are nice, oh praise God for the nice ones." She raised her hands up to the ceiling, and pumped them a few times.

Then she started to mumble again, but I understood the words as, "Lady, you have no idea," in a deeper more direct voice as if she was talking to herself at that moment.

Susie looked around the room and felt she needed to get it all out, while she had the attention of these fine ladies. The last time she was with these women, which was months ago, she did not get a chance to talk, so she was not going to let up.

The brief pause in her story had me thinking about the baby she had at age twenty-nine. As I sat and wondered about the story she had told me, my mind again began to drift, this time to the baby.

How do I know about the baby? "Think, think Amanda." I demanded from my memory. I could feel myself trying to drift away again to sleep mode, while I held back a big yawn.

Did she just now tell us? Was I not paying attention again? No……not us, it was only me? The baby, the baby, my mind wanted to know more, but I just didn't ask her at that time. But I can't ask her now. I've always been horrible at asking someone a personal question or for more information, if they don't just freely give it.

Again, I questioned my own mind. My fog brain couldn't think. My mind was so disconnected from the conversation. My brain was in a daze of some sort. Full fledge 'fibro fog' or something. Taking notes in the here and now yet trying to focus on the past conversation. In addition, I am oh so very sleepy. I cannot stay awake. I am so very tired. As you can tell, I am still complaining. Darn those sleeping pills!

"Stop…… Pay attention." I spoke again with authority to my brain. We all talk to ourselves right? Yes, I do believe we all do that. Some days, I can actually have a whole conversation with me, myself and I. Sometimes, I must admit I have these discussions with myself when I should be listening. And I do think it can even be more than just a 'squirrel' moment.

That is one thing I believe we all need help with. Just listening and not thinking of an answer or our own story, but just listen to others. It can be hard to do; focusing on them and the words that they speak. Humbling ourselves and thinking of them as being more important than our self.

But if you think about it, we all want to speak and be heard, after all that is why we speak right? But it is more important to listen. God gave us two ears and one mouth. If we could just remember to listen, we would be much better off.

I tried to sit and listen, like I'm supposed to but I am so tired. I felt a wave of spiritual battle, one that I have felt before. The one where it feels like I'm not in the battle personally but the battle is totally about me.

As I focused, and really concentrated my mind became clear. Susie had a baby that she didn't want. She had given the baby away. Was it a boy or a girl? She didn't know, she couldn't say or didn't say. She just signed the papers at the hospital and went back to the bridge where she was living. She told me this, I think the first time I met her, back in December. She is the one who told me directly, this secret that she seems to want kept secret.

I wasn't judging her, why should I? She acts as if I do judge her. I can feel her eyes staring at me. I didn't want to look at those almost cold dark eyes, daring me to say something. Yet, I only feel sadness for her. She has no desire to find her baby, even if she could. She seems to have no guilt or regrets about this either.

Ignoring the cold stare that I know was there, I backtracked in my mind to think more about that day. It was in the parking lot, after everyone else left. She was looking for money for her trip. It was a bit cold outside as we talked, well she talked and told me her story. I remember, I reluctantly gave her a twenty-dollar bill that I had in my purse and she seemed happy with that.

Susie says she is forty-six year old, but she looks much older. Maybe because of the Arizona sun that beat down on her fragile body or because of the hard life she has lived. Yet in her voice she does not seem old as she talked, she seems renewed, brave, courageous and energetic with a spirit to help those who are living on the streets. At least that is what I get from her.

Susie seems to have a purpose today in our meeting, wanting support and prayers and money from all of us, as she continued her story. "I won't be around for a while, maybe a couple of months, because I have information about my real mom and I'm going to Texas to pick up a packet of info. As I told you all, I was adopted and well they had rules that I totally disagreed with, I told you I left when I was fifteen, right? I ran away and lived on the streets. I lived in Texas, well mostly there and other places and I'm leaving next week or maybe the week after to go there." She said with excitement as she flicked her long braided red hair back.

"Hal and I" ……………there goes the mumbling under her breathe. I picked up a few of the words, "Oh you will never understand, pretty girl, never." She said in a deep voice, and I believe she looked at Valarie directly in the eyes, as Valarie was continuing with the "Oh no's". At least I think that is what Susie mumbled.

"What? Wait, What wh wh what did you say?" Valarie asked almost in shock with a scared voice. Valarie sat up straight in her chair and you could tell it was almost too much for her, she seemed uncomfortable, and in her voice you could tell she was almost ready to cry which isn't anything new.

Valarie fumbled with her bright blue pen as she shook her leg continuously and nervously bit her bottom lip. She was a nervous lady most of the time and just like Nell, she never really seems to trust any of us. She always sits with her face to the door and back to the wall. She herself talks about leaving Arizona almost every time we see her. She has had one foot out of the desert as long as I can recall these past three years.

At this point Silvia took advantage of the mumbling and questioning from Valarie and quickly added, "My daughter Ruth isn't feeling well, please keep her in your prayers....." is all she got out.

As Mary Jane also noticed the break in Susie's story and began again about her family that hates her. She continues where she left off, and raises her hand in a stop talking motion right at Susie.

"As I was saying, they hate me, I don't know why, they just don't want me around, and they wish I would die. My crazy daughter won't take me in, and I'm not well, all of you know this, I am sick with liver and kidney problems and I need help and I want to see my grandkid, and............." She was speaking in a huffed voice and I thought for a moment that she also was going to cry.

Silvia chimes in knowing without a doubt that they probably didn't hear her prayer request for Ruth, and asks, "Why do they hate you so much?"

Mary Jane mockingly looked at Silvia with a look like, 'Are you not listening?' As she squinted her eyes and shrugged her shoulders. "I told you, I DON'T KNOW!" She then throws her

June 2027, Amanda and the Ladies

hands in the air almost hitting Valarie who was on her left. She then starts asking for prayers for her health.

I really did want to laugh or maybe even cry myself. It seemed today was totally off for all of us, with a little bit of chaos thrown in the mix too, that was for sure. At that moment, I wished for the AC to click on and cool us off.

"I'll pray about that, your name is Mary Jane right?" Susie quickly said and then continued to say that her and her husband Hal would be going to Texas soon to receive the information about her real mom.

"Pray for me, that the court records are still open for public viewing. I will be paying someone money to give me the information, did I say I'm going to Texas, far away from here. I have lived there before, when I was homeless and I am looking for donations to help me out. So, if anyone wants to help me, I could really use the help. I really need for you to pray also, but I really need money, I need it today if you fine ladies would like to help me." She said as matter of fact.

"Oh Father pleaaasssseeeee help me stay awake, help me focus!!!" I prayed as I tried to concentrate, but all I really wanted was a nap. A long and quiet, deep nap.

Normally I would be hesitant, and question a little bit more about this opportunity. Telling her to be careful and warn her about all the scams out there. But I was just too tired.

All of these women are willing to help each other. We do things all the time. One thing about these women, they are truly great givers of their time and money. I did honestly hope that Susie would get the help she needed financially today.

Today I remained silent. My eyes closed almost asleep this time. I could imagine the look on Mary Jane's face as Susie interrupted her again, just priceless, as many times before, it is usually Mary Jane, that is the one that is interrupting the others in order to talk. I felt her quickly turn to me as if to say, "Did you see that, she rudely interrupted me, AH GEN!"

My eyes stayed shut and I took a deep breath as I counted to ten in my head, knowing exactly why her family had disowned her the way they did. I felt the glare on her face, it was too much to respond to so I just ignored her, knowing it just didn't matter today. I had no energy to fight or to control the ladies. I couldn't even roll my eyes. If I rolled them, I more than likely would have tucked them in and off to lala land, over and out. I laughed at the thought. I had no control today, and my eyes were almost seeing the zzzzz's. Maybe I shouldn't have taken those sleeping pills. A mental note to myself, 'do not ever take sleeping pills the day before a lesson.'

In the distance I could hear beeping and it seemed to shake me awake enough to listen again.

Silvia herself was just as quiet, as others spoke over her. She gave up even trying to add anything or even ask any more questions.

Beautiful Silvia is a sweet petite lady, who is always so caring and concerned for everyone. She and her husband Grant, who is just as sweet as her, are foster care parents.

Silvia and Grant fell in love with Ruth when she was a newborn baby and adopted her. Ruth has been coming with her for the last year or so to Bible study, but not today. Ruth has cancer. She really needs our prayers, as well as Silvia and all her family needs them. Ruth is supposed to be doing better; in remission is what Silvia tells us. But she isn't. She needs a miracle; she is in the hospital as we talk. Ruth does not want anyone to know how extremely sick she is. Oh, how I wish Ruth was here reading the Bible. I love her sweet innocent voice as she reads.

"Please God, help me pay attention, please help my brain focus on each of these ladies, I pray that through all their talking that you will hear the prayers that are needed for each of them. I just can't sort it out today." I said a quick prayer to God again for the hundredth time this meeting and as you can tell I am about to fall asleep, sorry I keep complaining about this.

Just as I said Amen, I realized Valerie sounded like she really did want to cry.

Valerie

Valarie nervously stood up and walked over to the coffee maker in the corner of the room. She felt almost ready to cry as she poured herself another cup of coffee and added some vanilla creamer that she had brought from home. She grabbed two cookies and continued to stand there eyeballing the other ladies. She too asked for prayers about a new job that she was trying to get at the hospital cafeteria.

"Ladies" she sighed deeply. "I have been texting you all my prayer requests the last few weeks for a new job, and thanks, I do appreciate you praying for me....." she lets out a deep breath. "I really do......the job is finally open and I find out about it soon." She straightened up as she leaned on the wall, feeling a little bit better she continued, "I do have an in, because my son works in the Radiology Department. The only bad part is that you have to get the CHIPS and I'm not sure about that or the flu shot that is required. I can't make up my mind if I should just stay where I'm at, at the school cafeteria, since I'm going to be leaving Arizona soon anyway……..I just don't know, pray that I get answers." She looked around as she was explaining and it appeared that no one was really paying attention to her except maybe Silvia. Mary Jane and Susie were still talking over each other as they explained their own stories.

Valerie looked down at her phone and decided she would just text all of us her prayer request again when it got closer to the time of the second job interview. As she thought about the CHIPS that is required for all new hospital staff without exceptions she shivered with a chill. Was it the AC or something more?

Valarie had worked in different school cafeterias since she had graduated high school but never in a hospital cafe. She was a young mom, only fifteen when she had her son, and from what she says, a single mom all these years.

She had finished high school and had been so grateful to be able to support them both by working as a cafeteria worker her whole life. She always tried to make a great home environment and helped her son with his schooling. He graduated college with honors and now resides in Arizona as a Doctor of Radiology.

Valarie in her young old age thinks that if she worked in the hospital cafeteria, she would be able to see her son more, because he works such long hours every day. It is as if the two of them only have each other and their jobs in this life and they would be lost without the other. Oh the love between a mother and a son.

June 2027, Amanda and the Ladies

She tries again. "So please pray I get this job at the hospital in the cafeteria, please pray for that." She added as she took a bite of her chocolate chip cookie, still from the corner of the room by the coffeemaker knowing that no one was really listening.

She felt a little safer standing up and watching the ladies. She was at least able to compose herself. That new lady Susie was giving her chills and kept mumbling at her and staring her down. She felt on high alert and was ready to run out as soon as she got her chance.

As she ate her cookie and watched the women she had to chuckle to herself for a moment, at the glimpse of memory. She thought about how she used to love talking to her parents, her boyfriend, and coworkers when she knew they were not really listening or paying attention, just so she could be truthful when she said "I TOLD YOU."

As she was laughing to herself, she suddenly focused on Mary Jane in shock. Mary Jane had stood up, kicked off her pink flip-flops and then sat down on the back of the chair with her bare feet on the seat of the chair. It was a sight that I believe caused all the women to look on in surprise and almost scoff in disbelief. Was it the act of what she was doing or the flip-flops?

Valarie then wondered where Nell was. She thought for sure she would be here after her meeting with her. Nell is the only one who can really control Mary Jane.

Mary Jane

Mary Jane started to get impatient with Susie so she stood up, kicked off her pink flip-flops, which is weird to see on any given day, because she normally wears her pink cowgirl boots with everything. Then with her bare feet, she stepped up on the seat of the green padded chair and sat on the back as to make herself appear even bigger and in charge. It was actually kinda crazy, I mean she is sixty-five years old not ten.

"Oh, it is 11:10, time to leave," she says in her bossy voice, not caring if anyone had anything more to say. "I'll say the closing prayer." She bowed her head and began to pray the closing prayer.

In a take-charge way she begins, "As we sit here together with our dear friends in faith, we know You will hear our prayers. Show us in a way that would be unbelievable to everyone the healing power of physical healing for all of us and for the other requests, we have. Give us some assurance that You will heal all of us completely. Send peace and comfort to our family and all our sisters in Christ. Walk along beside us and carry our fears and our many tears. We believe that You are powerful and capable of stepping into our situations and completely alter the outcomes. To You, all glory and honor is given. In Jesus name Amen."

It was quite a fancy prayer for her. She then looked up and then quickly back down, "Oh and don't forget, Nell always has her prayers for the babies, and now she can't make anymore hats for them, please hear our prayer about that too, Amen." She added in an almost 'who cares really' voice and proceeded to get up and head for the cookies. She grabbed about eight of them, wrapped them in a napkin then went back to grab her stuff and headed for the door to leave. Everyone else said "Amen" and stood up in total amusement, shaking their heads to the rush rush gotta go attitude. Susie quickly followed Mary Jane out the door.

Amanda

My mind was still wondering off on its own, trying to blink and stay awake. Today was a crazy almost out of control day for the ladies, not normal, and not patiently waiting for their own time for their prayer requests. It was like they were just hanging out, with many conversations going on all at once.

I focused my thoughts on how I love that about Nell. She has always asked for prayers for the unborn children, and for the moms of those babies. Mary Jane was right in reminding us that Nell wanted prayers every time she is here for Bible study. For a moment, I truly missed her today. If anyone could control Mary Jane, it was Nell, or at least Nell's look that would pierce your soul if she were trying to get you to behave. Those green eyes of hers were almost spooky when she was not looking far off in the distance and would decide to look directly at you.

I could almost hear her voice even though she wasn't there. Her prayers entered my mind as I considered all that I knew. I saw into her heart and the sadness and understood why she seemed bitter and cold at times. It all made sense that I knew, but how? How today of all days did I know more? I knew her grief. She did want forgiveness but she does not know how to ask or even believe it was possible.

She didn't want to take responsibility for her part. She just wanted to blame God for what happened. What she did was wrong but she still does not regret it because at the time she believes it was the right thing to do. She is so confused. Why *did* she tell *me* this? Isn't Mary Jane her best friend? I have the whole story somewhere in my brain, but for now, sleep is what I need.

So as everyone leaves and that loneliness inside my own heart overwhelms me again, I realize I had no voice and no prayer given. Again, I was overlooked, like the last few months. And the lesson went unlearned. Romans 1:12 came to mind. Paul wanted to encourage and be encouraged by the faith of the Christians there in Rome, so that they could be a blessing to each other. That was exactly how I felt as the ladies left the room.

Our faith as we walk with Jesus is what gives us life. Our faith has purpose. God has put His truth in our hearts. He is who gives us this faith. We have no excuse for not knowing God. The question is will we walk with Him through this life and will we choose to get right with Him through what Jesus did for us? Have we all gone through the process of getting right with God? I think it is time I step up and find out. My mind felt determined as I searched it for Bible verses for each of the women, something that would help each of them personally.

Colossians 2:6 (NLT) And now, just as you accepted Christ Jesus as your Lord, you must continue to follow him.

Philippians 2:3 (NLT) Don't be selfish; don't try to impress others. Be humble, thinking of others as better than yourselves.

Romans 1:18-20 (NLT) But God shows his anger from heaven against all sinful, wicked people who suppress the truth by their wickedness. They know the truth about God because he has made it obvious to them. For ever since the world was created, people have seen the earth and sky. Through everything God made, they can clearly see his invisible qualities—his eternal power and divine nature. So they have no excuse for not knowing God.

Chapter Eight

July 13 2027, Carrie

Carrie picked up the Bible she had brought with her. The one that her mom's best friend Debbie had given her a few days ago at the funeral they all had gone to and out fell a printout paper. It was only three inches tall and about five inches wide with jagged edges. It was a little bigger than a register receipt, but instead of the writing going long ways, it went sideways, like an old scroll.

"Cool technology. I wonder if this is from my mom's new voice activated computer?" She said to no one as she laughed, "I sound like you mom, talking to myself…..although I totally refuse to start answering myself." She laughed some more.

The paper was thin but so strong at the same time. The cursive handwriting was beautifully laid across it. Almost like a beautiful secret finally out in the open.

She decided to grab the Bible and the binder and headed to the kitchen table. She felt a little restless so she made a cup of coffee with lots of creamer, just the way she likes it. She smiled as she walked back to the table and began to read again, starting with the note that fell out of the Bible:

Small room. Writer's table. Paper. Gold pen. My thoughts. Stop me. Not safe. Time. Back when safe. March 5, 2027

Carrie was confused as she read the words. They made no sense to her. She wondered why her mom's handwriting was on this paper. At least it looked like it was her handwriting.

Finishing the cup of coffee, Carrie decided she needed more. Maybe if she just keeps searching and reading her mom's secret writings she will be able to make some sense of this note.

Although, maybe the handwriting was not her moms after all. It could be anybody's, maybe even Ruth's. Whomever it belonged to, what did it mean? Carrie was excited, after all she always loved a mystery.

Behind the Scenes

Debbie wondered if anyone else had seen the machine work. As far as she knew, the machine wasn't even to be used yet. It was still under review and the results were not very positive as it could cause more damage. Could it be that the machine is somehow programmed with God's morals, God's standards and God's principles? After all, Bible verses were coming from it. Maybe the committee didn't want it programmed in this way. Debbie was curious as to why it printed out simple Bible verses and such random words that appear as thoughts. She made the choice again to turn it off, at least for now. She decided she better do some more research in secret because she knows that the one in charge was not to be trusted.

Psalm 119:130 (NLT) The teaching of your word gives light, so even the simple can understand.

Chapter Nine

Roxie

Roxie loved Fridays all year round. She was a teacher and she loved her job just as much as she loved Fridays. Friday was her time away from normal activities. She always chose to make the day different, and she always made the day fun and relaxing for the kids as well.

She works at a public charter school, one of the few that are left in the city of Tucson. Thankfully, she is able to teach what was once called, a normal curriculum. Her school tries to stay on the down low and not make any waves with anyone. Although from time-to-time, there have been parents who tried to disrupt the good moral teachings. It has always amazed her how some parents and even people with no kids try to change what they are doing and how they teach at her school.

Her job as a fifth grade teacher was fulfilling and exhausting. Her goal is unspoken; it is to teach the basics, but in a Godly way. There is always a reason to do that.

Roxie was looking forward to teaching summer school this year. She has never had a helper before in her classroom, and this summer was going to be different. She had talked Mary

Jane from the Bible study class into helping her a few days a week and really thought it would prove to be helpful.

Roxie was extremely excited and was looking forward to the more one-on-one time she would be able to spend with the children, helping them with the basics. It was so fulfilling for her, and with the extra help from Mary Jane, it will be a delightful summer break.

The school mostly had less fortunate children who were in need of so many things. Summer school not only helped the struggling students but also gave the parents that couldn't afford childcare while they worked, a safe place to send their kids. The one thing Roxie could provide was her time in helping them with the basic schoolwork. Reading was her favorite to teach as well as math. The kids were her main goal, but she also had another motive for asking Mary Jane to help her.

She felt a little guilty that she hadn't said a word to anyone involved, but she wanted to help with a prayer request that had been prayed repeatedly for a friend, a sister in Christ, Mary Jane.

Today was the first day of summer school, June forth, 2027. It was a Friday, her favorite day of the week. The plan was to have an easy day getting everyone signed in, meet with the parents and go over the schedule for the summer, as well as a tour of the classroom and playground, before the real first week started. Some of the parents may have thought it was redundant to go over everything since they just finished the regular school year, but Roxie felt it was needed to give everyone a reset and remind them how special this school was.

It was the first day of summer school and Roxie was happy that many of her students would be there as well as some new ones.

However, the day ended up being somewhat more challenging then she had expected as Mary Jane showed up early and was bossing *her* around and behaving like a child herself. Roxie felt a twinge of hopelessness before the kids even got there, as she wondered if she really was making a difference at all, and will it even be worth it, her doubts began to seep in.

Mary Jane, just ten minutes in, was already a handful. Roxie was not sure at this point, first thing in the morning, she was going to be able to handle. She quickly grabbed another cup of coffee and downed it before the first kids began to show up.

Her plan to reunite Mary Jane with her daughter and granddaughter was perfect, in her own mind. She really thought it would be easy, but another fifteen minutes into it, she was no longer convinced of her plan or of herself being able to execute it.

She had hoped that if Mary Jane had helped her out, she would be able to connect Mary Jane with her daughter and they would be on their way to resolving their differences. Mary Jane's granddaughter was in her fifth grade class and was going to be here for summer school as well. Roxie thought that if Mary Jane could spend time with her granddaughter that her daughter Cindy could see how much she loved and missed them. Then maybe they would be able to reconcile their relationship.

She was playing 'Ms. Peace Keeper', which is what most of the other teachers called her, and she believed it has always been her superpower. She has always joked about being a superhero in a way. Roxie had a knack of connecting people and keeping the peace, no matter what. She has had much practice in her own life and keeping the peace is what she did.

About six month ago, Roxie had discovered that Darleen was Mary Jane's granddaughter and that she never gets to see her any more. Darleen had told her that three years ago her grandma Mary Jane had been kicked out of the family. She did not say why, but said she no longer had a grandma.

Roxie became curious about the name 'Mary Jane' since she only knew of one Mary Jane from Bible study who over the years has always asked for prayers for her family, saying she did not know why they hated her but they did. She has always talked about how she missed her granddaughter Darleen, and has felt very sad about not being able to have a relationship with her.

Roxie's brilliant idea to get them together had not panned out yet. The moment Darleen and her mom Cindy came into the classroom and Cindy saw Mary Jane they immediately turned and left with no words spoken. Roxie had no idea if they would return.

Roxie felt stressed as she watched Mary Jane rearrange things in her classroom and go through her desk drawers. She shook her head in disbelief not sure what she should say. Luckily, Mary Jane was cleaning out cubbies and moving stuff around the room that she did not even notice them walk in or walk out. It was obvious that her daughter did not want to see her.

"Father Lord, I have prayed about this, over and over and I thought maybe it was a good thing, but right now I feel helpless and discouraged. Please God please let this pass." She let out a sigh after her prayer and continued to watch Mary Jane.

Day one was not going as Roxie had envisioned. She was already exhausted and not because of the kids, her thoughts were on Mary Jane and the six more weeks of summer school, she had to endure. At least it was Friday, her favorite day of the week.

She decided right there and then, that she was definitely going to stay home on Saturday and not go and meet with the other ladies from Bible study. She hated to miss her time with Amanda and the women and of course prayer time. Nevertheless, at this moment she did not want to spend any more time with Mary Jane. She needed a break already.

She had such great plans for the summer, but babysitting Mary Jane was not included in those plans. The day had just started, and Roxie was on her fourth cup of coffee, wishing it were a beer, even though she did not drink. She excused herself to the restroom and began to pray again, in a more private place this time.

"Lord, not only do all these kids need extra help, but I wanted to help reunite sweet Darleen and her mom to Mary Jane...... and help out my friend from church....but why, why Father Lord? Why does it have to be so hard? I do have good intentions You know I do right? And in spite of the fact that Mary Jane is a handful, I do really want her to have a relationship with her family. I have prayed about this very thing. I thought my plans were Yours as well, I know that Your timing is best but I thought the best time was now." She questioned, then after a short pause she continued .... "and God, I really do want to spend good quality time one on one with my students.......please help me, I really need You, Amen."

Even as she prayed, it all seemed to go straight to the trashcan. The plans she had that would give her some real purpose failed on day one, or so it seemed. Roxie, again decided, she was going to stay home and recoup from this day before it even got started.

Just as she finished saying Amen, Mary Jane started knocking on the door to hurry her up. Roxie rolled her eyes and as she did, she quickly apologized to God.

It was not until Sunday night that ten-year-old Darleen's mom called and left a message to let Roxie know she would not be bringing Darleen to summer school. No other explanations. Just a simple "Hi Ms. Roxie, I want to let you know that Darleen is not going to be coming to summer school. I know she needs it, and you are a wonderful teacher, the best there is." Then she added, "Hopefully we will see you in the new school year. Thank you for everything, have a nice summer."

Roxie felt horrible as she sunk into her old worn out couch and re-listened to the message for the third time. Defeated was what she felt, as she looked down at her arm already starting to bruise from the hard grab of her husband the day before when he had grabbed her and threw her across the room, for burning his toast.

His drinking and his anger had been getting worse. She silently wished she had just gone to meet with the women yesterday. At this point, she was not sure if putting up with Mary Jane was worse or better then what she had to endure at home.

"Oh Father God, please help me, I believe and trust that You will help me to just make it through one day at a time." She silently cried and fell asleep on her bumpy worn out couch.

Her husband Kevin was already awake Monday morning when she arose. Angry that his favorite cup was dirty in the sink he yelled at her and she began to cry which made him even angrier.

"QUIT YOUR CRYING YOU'RE SUCH A BABY." He shouted.

She walked to the kitchen and as she grabbed the cup to wash it, it slipped right out of her hand onto the floor and broke the handle into two pieces. The crash was loud. World war three began right there and then. Slamming her into the refrigerator, he growled at her clumsiness and told her she would never amount to anything.

"YOU'RE LUCKY I PUT UP WITH YOU, NO ONE WOULD EVER WANT A CLUMSY GOOF LIKE YOU." He shouted and stormed out of the room.

She noticed his cigarettes had fallen into the water. She quickly grabbed them and shoved them into her purse that was lying on the table. She will have to throw them away at the school so he did not see them soaking wet.

Looking at the broken pieces as she picked them up off the floor, she wished God would mend and repair the broken pieces of her life. She felt so broken and so lost at that moment. She didn't dare cry any more, not yet at least. She just dropped the pieces in the trash and went to get ready for the new day. She would have to search for a new purpose, search for new hope and search for a better new life at some point.

Today, she felt no peace. Her life, her thoughts, her soul was broken more than the ceramic mug. She tried to grab on to the picture in her mind, of the lighthouse built up on the rock with the raging water all around it that hung in the bathroom at her church. The picture had a man standing peacefully in the doorway, in the middle of a storm. She recalls her Pastor telling her that we can have that peace, God's peace in the middle of the storm. But today, she had a feeling that she couldn't no matter how hard she tried, her super power of Ms. Peace Keeper has been deactivated. She felt numb in her heart and soul. She had no peace.

The memory verse from a few months ago came to her head: Psalm 16:8…. "I know the LORD is always with me. I will not be shaken, for He is right beside me." She shook her head and prayed that it was true.

She was still shaking as she showered and got dressed. "Good bye." It was all she said as she walked out the front door and quickly walked to her car.

She decided she must walk away at some point and never return. He was always finding faults with her, while she spent her time overlooking his. Another verse entered her mind, one she has told herself many times before: Proverbs 12:16….. "A fool is quick-tempered, but a wise person stays calm when insulted."

"Can you fix my broken life?" She asked but did not think the answer could possibly be yes.

"He's right ya know, I'm nothing, I'm a good pretender, but that's it." Looking up at the sky, she didn't wait for any answer as she drove slowly to the school, which was about seven miles away, planning her exit. "Please forgive me God for what I need to do."

Her heart sank as she pulled into the school and saw Mary Jane standing and waiting at the door. The tears in her eyes could not be contained anymore, as they rolled down her cheeks.

As if the Lord heard her, the DJ on the radio read the Bible verse for the day. "Psalm 56:8 says…..You keep track of all my sorrows. You have collected all my tears in Your bottle. You have recorded each one in Your Book."

The DJ then reminded his audience that God see's every tear. She put her head down on the steering wheel afraid she couldn't move or even get out of the car as she tried to wipe away all the tears. She paused for a moment, as she pictured God grabbing each tear and putting them so gently into a clear bottle that was almost full.

Roxie had always felt like she was a prisoner in the middle of a war, but she knew her struggles did not go unnoticed by God. God was by her side and she felt His strength and trusted Him but felt none of that trust in herself. Not yet anyway. She wiped the remaining tears to the side and stepped out of her car. She pictured a woman in battle gear, knowing that her strength was not her own, but it was given to her by a loving and caring Father. She walked into the classroom with Jesus by her side, as well as Mary Jane.

1 John 1:5 (NLT) This is the message we heard from Jesus and now declare to you: God is light, and there is no darkness in him at all.

Chapter Ten

July 13 2027, Carrie

Carrie continued to read as she waited: The next writing was called 'The Void' and it was written back in 2000. Carrie knew her mom loved to write, but she hadn't realized that she had been writing many words for so many many years.

The Void

The void....I try to fill it........yet it's still there.....something is missing....something is gone...like a void....like a hole....a hole so deep...I cannot fill it....no matter how hard I try....it remains empty.....seal the cracks......make it whole.......let it be filled.....let it hold......let it hold Your word....let it overfill....let it run over.....let it seep with joy.....joy for You Lord....joy for life....a life worth living.....a life for You.....let there be a reason.

The void.....is hollow....filled with nothing.....but You can fix it......You're the potter....I'm the clay....mold me....shape me...renew my mind.....renew my heart.....use me for Your glory.....purify me......cleanse my soul.....with Your touch.....

July 13 2027, Carrie

You can make me whole…..help me to see…..help me to hear….help me to feel….that You are near…..guide me….protect me….call me by name…..my life is Yours…..it will never be the same…..let there be a reason.

The free will you give…..is so we can live….Your precious perfect plan…. cannot turn into a void……You saved my soul….to serve for You…….only You can fill the void……only You can fill my empty heart……..make me Your masterpiece…..to have and to hold…..my Lord and my Savior……..forever and ever….. to Eternity…..let me be void-less….let me be whole…..
Let there be a reason.

Carrie closed her eyes for a moment trying to picture her mom writing these words. She then decided to read them again, knowing that God was the answer to all the voids in our heart and in our life. He is who makes our life worth living. He fills the empty voids in the hearts and souls of His kids. He is the reason we can move forward. His perfect love fills those voids.

Carrie felt those voids at times in her own life and as she sat there and reread the poem for the third time. She pictured God filling them all with His peace. She focused on the love of God and not the ugliness of the world around her. She has always been aware of the evilness, but her mom and dad had always told her to focus on God and His goodness, His blessings and not to give satan with a little 's' as they always say, any power. See the good and be the good in the world.

Carrie has always felt like she was in God's ark of protection. He seals her in and closes out the world. It's what she prays for every day. She is sealed into His safe place, His ark of protection, and she is so thankful that He fills every void. She knows she walks in His presence and she is on Holy ground with Him. As she thought about that, she decided to remove her shoes, she wasn't sure why, but it gave her a sense of calmness and a peace and she could feel His protection around her. She could almost hear the words, "It's okay Carrie, I'm here with you, everything's okay."

Behind the scenes

Everything Debbie reads about the experimental brain machine points to 'scrapping it' for now. It's not safe. She tears off more printouts and takes them home. Why do they seem so personal to her and the other ladies? God's Word seems to have that living touch as it reaches our soul.

She smiles as she remembers the Pastor at church teaching that the Word of God is living and active. Many verses from the Bible were given that day. Her favorite was Psalm 119:105. She had made it one of her memory verses. A go-to verse when she felt lost, which thankfully didn't happen much. She has had a very blessed life, one that she knew came from God. His Word is the lamp for her feet and a light for her path, just like what He says in the Bible.

Hebrews 4:12-13 (NLT) For the word of God is alive and powerful. It is sharper than the sharpest two-edged sword, cutting between soul and spirit, between joint and marrow. It exposes our innermost thoughts and desires. Nothing in all creation is hidden from God. Everything is naked and exposed before his eyes, and he is the one to whom we are accountable.

Chapter Eleven

The Day Before Continued

Finally, Amanda was ready to go to the store and pick up the needed ink for the printer. It was 12:15 as she walked out the door with her purse and phone in hand. She locked and shut the door behind her. Just then, she realized that her keys were not in her hand. You guessed it; the keys were behind the door, yup, the locked one.

It was an unusually hot day for March; already sweating she sat down on the porch chair and called Chris. He was not very happy to have to leave work and come home to let her in again this week. He too was having a very busy day. He had many projects that needed his attention.

Thoughts flooded her mind as she remembered the last time this had happened. That time she didn't even have her phone. She sat there and tried to remain positive.

"What a blessing that at least today, I have my phone" she said out-loud. "Thank you Lord". Aha, the silver lining.

As she sat and watched a lady walking her dog by their home, it made her think about the crazy dog she used to pass on her way to work when she was working for the school.

She chuckled and quickly dismissed the thought. She was too anxious to laugh at this moment. Deciding to use the time wisely, she decided to pray for each of the women of her class. Focusing on the prayer requests over the years, she sat in silence as she talked with God.

After about twenty minutes outside, she felt thirsty as she waited for Chris to get home, which should only take about a half an hour. The water spigot on the side of the house had no hose on it but she was able to get a drink by cupping her hands after waiting for the water to cool off as it was coming out fairly hot, even for March.

She decided then that she would have a copy of her key made at the store so when this happened again (and she knows it will) she will be ready, prepared and armed with a spare key. She looked around for a good place to hide it.

By the time, her not so happy husband got there, about an hour later, she was almost in tears, in spite of her praying, she felt anxiety and stress mixed with calm and comfort. I know, it is a weird combination, but life sometimes brings both at the same time.

The look on Chris's face was filled with disgust and disappointment. She couldn't help it now, and sure enough, here came the flood of real tears. Amanda couldn't take anything more; her morning was already full of setbacks. Maybe it was just the heat of the sun and the stinky garbage can plus the fact that she was so hot and sweaty, that she just wanted to go back in, lie down and go back to sleep.

"Why didn't you tell me you needed ink?" Chris yelled at her. "I can get it much cheaper online."

"I did, but you didn't get it....remember when I was making copies of my lesson last month, I told you then." She yelled back, knowing it was not only his fault. She was going to remind him, but he had been so grumpy lately. She knew she needed it, she just kept forgetting to buy some back up ink when she shopped for the weekly groceries.

Her tears were quickly turning into streams of anger and his attitude was putting her in a bad mood as well. "Since I'm here, what's for lunch?" He questioned her.

Amanda felt angry at everything at this point and she was in no mood to make him lunch. She just wanted a fan blowing directly on her, some rest and possibly a nap before heading to the store. So when she got into the house she sat in front of the fan just to think about it for a minute, and to rest and cool off.

Impatiently Chris blurted out "FORGET IT!!! I'll stop and get something on my way back to work."

"Give me a second," was what she was thinking as she stood up and instead yelled "FINE" and walked to the bedroom, shut the door and flung herself on the bed.

A few minutes later, the front door opened and closed and he was off.

Amanda felt like her life was falling apart, and today was just another small piece added to her setbacks. "God, where are you?" She whispered as she fell asleep. It was 4:30 pm when she awoke. Sweaty and so hot she struggled to pull herself up off the bed and into the bathroom. Her eyes looked puffy and red even though she just slept for another three hours. She wanted to just lie back down and disappear.

Somehow, she mustered up the energy to grab her keys and her purse and headed out again to get the ink for the printer. Feeling the need to hurry, as it was not always safe anymore to be out when it was dark she started to drive a little faster than the posted forty-five mile per hour speed limit. She was hoping to get to the store and back home again before the darkness of the night sky fell upon her.

She does not go far from home anymore and she never travels anywhere she is not familiar with in fear of being lost or possibly attacked. Her sense of direction is horrible and she has developed a fear of most people. The world has gone crazy and most people have no concern for anything or anyone anymore. Chaos, destruction, and evilness are everywhere so it seemed.

Jesus didn't trust people so why should she. Okay well maybe she is interpreting that verse in a way to fit her own situation, but Jesus knew people and He didn't trust them either in John 2:24-25. She uses that verse to justify her fears sometimes. There are so many reasons to be afraid on this earth because the Bible is clear that it's satan's domain.

She must choose to focus on John 10:27-28 where Jesus says, "My sheep recognize my voice; I know them, and they follow me. I give them eternal life, and they will never perish. No one will snatch them from me." Amanda reminds herself that the little 's' man cannot harm her soul, because she chooses Jesus. She belongs to Him.

A small part of a lesson came to her mind. How will they know if we don't tell them of Your complete and marvelous love? How will they know if we don't speak up about Your precious love that draws us close? How will they know?

"Please be by my side Jesus. I can't do this without You" was what she was thinking when her red four-door Sonata began to limp. "OH…… NO……..NO. WAY……..feels like a flat tire???" She questioned the air in a defeated voice as she pulled into the parking lot of the corner gas station and convenience store.

The Day Before Continued

Amanda reached for her inhaler as she scanned the area around her before exiting her car. She began to look at all of her tires. The last one she looked at on the front passenger's side was totally flat. At this point, she started to just laugh....... "Of course" and then the tears started to well in her eyes. She tried to blink them away, but couldn't control the flow, again for like the millionth time this day.

She walked around and got back into the car, locked the doors, used her inhaler and sat for another few minutes.

When she finally stopped crying, she considered changing the tire herself. She has done this before, a long time ago. She is perfectly capable of doing it. She looks around at her surroundings and then she decides she is going to call Chris.

He's already mad at her today, and he will come and help her. He is a good man, just grumpy lately, probably due to the unexpected hot sunny days of March, and the fact that he's married to such an airhead as she.

She searches her purse and realizes she had put her phone on the charger before her long nap, and now that is where it sat.

She sinks into the seat and puts on the AC full blast. Trying to remain positive and look only at her blessings she bravely prays, "Ok, Lord, we got this, and there is water at least here at the corner store, it could be worse."

Amanda fearlessly sits up, thinks through it for a moment, grabs her credit card and heads into the store for some water.

There was a young woman that looked like she was in her twenties, outside the door smoking a cigarette and talking on her phone. And for a moment Amanda paused and thought that maybe she would wait and ask to use her phone, but quickly changed her mind as soon as she made eye contact with her and she gave Amanda a dirty evil look as if she was saying "Don't even think about it, get away from me, I hate you!"

Amanda flashed a quick smile and went inside. She decided to grab three waters so she would not need to go back in. She just wanted to fix her tire, go get the ink and hurry back home.

As she stood in line with her water the cashier, a thirtyish year old short guy with huge muscles and the voice of a New York mobster was yelling at the very old man in front of her to hurry up. The poor man was having a difficult time counting his money as his hands were shaking uncontrollably.

"Yo, come on old man, hurry it up, we ain't got all day, let's go."

Amanda decided that she would ask him if he needed some help as she reached out and tapped him on the shoulder. She looked at the cashier and said, "I'm in no hurry."

The old man turned around and she asked "May I help you?" in a sweet almost shy voice.

He looked her in the eye and then handed her a handful of money, dollar bills and change.

Annoyed, the New York mobster yells, "TODAY!!!!!"

Amanda looked at the man and said almost in a whisper, "Put all your money back in your pocket, I'll get it for you...... please let me" as she pushed it all back to him. He decided to let her and he moved to the side and let her up to the counter as someone else walked up behind her.

She started feeling nervous, as there were now too many people inside her space bubble. She could not make eye contact with the cashier because he looked like he was going to explode at any moment, as he tapped his hand impatiently on the side of the register.

The person behind her felt so close and something did not feel right. Immediately her breathing changed, her heart rate was increasing, and she could feel it beating faster and harder. A lump formed in her throat, and a sick uneasiness filled the pit of her stomach. She froze as she pictured herself floating out the door. She had to do a fast quick shake of her head to make the feeling pass. She instinctively knew she needed to be on guard and ready for flight or possibly even fight. Her fear increased as she struggled to remain in control and stay calm.

She then noticed a small selection of printer ink on the wall behind the short mobster man. "Do, do do......ahem" she cleared her throat. "Do, do you have an ink cartridge for a 952XL in in....in black," she nervously asked, knowing that at the corner store, it was going to be even much more expensive. Luckily, they did have one, and as expected, it *was* much more expensive. She bought it anyway with her credit card.

With anxiety and fear in her mind she felt as if the day was going by way too fast and it was going be getting dark very soon. She needed to hurry. The man behind her was still standing so close, she felt trapped and it freaked her out. She questioned, "What happened to the six foot rule?" Only to herself of course.

The old man grabbed his coffee and candy bar, she grabbed her waters, and her ink cartridge and they both walked out together, a little slower than Amanda wanted to go. Amanda began to cough as she walked out the door and finally took a breath of air.

The evil eyed woman on the phone was still there smoking. It had to be her third cigarette by now, Amanda thought. She was almost standing in their way as they walked thru the door to the outside. "EXCUSE YOU" evil eyes said with smoke drifting from her mouth and nose.

"Sorry" was all Amanda could say as she began to head toward her car, while trying awfully hard to not look directly at her.

The old man followed Amanda to the side of the building. He was parked next to her and said a simple, "Thank you" as he slowly walked past her and then came back around again. "You have a flat tire." She nodded her head yes that she knew and clicked open the trunk.

"Do you need some help?" He asked of her with an almost boyish flush in his face.

Amanda smiled and asked, "Do you have a phone I might use?" In the most upbeat voice she could muster and slowly out came an old-fashioned flip phone.

"I remember those" she squealed…. "I loved my flip phone…..I didn't know they were still around…..do you mind if I use it to call my husband?" He handed it to her along with a smile and she made the call.

Proverbs 29:25 (NLT) Fearing people is a dangerous trap, but to trust the LORD means safety.

John 14:27 (NLT) "I am leaving you with a gift—peace of mind and heart. And the peace I give is a gift the world cannot give. So don't be troubled or afraid.

Chapter Twelve

July 13 2027, Carrie

Carrie glanced at her watch, it was still early. She flipped through a few more pages, thinking about the words written in her mom's binder. These writings should be shared. She decided that she was going to help her mom get them published someday.

Just then, an alarm on her phone went off. It was nine o'clock and time to pray. A few months ago, Debbie had asked everyone to pray every day at nine in the morning. So she stopped, bowed her head and said a heartfelt prayer.

THE LESSON IN THE HYSTERICAL LAUGH was the next story she stopped at. The story was typed all in caps. Carrie recalled the discussion she had with her mom about typing in caps.

"Mom, cap letters? Looks like you're yelling."

"Carrie, I love the cap letters, if I'm yelling..... I'll put it in bold. To me, the caps mean I'm excited and happy, and plus it's easier to type, now bold, bold would mean I'm yelling."

"Yeah, but to everyone else, your letters in caps looks like you're yelling" she said as she laughed.

"Well Carrie, some people like it, they even say it's my signature writing."

"Okay mom, whatever you say." She just rolled her eyes and let it go.

THE LESSON IN THE HYSTERICAL LAUGH

I AM STILL LAUGHING.

I WAS DRIVING ALONG, A LITTLE UPSET WITH MYSELF, BECAUSE I DIDN'T GET UP EARLY ENOUGH TO SPEND TIME WITH MY FATHER, MY LORD, MY FRIEND, BEFORE LEAVING FOR WORK.

AS I WAS DRIVING, I WAS TALKING TO GOD, THEN WHAM….IT FELT LIKE GOD WAS TALKING TO ME THROUGH THAT DOG…. YEAH A DOG…..THAT'S WHAT I SAID….. OK BEFORE YOU GO ALL CRAZY ON ME, I KNOW THAT GOD WASN'T TALKING TO ME THROUGH THAT DOG, IT JUST FELT LIKE IT.

I DROVE BY A LADY WITH A DOG….. SHE WAS TOTALLY WORKING OUT….WALKING OR RUNNING, I'M NOT SURE BECAUSE AT THE MOMENT SHE WAS JUST STANDING DRESSED IN HER WORKOUT CLOTHES, HAIR IN A PONY TAIL AND A HEADBAND ON, AND SHE HAD ON BRIGHT YELLOW TENNIS SHOES.

SHE WAS HOLDING A LEASH…..YEAH HER DOG'S….HER BIG 150 POUND DOG WAS LAYING ON THE GROUND, TONGUE HANGING OUT…….ALMOST WITH A SMILE ON HIS FACE.

HE WAS LIKE…. "NO, NOPE, NADA, I AM NOT GOING ONE STEP FURTHER, I'M DONE, AND I NEED TO REST……. YEAH TRY AND

July 13 2027, Carrie

CARRY ME IF YOU CAN, BUT I'M NOT MOVING, I'M NOT GOING ANYWHERE, NOT NOW OR ANYTIME SOON!"

HE HAD THIS LOOK ON HIS FACE AND I SWEAR AS I DROVE BY, HE LOOKED RIGHT AT ME IN THE EYE AND I JUST STARTED LAUGHING.

I WASN'T JUST LAUGHING……. I WAS HYSTERICALLY LAUGHING THE REST OF THE WAY TO WORK.

IT'S STILL FUNNY. HIS LOOK……. HE WASN'T GONNA BUDGE, NOT ONE MORE STEP.

THE LADY, SHE WAS STANDING THERE HOLDING THE LEASH WITH HER HANDS ON HER HIPS LOOKING DOWN AT HIM.

"REALLY, REALLY, YOU'RE GONNA JUST LAY THERE, I'VE GOT WORK TO DO, AND YOU'RE HOLDING ME UP, NOW GET UP LET'S GO, REST TIME IS OVER!"

OKAY SO I DON'T KNOW WHAT SHE WAS SAYING, BUT SHE DID LOOK DISAPPOINTED IN HER DOG. BUT IT WAS LIKE A PATIENT DISAPPOINTED LOOK. SHE SEEMED TO BE LOVING AND CARING WHILE STILL DISPLAYING A REAL DISAPPOINTMENT IN HER DOG. AND HE WAS LIKE HE JUST DIDN'T CARE, WITH A SMILE ON HIS FACE, TONGUE HANGING OUT. IT CAUGHT ME AS SO FUNNY.

I'M LIKE THAT DOG SOMETIMES. I JUST WANT TO REST, AND SOMETIMES I REST TOO LONG. YA I KNOW IF WE REST TOO

LONG WE BECOME LAZY AND WE DISMISS YOUR LEADING, YOUR PATIENT KIND LEADING GOD.

YOU GIVE US REST, AND IT IS WISE TO FOLLOW THAT GUIDANCE….I DO NOTICE WHEN YOU GIVE ME REST, REST THAT I NEED ……I AM SO THANKFUL. AND IT MAKES ME SMILE, LIKE THAT DOG WAS SMILING.

BUT I MUST NOT TAKE IT FOR GRANTED, BECAUSE YOU HAVE WORK FOR ME TO DO.

SOMETIMES I WANT TO CONTINUE RESTING AND JUST BE IN MY OWN LITTLE WORLD, OTHER TIMES I REST IN YOUR STILLNESS TO REALLY HEAR YOU, AND OTHER TIMES I'M RUSHING THROUGH THE DAY AND MISSING YOUR LEADING, AND THEN THERE ARE TIMES I DON'T REST AT ALL.

HELP ME FIND THE BALANCE….HELP ME TO NOT DISAPPOINT YOU WHEN I DON'T FEEL UP TO THE TASK….HELP ME TO HAVE PERSEVERANCE AND STRENGTH AND ENERGY TO FINISH STRONG.

THANK YOU FOR THE "HYSTERICAL LAUGH" REMINDER TO REST WHEN YOU GIVE ME REST AND MOVE AND WORK HARD WHEN YOU LEAD ME…..THANKS FOR HOLDING ON TO ME DURING BOTH, LIKE THE LADY HOLDING ON TO THE LEASH.

NUDGE ME WHICH WAY TO GO, LIKE I'M SURE THAT WORKOUT GIRL WAS TRYING TO DO WITH HER DOG THAT DAY. THANK YOU. THE HYSTERICAL LAUGH GAVE ME REASON TODAY TO MOVE FORWARD.

July 13 2027, Carrie

Behind the Scenes

Debbie again ripped the printout off as quickly as she could and shoved it into her coat pocket just as Nurse Izzy walked in. Startled, Nurse Izzy looked down at her clipboard and ignored Debbie as she turned quickly to leave. Just then, another printout spit from the brain machine. It read: "Possible evil is among us………. WATCH OUT." Debbie again tore it off and left the room a little rattled and suspicious of Nurse Shady (As she referred to her). What was she doing in here? This is not her patient.

Hebrews 4:9-11 (NLT) So there is a special rest still waiting for the people of God. For all who have entered into God's rest have rested from their labors, just as God did after creating the world. So let us do our best to enter that rest. But if we disobey God, as the people of Israel did, we will fall.

Chapter Thirteen

Nell

Nell decided the hateful rudeness from the woman on the phone back on January 12, 2027, only two months ago, was too much. She had been making baby beanie hats for the hospital nursery for years now. They even distributed them to other hospitals.

The woman was so non-caring and rude to her. "No more hats Nell, we don't need them anymore. We hardly have any babies being born here. Nell, stop making the hats. DO. NOT. BRING. ANY. MORE. Do you hear me *Old Lady* Nell?" She put a big uncalled for emphasis on the words 'Old Lady'. It angered Nell to hear this woman who had no idea what it means to her to make the beanies, command her to stop.

She hasn't had much thought or dialogue with God over the years about the situation she found herself in. She tries to just forget, but she still feels the pain, the guilt and so much grief. And even though she hears all the teachings and lessons at church, she doesn't believe God could ever forgive her. She can't even forgive herself after all these years.

Two months have gone by and she still cannot stop making them. She stays home all day every day making pink and blue beanies. She hasn't gone to church since the phone call. In her mind, God was punishing her and causing her to struggle and feel defeated.

"Why do I need to stop, why are *You* making me stop?" She questions God.

Just then, Nell remembered the lesson on forgiveness that her Bible study group did about eight months back. She almost believed it. "All you need to do is just ask God to forgive you, just ask." That part kept running through her mind.

"They don't understand, how can You forgive what I did, I sure can't."

Nell looked down at her old worn out hands that have worked so hard all these years trying to make up for the wrong decision she had made forty-six years ago. Even though, it felt like only yesterday. It was a decision that had almost caused her to lose her mind. She had to fight hard for years to concentrate on each day at hand. One day at a time and one foot in front of the other. The beanies gave her comfort and helped her find reason to move forward.

Nell stood up and went to the shelf where her Bible laid closed and stared at it for what seemed like ten minutes, before picking it up. She then opened it to one of the pages her grandmother had highlighted for her many, many years ago. Psalm 118:24 was highlighted on page 949 and she read it out-loud, "This is the day the Lord has made. We will rejoice and be glad in it." She could almost hear her grandmother's sweet tender voice after all these years, uttering to her God's word from memory.

Nell has almost sleepwalked through her entire life. She just follows the same, well worn out path. She wasn't sure she could change her routine and definitely knew she could not stop making her beanies.

Nell flipped back a few pages to Psalm 32:8, which she had highlighted in pink and felt the need to read it out-loud. "The Lord says I will guide you along the best pathway for your life. I will advise you and watch over you."

She walked to the window and stared out at the big tree in her front yard. She held the Bible up to her chest as she thought of the day when Ruth had asked her about the beanies.

Ruth had been sad that day because she felt like she would never be able to have a baby, because of her cancer. They had talked for a good twenty minutes while sitting at a table by the food court at church.

Nell gave Ruth two of the baby beanies she made. One pink with diamond like speckles throughout, it was one of her favorite ones to make. And a blue one just in case Ruth someday had a boy. Nell encouraged Ruth to keep moving forward and she told her she would pray that she would get married, have a child and be a mother someday.

Nell has prayed every night for Ruth to be cancer free and for her to get married and have children. Nell loved seeing Ruth. She loved the time they were able to spend together. Ruth was always so kind to her in a most precious and pure way. Her heart felt so much love for her, love she has never really felt for anyone, except for her own grandmother, whom she still missed so much.

Nell believes that God has a plan and purpose for everyone else, and prays for them too, she just has a hard time with her own life. What does God want? What is her purpose and reason?

She listens at church and she knows He wants her to trust Him and do good, obey Him and commit her life to Him. She has heard that if she commits her life to Him, He will direct her path.

"No more beanies Old Lady Nell," has been etched into her brain for months now. She really couldn't stop herself as she sat back down and picked up her knitting needles again.

Nell's deep thoughts of her own child filled her mind. It had been forty-six years ago (1981) and the choices she made were the best ones she could at that time. Abortion was not really an option, at least not by many. It was unheard of and wrong, at least in her circle of acquaintances. Plus, there was no way she could have done that anyway.

She was only sixteen. What seemed like just yesterday has been her lifetime. Oh how the world has changed during her short life here on earth.

She sat on her couch lost in thought thinking about how these days abortion is used as a crazy birth control on an 'alter of convenience' for so many girls. It seems as if many have no value for life in the world today.

It is the worst it has ever been in her lifetime. Laws have been passed in many states to make it legal but she knows that it is not a good thing. There are women out there marching and fighting for the convenience to kill a baby, all the way up to birth. It is really so disgusting and bizarre. There is nothing right about that.

"It's just not right." Nell thinks as she shakes her head, it really angers her. With so much 3-D technology we now have, we can know for certain that a baby is alive and growing into its own person. Nell focused on a lesson that she heard about how God formed us in our mother's womb. Psalm 139 was all about how God knows everything about us, but at the time of the lesson, it had given Nell more ammo to blame God.

"If You knew, then why didn't You stop me, why didn't You guide me and give me strength, why?" Nell felt her heart twisting into knots. She couldn't hide, even in the darkness, if only she could. Hide and wish it had never happened.

"Freewill is overrated....You give us all that we want....but I don't want it.....I really want YOU to show me the path!" Her anger was rising again at God, blaming Him for her decisions. She was only sixteen at the time. Why didn't He give her better direction? She just couldn't understand. If all good things come from God then why did this turn out so bad? Even in her pain, she could answer her questions herself, because she knows full well, she never even asked or considered God's direction back then. She knows she didn't even think about it.

Making baby hats for the little babies is the one thing that helps Nell forget about the past and focus on the new life about to be born. In a way, it helps her feel less guilty. These days it seems there are only two options for women; have and keep the baby or kill it. The world has gone extremely mad. The more Nell thinks about the option that she chose, the more she knows, she is just as crazy.

Nell doesn't really try to know much about God, even though she goes to a great church. She has built up a wall of anger, bitterness and regret. A thick wall against His truth and she knows He would not approve. She prays for everyone, but not often for herself. In fact, she doesn't even pray for His forgiveness, because she doesn't feel she deserves it. She is not even sure He hears her prayers although deep down she believes He does.

"Oh God, I do want forgiveness, I just don't deserve it, do I? Don't forgive me, I don't. I just don't think I deserve it." She prays angrily at herself and almost talks her way out of being forgiven every time, she prays and answers herself, as if it was up to her.

"Please just make sure my baby is safe." She has prayed the simple prayer daily for the last forty-six years. If only she had done things differently. Her guilt weighs her down almost every time she prays.

She remembered her grandmother telling her how much she loved her and how she would hold her hand and tell her what a gift she was. She would quote Psalm 127:3 "Children are a gift from the LORD; they are a reward from Him."

Nell thinks about her life and realizes she is now of grandmother age herself. And for the first time in a very long time she can't stop hurting or missing her own grandmother, as she knits the next beanie.

Little did she know, this very moment, Mary Jane of all people, was praying for her, asking God to heal her broken heart, and praying about the beanie hats and for Nell to come back to church. Mary Jane has always thought of Nell as her friend, they have always fought and loved like sisters and she was missing her.

Several hours had passed when Nell realized it was getting late. She picked up the phone to call Amanda. She felt a tugging on her heart but she had made up her mind, she was not going to go to Bible study this month either.

She had told her friend Mary Jane about the beanies and the hospitals request for her to stop making them and asked her not to say anything. But she knew that she had when she saw Silvia at the store and Silvia expressed sadness for her. She felt angry and a little hurt that Mary Jane had said something, even if it was in a prayerful request way.

Sometimes, a few of the women used prayer request time as a way to talk about things, even gossip at times. She didn't mind knowing things, but maybe in a different setting, and not during the prayer request time. Prayer time is precious and she knows this for fact. Her grandma used to pray with her and it was always so special and holy to her, as they would pray and talk directly to God. She loved to pray with her grandma. If only she had the faith that her grandma had. If only she had continued to seek God's guidance.

She started to dial Amanda's number and then looking back down at her Bible that was open, she glanced at a verse her Pastor refers to often…… 1 Peter 5:8. She had highlighted it years ago. She knows full well satan attacks the people who are alone, and that he prowls around like a lion, looking for someone to devour. She knows full well God is not to blame for her bad choices. She knows full well that satan is in charge of this world and that she doesn't need to live under his thumb. She knows it all but just can't make it part of her life. If she did, she would have to forgive herself, and that was one thing she could not do.

Nell had been baptized. It had been the week after her eighteenth birthday. She knew that God had forgiven her at that time. She knows that satan continues to use her past against her. She knows all of this, but over the years, she has pushed all the forgiveness to the side. Her guilt and shame eats away at her heart. Why does she let it? Her path is so rocky and so thorny.

It seemed easier to have someone to blame, it was easier to blame then forgive herself. Nell knows the blame is not to be directed at God, He is not the one for her problems. How can she know so much and not apply it to her life? She has had a block wall up between her and God for so long that she just can't see.

For the next hour she recalled the many times her Pastor talked about satan. How real he is and how we are on the enemy's territory. She pulled out the slip of paper she kept in the front of her Bible. The one with the Bible verses her Pastors wife had given her about how the whole world lies in the power of the evil one. It was a huge list. She started to look up the verses as she hung up the phone without dialing.

1 John 5:19, 2 Corinthians 4:4, Galatians 1:4, Ephesians 2:2, Luke 4:5-6, John 12:30-31, John 14:30, James 4:7, 2 Thessalonians 3:3, Proverbs 19:3. She flipped through her Bible and read each one. Each one telling her where the blame needed to go, then as she set the Bible down it opened to 1 John 1:5, she started to read it and continued on to 2:6.

She stopped and went back to 1 John 1:9 where it said, "But if we confess our sins to Him, He is faithful and just to forgive us and cleanse us from every wrong." She has heard this so many times in her life, especially since she started going to the CCC church. "CCCCCCCC you at church" jingled through her mind.

She then reread it word for word slowly...... "But. If we. Confess. Our sins. To Him. He is faithful. And just. To forgive us......To forgive us," she read again. "And cleanse us. From every.......every wrong?" She questioned it.

"Do You forgive me God? Can you really forgive me? I'm asking You to please forgive me. It will never be right.....but, but can I forgive me too? I need Your help Lord, please help me to forgive myself. Help me to know. I need to know." She then picked the phone up again and dialed Amanda.

2 Corinthians 4:4 (NLT) Satan, who is the god of this world, has blinded the minds of those who don't believe. They are unable to see the glorious light of the Good News. They don't understand this message about the glory of Christ, who is the exact likeness of God.

Proverbs 19:3 (NLT) People ruin their lives by their own foolishness and then are angry at the LORD.

Chapter Fourteen

July 13 2027, Carrie

Carrie was searching for something in her mom's writing. Something that spoke to all of the ladies from Bible study, something she could share, she came upon this:

My Hands

"My hands are weary. They hurt, they are crippled. It's hard to do just easy everyday stuff. I pray to you oh Lord; please do not let them fall from worship. Don't let them be limp, but lift them high in the air up to You in worship and praise. You are the one who steady's my hands. You keep them from shaking. Please give them strength to finish the task.

As I look down at my hands, they look so old and wrinkly. I remember when they were young and strong; but now I only see they are so old and dry. Even my fingerprints seemed to be gone. The veins are popping out from the backs of my hands, so sore to the touch. My fingernails look so brittle and rough. I never did take time for them to look nice. They look very un-kept as they did for most my life.

A lot of work has taken place with these hands and a lot of prayer as well. I don't always close them as I pray; I like to hold them open, ready to catch Your blessings that You always provide. Oh Lord, I stretch out these weak dry hands and expose them to You, please renew them, please give these lifeless tired hands a renewed strength.

Let my hands be the pencil in Your hands as You write out the next adventure. It is with pleasure I get to write for You. My life is in You, Father Lord. Give me the enthusiasm and the patience as You write our story through these old weary hands on to the paper before me. My hands are not crippled when You guide them and accomplish what You need done. They are willing, they are excited, and they are thankful for the opportunity to serve You in ways that are meaningful. So I lift my hands to You. Let me receive Your blessings through these old and worn out hands to the paper that waits for the words. Thank you."

Carried smiled and looked down at her own hands. Her mom always told her to be strong and happy about God's work, because you know that nothing you do for the Lord is ever useless. She thought about that for a moment. How could God use her? She stood up and stretched her legs, then immediately sat back down to read some more.

She chuckled as she remembered she had read ten books once, in one week. She had done a stay at home vacation, read the entire time, and loved it. She has always loved reading. It took her many places.

July 13 2027, Carrie

Behind the Scenes

Dr. Prong was angry as he spoke to Joe his assistant, "Why isn't this working, you need to change it up, get it to work.... this is on you, not me....understand....?"

"Actually, this is on you....*you're* the one that is rushing this....besides, I can't change it up....if I do anymore, this experiment will pass.....*YOU* understand?" Joe barked back.

"Listen Joe, I need you to mix the drugs. They need to keep her in a coma, but not so much that my machine doesn't work. Do you even know what you are doing?" Dr. Prong sarcastically questioned Joe knowing how much it angered Joe.

"Shut up, we both have a stake in this, you do your part and I'll do mine." Joe wanted to slug him but held it back.

John 3:16-21 (NLT) "For God loved the world so much that he gave his one and only Son, so that everyone who believes in him will not perish but have eternal life. God sent his Son into the world not to judge the world, but to save the world through him."There is no judgment against anyone who believes in him. But anyone who does not believe in him has already been judged for not believing in God's one and only Son. And the judgment is based on this fact: God's light came into the world, but people loved the darkness more than the light, for their actions were evil. All who do evil hate the light and refuse to go near it for fear their sins will be exposed. But those who do what is right come to the light so others can see that they are doing what God wants."

Chapter Fifteen

The Day Before Continues, Amanda

I handed the phone back to the old man at corner store with tears in my eyes. "Thank you, he's on his way. I appreciate your kindness."

The old man looked at me intently and said, "No, it is I that appreciates your kindness, you don't meet many of you around anymore, thank you." He then turned and got into his car and drove away.

I got back into my car, locked the doors, drank some of the water and waited. I wondered if the old man was an angel. He made me smile and I think I will make him my main character in my next book. The old man with the flip phone, I love it.

I glanced at the clock on the dash, 5:06 pm. The evil eyed cigarette lady on the phone seemed to purposely stand in the way of everyone walking by, blowing smoke on them as she ignored them and talked on her phone. Her clothes were almost too small for her. Her cut-off tee shirt was very tight and the cut off shorts were so short that they barely covered her bottom.

Even though it was a hot day for March I wondered, when would decent clothing be acceptable again?

"Father, if she only knew the gift of Jesus, a treasure that is so precious........ if she only knew how precious she is to You, if only." I let out a sigh.

She was about the same age, maybe a little younger than my daughter Carrie, although my Carrie is a much different girl in her twenties than this one. As I sat and watched her, I wondered if the young woman rebelled against her good parents or if she just had bad parents.

The lesson at church a few weeks ago was titled, "Teach your children about God, Jesus and the Bible or the world will teach them not to believe," ran through my mind.

From where I was parked in the first spot on the side of the building I could see the front door clearly. I really didn't want to be judgmental of her, but she was acting so rude to others, and it really troubled me. Her behavior was so disturbing. "I'm sorry God, please let me see her with Your eyes.... she is lost.... so very lost.........no matter what she is wearing or how I see her, she is created in Your image, she matters to You and she should also matter to me....... but how will she find You in this world?"

As I watched more eagerly, the young girl's actions and behavior unfortunately was kinda entertaining to me. It made me think of a new story like life of her. I decided I might even use the story in one of the many stories I love to write.

It was then, as if the woman could sense me staring at her, she turned to look right at me and flipped me off. How rude. I quickly looked down, away from her, rechecked the locks on my car door for the millionth time, and then fumbled with the radio station.

"Thank you Lord for Christian Radio." I smiled as I turned up the volume.

I was so glad that it was still on the air, even though several groups have tried over the years to get it suspended or kicked off the air because it talks about Jesus and plays only Christian songs.

When I looked up again the woman was gone. I wasn't sure if she went inside or left in a car. The song 'I can only Imagine, by Mercy Me' was playing and I sang it loudly as if I was in God's band.

I then prayed for the woman that I encountered and hoped that she too would fall to her knees and praise Jesus. "How will she find you Lord?" I asked again with real concern, wondering if I had lost an opportunity to tell her. I grabbed my notebook and penned the poem: Will we rebel or will we grab hold of You?

The price of disobedience, the cost of rebellion
Did we miss the beginning or did we ignore
A Nation going under
Surrendering to the core
Will we allow it or will we stand strong
Punishment will no doubt come
It has in the past, it will be done
The price of disobedience, the cost of rebellion
A moment in history
A reset of each heartbeat
As we wait for Your return
We sit in the corners of time until we can meet

Let us be completely sold out and only to You
The price of disobedience, the cost of rebellion
Is much too high for us to pay
Come back to our Nation Father God
Come back to our core and stay
Lead us on Your path, and do not let us stray
Please bless us and fill our heart
And let not the evil touch us in any way
Keep us safe in the ark of Your protection
Those that are always Yours
The price of disobedience, the cost of rebellion
Discipline is sure
But let us hold fast, the time has come
Let us speak only of Your truth
Let us not go numb
For how will they know
Open our eyes, soften our hearts, for that is where the beauty lies
Let us put our wrong behind
And listen in the stillness for Your voice
Jesus, oh Jesus, may we treasure what we have always known and seen
As we rejoice and be true
All the way to Eternity, let us grab a hold of YOU ☺

It was 6:13 when Chris finally pulled up and the light of day was beginning to dim. I shoved the pen and the printer ink into my purse and got out to show him the tire.

"I'm sorry." I paused. "Today is not my day." It was all I could get out of my mouth before the tears began to fill my eyes.

Chris gave me a hug and said his day was not so great either. He then got started on the tire.

I stood there, watched and prayed that the spare tire was in good shape. I handed him one of the waters, which was not as cold as it was an hour ago and he drank it down and finished changing the tire.

"Let's drop off your car at home and then go get something to eat, okay?" He almost demanded in a nice calm way knowing that I do not like to be out at night. Nor do I trust eating out anymore, since food tampering had become such a huge thing.

I just nodded. I didn't want to argue and said, "Okay" and got into my car and he into his truck, and we both drove toward our home. Me, with my car lights on.

"I'll be right out, I've got to use the bathroom," I yelled as I got out of my car. I ran to the bathroom, fixed my hair and grabbed my phone that had finished charging. Then turned on almost every light I passed on the way to the front door. I was almost to the door ready to leave when Nell called.

"Amanda, oh sweet Amanda I am so sorry, but I won't be able to make it to your class tomorrow."

"Nell, are you okay?" Then a little louder. "Nell, is there anything you need?"

"No, no I just don't feel like coming. I have some decisions to make and I just don't want the ladies to try and solve them for me."

I told her to call me later if she wanted to talk or even come to class if she changed her mind.

"Oh darling Amanda, I doubt I'll change my mind." It was all she said and hung up the phone without even a goodbye.

Nell

Nell hung up her phone and decided to watch the TV Preacher. She grabbed a granola bar, lit a candle and turned off the light. The glow of the candle and the TV light was calming to her after all the reading she had just done. And even though she decided not to go to the Bible study meeting, she had a peace in her heart, one that she usually didn't let enter.

The TV preacher was in the woods broadcasting his sermon. Most of the TV church services were no longer on, but somehow this TV preacher was able to get his message out. He usually was in different location and on channel four almost every night at seven. Most people think he somehow hacks into the station for a live stream for about fifteen minutes than he is up and moving. But the truth is; he actually pays them to give him fifteen minutes to spread God's truth. So far, the station is run by people who don't care what he does, as long as he pays them they will run his taped sermon.

Nell has been watching him for about a year now, not really listening to his message but trying to figure out where he was broadcasting from. It had become a game for her. But today, for some reason unbeknownst to her, she decided to really listen and hear his message of truth. In a strange way, she finally understood that satan is out to destroy her and that God was not to blame for her own decisions. The Bible verses she read really helped her.

There Is A Reason

A Report of Amanda's Day Continued

Amanda noticed the TV was on as she walked out the door, wondering if she had left it on or if her husband had stopped at home before coming to rescue her, she glanced at the TV Preacher that was just coming on and she was able to catch some of his beginning prayer.

" ……….The light from Heaven is about to break upon us….."

Oh how she wished the light from Heaven would light up the sky as she walked out the door.

Amanda was so tired, so exhausted, as she locked the door and walked to her husband's truck in the dark of night. Getting into the truck, she looked over to her husband who just smiled at her as she silently put on her seatbelt.

Looking up to the sky as they pulled out of their driveway, she noticed the huge full moon. The eye in the sky is what she has always called it. She nodded her head like a bobble-head in agreement with God that He was looking after her. One of her memory verses, Psalm 32:8 made an announcement into her memory and she suddenly felt calm.

She felt a little more at peace as she said, "Sorry," again to her husband. He reached over, held her hand, and nodded his head.

They decided to go for pizza. It was always their favorite comfort food and it was only a few miles from their home. Jumping on the freeway, she was relieved that there were not many cars out. "Thank you God." She silently prayed. She tried to remain calm, not only were they driving on the freeway which has always made her uneasy, but it was getting darker by the minute. Again, she said another, "Thank You" to God for the full moon and the slow freeway.

The pizza place wasn't very crowded for a Friday night and they were seated right away. They decided to get an extra large pepperoni pizza so they would have some leftovers for the next day.

The server walked up, a twenty plus something year old girl. She looked familiar for a moment, and Amanda stared at her. She noticed and looked back as to say... "Take a picture, it will last longer." With a shrug to her shoulder as she flipped her hair back.

The rude look was the give-away and Amanda knew it was the same girl from the corner store. She was dressed in slacks and a blue button down shirt. A nice outfit if she would just button at least one more button so the lacey part of her bra wasn't showing in defiance. Amanda chuckled to herself, thinking that maybe it was to get her some bigger tips.

The girl was chewing on a huge piece of gum, probably trying to cover up the cigarette smell from her mouth, it didn't help much. As she took their order, she was partly occupied and pretty talkative to the earpiece that was in her ear. She continued to have a conversation with someone else as she wrote down their order. Sarcastically Amanda's brain interrupted her thoughts of pizza with a 'squirrel' comment that made her almost laugh out-loud, "At least she can multitask."

Amanda listened as the girl told the person on the other end that her motorcycle broke down and she had to get a ride to work. "Yea, it's just too far to walk at night, it's a good thing I was able to get a ride from my neighbor and he even picked up my motorcycle from the side of the road......pra........" She almost slipped and said "Praise God." But she caught herself in time.

"Well anyway……" Then looking at Amanda she said "……. your order will be right out." She then nodded and smiled at Chris as she walked away still talking to the person in her ear.

When she left, Amanda told Chris about her smoking and her standing in every ones way at the corner store. Then she told the story about the old man with the cool flip phone, and how she was going to use them both in the next story she writes.

The food was refreshing and much needed. Chris seemed to be in a much better mood by time he finished his third slice. He didn't talk much; she did all the talking and storytelling.

Amanda

"How would she know?" crept into my mind again, as Chris and I got up to leave. I decided I would leave a church business card to our church with the tip money on the table. The lady whose name badge read 'Pickles' picked it up and laughed at me and accused me quite loudly of being foolish.

With a spiteful smirk and an ugly chuckle, Pickles questioned me. "Really lady, what's this? Do I really look like someone who cares or would even consider your church or your God?" She waved it in the air but still held on to it with the tip money and then pocketed it into her apron, as she started to clean off the table.

Remembering the verses from the day before, I maneuvered myself around Pickles.

2 Peter 3:3-7 reads: Most importantly, I want to remind you that in the last day's scoffers will come, mocking the truth and following their own desires. They will say, "What happened to the promise that Jesus is coming again? From before the

times of our ancestors, everything has remained the same since the world was first created." They deliberately forget that God made the heavens by the word of His command, and He brought the earth out from the water and surrounded it with water. Then He used the water to destroy the ancient world with a mighty flood. And by the same word, the present heavens and earth have been stored up for fire. They are being kept for the Day of Judgment when ungodly people will be destroyed."

I stopped and turned back as she looked up from her cleaning. So I looked her in the eyes with compassion bravely wanting to say, "A day is like a thousand years to the Lord, and a thousand years is like a day. He is being slow at coming back so you can have time to make the decision to accept Jesus, but time is running out." The words froze in my mouth as Chris' hand gripped mine and led me out the door.

As we started to walk away, I bravely stared directly into Pickles eyes and for a moment, I felt almost like my soul spoke to this young lady.

I sat in the car hoping that when our eyes met they said something to her. Time was running out for everyone to get right with God and truthfully, I quietly wanted to hurry it along.

Pickles

Pickles real name was Riley, she had acquired the nickname 'Pickles' because she was always eating the big dill pickles from the jar. Riley started to feel sad, almost sick at how she just treated the nice couple. She looked around and she still fit in with the world. No one will figure it out as long as she continues to behave like them. Something about the look of the woman's eyes had her questioning her behavior. It was as if the woman's soul found hers and had a short conversation.

It wasn't easy being a Christian and most days it was much easier to blend in as a non-Christian. The compromise hurt, but it was what she needed to do in order to survive, or was it?

Her own dad was a faithful righteous man and was killed by a stranger who saw him bow his head and pray at a fast food place a few years ago. He didn't even see it coming, from what the witnesses said. As he lifted his head and said Amen, the punch was on its way to his jaw causing him to fall hitting his head on the table killing him instantly. Riley's mom had passed away when she was just five years old from breast cancer. She doesn't remember her much but tries to create a life with her from the photos her dad had on his phone.

Standing up against the pressures and temptations of society is never easy, she knows it is deadly to give in, but it is even deadlier if she didn't appear to. She is just trying to survive. The bad girl look with attitude fit in with the world, and in her mind, it was the one and only way to stay alive.

A few hours later, in private, in her own small studio apartment she asked for forgiveness and strength from God. And thanked Him for her neighbor, who drove her to and from work.

Her Bible was like manna to her. "Manna from Heaven." That was what her dad used to call it. And it was. It fed her soul. God and her Bible were the only real things she trusted. Riley looked down at the card that was left for her and placed it in the front of her Bible. There was a Bible verse at the bottom of the card that said, Isaiah 40:8....... The grass withers, but the Word of God stands forever. She smiled with tears in her eyes as she read it. It was her dad's favorite verse.

Riley turned on her TV to watch the news she had recorded for the day, channel four. She loved to listen to the hacked in TV Preacher that would talk for fifteen minutes and then to the news and weather. As she fast-forwarded through the worldly stuff, she thought about the lady and how brave she was to give her the church invite.

She stopped fast-forwarding when she got to the TV Preacher. He had the same look in his eyes as the woman had in hers; as a matter-of-fact, they were the same color too, as he stared right at her through her small TV screen.

He began to pray with his eyes open. "Because of Your tender mercy, I know the light from Heaven is about to break upon us. It will give light to those who sit in darkness and in the shadows of death. Please guide those who are Yours to the path of peace. Amen."

He was sitting in the woods somewhere, but Riley couldn't pay attention to that. She couldn't take her eyes off him as he spoke.

"Yield to Him. Receive and respond to Him, wholeheartedly. We are not to surrender to the world." He held up his Bible and shook it. "Nowhere in here does it say to surrender to the world!!!" She swore he was talking directly to her as he said, "Surrender to Him, not the world. Receive His message and respond to it."

She dropped the pickle she had been eating as her mouth stood wide open with words that would not come out. And then she prayed.

"God, You want me to be restored. You love me, and will take the brokenness of my heart and make it whole again....I must yield to You, but how?" Riley reached up, shut off her TV and began to cry her real first tears since her dad passed away.

It took her awhile to compose herself, the tears felt so good, almost cleansing. She then turned him back on and listened some more. She sat still as she prayed for the woman who gave her the card. She was brave that's for sure; she prayed that the nice woman did not end up like her dad.

The billboard on the highway changed, with new lights flashing in all four corners, it now read, "A NEW EARTH IS COMING....BE PREPARED.......GET YOUR CHIPS TO LINCS TODAY."

Amanda's husband looked at her knowing she read it, shaking his head he said "If they only knew........ We need to shine the light in the darkness no matter what Amanda. The enemy wants to keep them blind to God's truth. Somehow we need to reach our neighbors."

Amanda felt sad for the world of fools. The result is disaster for them. Remembering her Pastors teaching and his words stood out in her mind. "Twisting God's Word they speak lies and half truths. Being spiritually alert is hard work for every Christian with all the reminders everywhere that He is rejected and irrelevant at every turn in the hearts of evil wicked people." Those words rang true at every turn for years now.

Amanda tried hard not to be judgmental but lately she found herself at odds with almost everyone. She knows she isn't perfect herself. Her own spiritual life journey has challenged her faith for many years now. Uncertainties stumble into her mind like dark clouds rolling in, blocking out the sunshine.

She silently prayed as she saw her home coming closer in view. "Lord, I pray there is more FOR You and WITH You then there are against You. I pray that the many that want to destroy

You and Your standards and morals are few, a small fraction compared to those who believe. Please keep us safe, safe in the ark of Your protection. I know the harvest is huge and You need me to be strong and brave and bring people to You, but how? I'm so afraid. What about Pickles, she scared me Lord? I froze, I couldn't say a thing............"

Amanda knows that faith is a gift that grows when she uses it. She turns and looks at her husband as she grabs his hand, feeling blessed she smiled and let out a sigh. She is so happy that her husband, even when he is grumpy, loves God. And he serves God no matter what. How did she get so lucky? She sat there with a thankful heart. The eye in the sky shined right above her and was bright in the sky and it calmed her anxious thoughts as they parked the truck and got out. She smiled as she watched Chris open the front door to a well-lit house.

Pickles

Pickles glanced again at the church business card and decided that maybe, just maybe she will give this church a try. She knows her dad would approve. Can she be fearless? Will she be okay?

The teaching on TV hit her hard, as well as the woman's eyes that stood still and talked to her soul. Yes, she will check out her church. As she thinks about the church, she is pretty positive that her neighbor John and his wife go there as well.

He had offered to fix her motorcycle tomorrow. Maybe she will ask him about his church. If he is able to fix her bike, she will be able to go on Sunday. She felt a peace come over her and felt good about her decision. "Thanks God."

1 Corinthians 15:58 (NLT) So, my dear brothers and sisters, be strong and immovable. Always work enthusiastically for the Lord, for you know that nothing you do for the Lord is ever useless.

Proverbs 1:7 (NLT) Fear of the LORD is the foundation of true knowledge, but fools despise wisdom and discipline.

Chapter Sixteen

July 13 2027, Carrie

Carrie moved back to the recliner and noticed a small purple piece of paper on the floor. She reached down to pick it up. It looked like a list of some sort:

Change of heart
Get right with God
Live right for God
Obedience
Don't give anyone an excuse for not accepting God
How will they know?
And on the back, it read:

    Hundreds, thousands, billions have walked this earth. Some have made the decision to get right with God, others didn't. The fact is, they are all gone from here and are either in a good place with God or they chose against Him and are separated from Him forever. Either way they are no longer here on earth. Had anyone reached out to the ones that are gone, before that day?

Behind the Scenes

It has been a few months and what appeared to be initials began appearing at the top of the printouts. Plus a few names she knew as well. But how could that be? The information from the Word of God would be helpful for her friends, but Debbie couldn't risk it, not yet.

She had noticed the two talking in frustration the other day. She tried to move closer to hear, but could only tell the tension was stretched tight and only heard the words "Brain surgery" before she was spotted and they moved on down the hall.

Luke 10:2-3 (NLT) These were his instructions to them: "The harvest is great, but the workers are few. So pray to the Lord who is in charge of the harvest; ask him to send more workers into his fields. Now go, and remember that I am sending you out as lambs among wolves.

Chapter Seventeen

Friday Night Continues

Amanda put the ink into the printer as soon as she got home and started printing off twelve copies. She scribbled a quick note on her purple note pad, tore it off and threw it into her binder, as thoughts for another day.

Locating the box on wheels her husband had bought for her years ago to put all her stuff in for Bible study reminded her of how blessed she was. It was a yellow 18"x 18" plastic box with a pull up handle, much like traveling luggage with wheels. It made bringing all her stuff back and forth to class so much easier. The two coffee pots, cups, coffee, powdered creamer, sugar, spoons, dry erase markers for the board and all the other stuff she decided to bring each month, like her Bible, the lessons, and pens all fit perfectly inside plus of course, some yummy desserts.

Amanda felt like a robot as she scurried around the house putting it all together. She has done this many times before, and probably can do it in her sleep.

She was already exhausted when she finally sat down in the comfy recliner and stared at the TV her husband was watching. She knew she needed to wind down and relax. But the exhaustion almost energized her. I know crazy right? Her mind would not rest with the day's activities still playing in her brain. Like many times before, she got up grabbed a sleeping pill and went to sit back down in the living room even though she knew she should go straight to bed instead.

Tuning out the movie on TV, she concentrated on the one playing in her head. As the Day Turns was the title. The soap opera of her life played over for a rerun of the day. From printer problems, to stubbing her toe, to sleeping and crying and locking herself out, to the sleeping and crying again, to the fight with her husband, to the flat tire, to the old man with the flip phone, to the mobster cashier, to the man standing very close to her in line, to the girl outside of the corner store named Pickles at the pizza joint, to the billboard, to the dark sky with the full moon, to the girl again and her rudeness, to her own life, to her husband and her own daughter and son and then finally it rested on God.

About two hours later she was in the kitchen grabbing a cold piece of pizza and forgetting she had already taken one, she took two more sleeping pills as she watched her husband asleep on the couch.

"Thank You God for him." She said it out-loud and then flashbacks about when they first met kept her thinking as she rested in the bed. Once she pulled up the covers, she was out. Out like a light in the dark dreams of her life, swirling around in the depths of her conscience she recalled the new beginning.

Chapter Eighteen

July 13 2027, Carrie

Carrie went to the very first story at the beginning of the binder. Looking at it, as she flipped through the pages, it appeared to be a long story. She was excited to read it. It had been written some time ago, twenty-six years to be exact. It was titled 'The End' by Amanda....... My own story starts like this:

The End

This story begins in a place where it was all about to end. The Place? Well, the place was somewhere I found myself in. It was ugly, it was dark, it was cold, it was scary and I was alone, with no hope and no future.

As I look back on that place, I realize how far I have come. It's like I'm at the top of that mountain, only now it's different. It's no longer a mountain of fear. Before, it was easy to climb that mountain, it didn't take much, and I really didn't fear it. Although it was fear that led me to it.

My goal was to climb to the top, close my eyes, and just fall. At the time, it seemed to me that it would be so…'freeing'. You know, like, like an accomplishment, to fall and fall, until it was over.

It was really easy to find myself up there on that mountain, looking down, closing my eyes and wanting to just 'freefall'. Not looking back….no past. Not looking ahead….no future. I just wanted it to end. Just disappear over the edge.

I was there at the top of that mountain quite often. Actually, to be honest, I was there most of the time, for most of my life.

This is where my story begins……One day I found myself, stepping over that edge. I was falling and falling and falling, it was getting darker and darker and colder and colder. I felt scared and so alone. And guess what? I made it to the bottom……. but……..it wasn't over. Imagine that, I took the step, AND IT WASN'T OVER!! Here I was, sitting at the bottom of this deep, dark, cold, scary place, in a big empty hole and nothing…..so……I stood up, wanting to fall further, looking for the edge, the end…. only here I was…..rock bottom……AND IT WASN'T OVER.

As I stood there crying, yelling and feeling like such a failure, feeling sorry for myself and feeling like I just can't do anything right. I realized that I chose to step over that edge….I wasn't pushed; I chose to fall….but I also chose and WANTED IT TO END. That was my choice.

BUT GOD SAID "NO……HE HAD A DIFFERENT PLAN FOR ME."

As I stood there unable to truly focus, I wondered why He would deny me this. Why? Why? WHY?

I also realized I had more choices to make. Two really. I could, stay where I was, in this deep, dark, cold, scary place. I could ignore God. I could hide and be invisible to both the world and to God (Who would notice anyway?) I could live this way, after all I already lived there sort of and it didn't take much effort, it was familiar and I was actually getting used to it………or……..I could, if I chose to, I could look up, reach up and ask God and trust God to lift me out of this place. I was sure He would, well pretty sure He would. MMMMMM. I had two choices, you would think it was a no brainer, I mean on one hand I had a dark, cold, and scary place and on the other I had God and all He had to offer.

Well in some ways, it seemed easier to stay put. I had convinced myself that it just made sense. I mean, I wasn't stupid and I did know things about God, Jesus and the Bible. I knew God was loving, caring and forgiving……..but……but……I didn't feel worthy; I didn't feel worthy at all. I didn't feel accepted in this life, so why would God think I was worthy? Why would God accept me? Out of all the people in the world, why would I matter? Why would He even take a second look at me?

Well, anyway, I had heard all this talk about God, Jesus and the Bible and about being baptized and about living right for God…..so, I said to myself….. "Ha that's it. I will get baptized and then God will forgive me and He will put an end to all of this, the next time I step over that edge."

Ya know I still didn't get it!!!!! And again, I found myself at the bottom of this cold, dark, deep, lonely, scary place and IT STILL HADN'T ENDED! Again I stood up, wanting to fall further, and again here I was, 'rock bottom'. Only this time it seemed worse. I didn't like it, yet I found myself there again and again and again. And each time I didn't feel quite right.

I thought of all the things in my life and all the choices I had made that had brought me to this place. I could name quite a few circumstances that had landed me right where I was. All the decisions and choices I myself had made. Bad choices. The IF ONLYS and the WHAT IFS. It didn't matter, I chose it and I wanted it over. (One thing I am; is stubborn. If I put my mind to something there is no changing it.) Well again, God said "NO…….HE HAD A DIFFERENT PLAN FOR ME!!"

I was so confused, I laughed, I cried and then like most stubborn people I started to argue and question. "How can You use me? I have no purpose, I'm worthless, I'm nothing, and I'm a nobody." I argued. "I want to be invisible, I'm here, but I don't want anyone to notice me, not like they would anyway." I said in a matter of fact sarcastic statement.

Then I dropped to my knees, exhausted, and oh so tired. God gave me some rest. And I rested. Then one day I opened my Bible. And God said it all to me. He spoke through the pages. As I flipped from page to page, I saw so much. God spoke to me and was telling me….. "Oh my child you have so much to learn, you have so much value to Me. You are worth everything to Me. I have a plan for you. I love you and I care for you. I will rescue you and I will teach you. You will be strong. I will give you courage to face each day. You, my child are never alone, you are not an orphan, I Am your Father, and I love you dearly."

As I sat there reading and listening to God and His Word, I started crying (I know, shocker right….I mean I cry at all the little and the big things in life.) As I cried, I started to believe the words written to me. Could this be true? Could God love me this much? Could He use me for His purpose? Do I really have value? Does He really have a plan for me? So many questions, and I had all the answers right here, in this Book, in His Book, the Bible right here in my hands. But how do I begin to let it impact me? Where was my hope, my faith, my future?

Then as days went by, I began to notice all the people God put in place. He sent people into my life, into my path. Some just talked with me, others prayed for me, some pointed to scripture and other just smiled and nodded. I began to see the light, just to fall back down again, and like I said, it didn't take much.

God didn't give up on me. I had gotten right with Him, by accepting Jesus as my Lord and Savior into my life. I was baptized, submerged under the water and raised to live a new life. God held on to me. He never left me, even in my doubts He kept showing me, in His words and in His love. He kept sending people into my life. He even used strangers and people I hardly knew to guide me. He was working very hard to rescue me.

As I struggled, I noticed something else, something so real. As God worked so hard to save me, I was fighting with something else as well. Actually, to be honest here I was being pulled in two different directions. One was pulling me up and the other was pulling me down. I was drowning. I would reach up and grab His hand, get a breath of air, only to go back down. I was in a battle for my soul, a battle for my life.

It was strange, I began to not only know who God is, but I also began to know who satan is and what he wanted. And what he wanted wasn't pretty; satan is pure evil, and he wanted me, and he wanted me bad. He is a liar, a cheater and a murderer. He really is that roaring lion, seeking to devour God's kids. He loves to go after the weak and he had his eye on me. Actually, he had a firm grip on me. He wanted me to end it all. He wanted to win and he wanted to win badly; and he had convinced me that I wanted it too.

As I sit here now reflecting on that battle, I feel a sense of victory, a victory that goes to God. God is like my shining knight, riding on the white horse, coming just in time to scoop me up and rescue me, satan is no match for Him, the Almighty, our Lord, our God, and our King.

Once God showed me who satan was and what he wanted, I made the choice, the choice to really follow and obey God. I won't kid you, it hasn't been easy and satan still tries to trick me and confuse me, but God has made me stronger just like He said He would do. Even when satan tries to throw my past at me, I now remind him of his future.....burn baby burn!

Carrie took a deep breath. Her mom's story was so horrible and wonderful at the same time. How come she never knew this about her mom? Her mom always seemed so put together, so full of faith with positive emotions the whole time she has been alive. Her mom loved her and she was always telling her how proud she was of her. Why didn't her mom share this with her? Carrie picked up the binder and continued the story of The End.

It's funny how I sometimes view this. It's like I'm trapped in a room with a door inside my heart, lots of doors with lots of locks on them. If I unlocked one lock I'd feel less protected. And if I unlocked another I'd feel more vulnerable. Then another I would feel scared and insecure. I pictured God on the outside, knocking to get into my heart. I would slowly open the door, only a crack because the chain lock was still on. He could peak in, but couldn't quite get in. My room was empty, I felt empty until one day I decided to really trust God. I needed Him, and I unlocked the chain lock and let Him in.

Something unexpected happened. .... I thought I was protected in that room, no one could get in, and I was safe. But

July 13 2027, Carrie

it all changed when I opened the door and allowed God to enter. I suddenly felt more protected in a totally different way, like I had big arms around me, holding me, comforting me, loving me and caring for me. I felt more alive. I felt more at peace.

The room began to fill with windows, light shined in and soon God and I were dancing around opening more locked doors and filling those rooms with light and life. So much comforting light. More windows, more possibilities, more plans....it was all opening up to me. Rooms I didn't even know I had. I still have a long way to go and a lot more to learn, but I'm learning to love every day and enjoying every minute, as we open new doors.

At least I'm not where I used to be. These days I thank God with all my heart and all my soul. God is awesome. He loves me, He values me. And no matter what the world throws at me, He is there protecting me and caring for me. He is my hiding place. He has given me everything. He has given His Son to die for me and my sins. He has given me the Bible to read so that I can know Him and understand how to live my life. He gave me a very blessed life....one that I almost threw away. He gave me love and worth and I praise Him for that. He has given me reason to live. I love the place I am in now!

The Place? Well the place I find myself in now is warm, loving, bright and full of life. I can't express the joy and peace that I feel. Even when I mess up, which I still do, God surrounds me with His peace and understanding with His love and most of all, His forgiveness.

The journey was rough at first, but definitely worth it. I still like I said have a few roadblocks to overcome, but when I do encounter them, God helps me to get around them or over them or we just plow right thru them together. He is there all the way.

I give no thoughts to the one with the little 's' who tried to take this all away from me, the one who kept me blind, the one who was out to destroy me and my relationship with God.

I can feel God's love. HE WAS RIGHT, I AM NOT ALONE AND HIS PLAN WAS DIFFERENT THAN MINE. HIS WAS THE BEST PLAN.

I can now climb that mountain with confidence and 'be free' with no fear, but with hope and a future. I love how God works thru me, even on my bad days, He is always with me. (I'm not perfect, and still a bit stubborn.....well maybe a lot stubborn.) HE IS ALWAYS WITH ME!

I now want to be His light. I want to shine for Him to the world. Glory be to Him. God is the only way. Thank you Jesus. Good always defeats evil. There is always a reason to get up and fight the fight. Had I not done that, who knows where I would be?

As my story comes to an end, what I thought was going to be "The End" really was a "New Beginning".

Psalm 68:19-20 Praise the Lord; praise God our savior! For each day, he carries us in his arms. Our God is a God who saves! The Sovereign LORD rescues us from death.

Written in April 2001

Behind the Scenes

The words in the chart seemed to be coded, but from what Debbie could tell, he thought the brain machine was not working. She began to close the file to put it away before she was caught snooping and noticed that more tests were scheduled, and marked 'urgent'.

Chapter Nineteen

The World and The Church

Christian churches are being destroyed little by little, in fact the last few years had been quite challenging for all churches. So far, Amanda's church has been under attack but not destroyed. 2020 was devastating for many of them. Many had closed down because of the pressures and mandates the government had put on them due to a man-made virus. The little 's' man has won many battles over the last several years since that 2020 disaster. But in some ways, he has lost quite few as well. Eyes were opened. If you looked. For a short time, everyone was able to look behind the curtain and see some of little 's' man's tactics. Some did nothing, some did try to make changes and speak out, some just ignored what they saw and kept going the way they were before without any concern, and some just didn't care.

Amanda and her family have been attending the same church for over twenty-seven years now. It is 2027 and the world has been changing, right before their eyes. People are changing. So far, God has kept her church safe and they are still meeting there, although some are turning away, afraid of the violence against God's people.

Amanda's church, the CCC Church chose to step up and make a difference in their community and in their town. Even though they had always been helping in the community they stepped up their game in full force because as their Pastor puts it: 'this is their generation to make a difference in all areas.' Some of the congregation began working hard on the school boards, some chose politics and got involved in the voting and elections, some studied and taught basic history of America and of the Founding Fathers, and some got more involved in their community through helping with diaper drives and furniture drives for families with children who needed more. The ones that were teachers involved themselves in more hands on with the younger generation and teen programs, and some stepped it up on social media with short clips of how far we have gotten from God and how we can get back.

Over the last few years minds had been hardened and set against God everywhere. Like in the time of Moses, only worse. Why can't people see how God protects His people? Why do they not want the true and only God? Why is the world so blind? There are so many churches that are crumbling under the pressure and teaching lies instead of God's truth. They are compromising and rationalizing their stances. Thankfully her church, will not crumble in fear, they will always teach God's truth and never sugar coat it. Amanda knows that her Pastor is definitely a super brave-heart.

Amanda's personal fears of the world cripples her in many ways, she keeps it hidden so well that those around her don't notice, and much is unseen in her daily life. As a teacher of God's Word to women in her Bible study, she holds it together with an appearance of pure faith. Her husband sees her fears but doesn't talk about them. Knowing she has always been that way, especially after she had Carrie, their daughter who is now twenty-four and living on her own, only five miles away, and Christopher their son who is a few years younger and also living on his own.

"Ya know Chris, I wish we hadn't taught the kids to be responsible adults, living on their own."

"Why?" He scrunched his face, "It's a good thing. They are adults now, and we raised them right."

"I know I just want to know if they are home, safe and the doors locked every night."

"You know babe, God watches over them, like He does us.... you got to trust that, okay?"

"I know, I do....I just miss them. I know it's a good thing and I do know God is with them. We did a good job raising them............ but the world is scarier than when we were their age."

"Yaaaaa probably the same. It's not much different. We just know more, because of social media and the more truthful news stations. They are adults and they are okay. It is not good to worry. God says it's not good to worry, so stop okay!"

"I know....I know, it's easier said than done."

Amanda has gotten worse the last few years and her fears upset his life at times. But he loves her and he would do anything for her. He has told her over-and-over again to stop watching the news when he is at work, but she wants to know what's going on in the world yet she doesn't want to know, and half the time she wishes she would have just listened to him and not turned on the TV. It really frightens her and even gives her nightmares. He, himself only watches the news after she goes to bed.

The government doesn't seem to care about the Nation. They only care about the money they are making and the power it gives them. Amanda doesn't understand why they want the power, what does it truly do for them or their families? It's not like they will take the money and power with them when they die. And someday they all will die and then they will know the truth and they will bow down to an even higher power.

When Amanda does go out to the store, she hardly makes eye contact with people. She has trained herself to focus on their necks. Forever trying to figure out if someone is male or female is a game she plays; always looking for the Adam's apple. Much of the younger world has decided that there are no such people as boys or girls; there are only 'neutrals'. They try to look plain; they try to look neither boy nor girl. In addition, some do the opposite; girls dress like boys and boys like girls is another one of the 'new norms', the new fad with the younger generation. Males and females that choose to be what God created them to be, in their mother's womb, are considered to be the abnormal ones. Common sense seems to have disappeared. Welcome to crazy town.

Rebellion is good according to them and the more evil you are the more you fit in and anything goes. If you belong to a Christian church then you are the bad person, the intolerant one, and the hater. The world now accepts bad behavior and wrong doings without even a blink of an eye. It's very sad to see it in this downward spiral. Most Christians are silent and say nothing to the world around them. They are just playing the game and praying that Jesus comes back soon, very soon.

The world had changed so much in just a short time and it was only about three years ago in 2024, that Amanda had noticed that things were maybe too far gone. Abortions sought after, same sex lifestyles were on the rise, and the most sickening was that parents were choosing to change their child's gender at very early ages. Doctors, even checking boxes that say 'undecided' when a child is born, very sick and disturbing to say the least. Intolerance toward Christians and God's truth spit upon. The use of scripture in daily lives discouraged, reading the Bible, frowned upon. Tampering with food, open use of drugs and drug abuse, child endangerment, killings, rape, hatred of authority, and disregard for all life whether human or animal and much more are all orders of the day everywhere in the world. The farther people get from God the worse it gets. The world is in much need of a Godly Revival everywhere.

The Nation is falling into much sin and chaos, and now it's hard to tell if someone is a boy or girl, without looking for the Adam's apple. It's almost too much to take in. The change happened almost overnight, even though it was noticed decades ago as a steady decline in morals and standards.

A quote from her Pastor rings true, "Only those who know their sin and feel the brokenness when they repent will know the truth, and then nothing can separate them from God." Truth, God's truth is so important. God's truth will set you free.

Amanda loves that Jesus prayed for the disciples and for us. He asked God to teach us His truth, to make us holy by His truth, to teach us His word, which is truth. It is only through His truth that we can see the right way to go.

Amanda knows that if good people do nothing then evil will triumph. Evil will accomplish its purpose when we do nothing to stop it. Many are trying, but the wrong side is so corrupt and they cheat and lie.

God knew what he was doing Amanda thought with almost a chuckle as she thought about the 'neutral' at the store last month. What she thought was a guy, with a butch haircut ended up being a gal in the feminine hygiene section of the store picking out sanitary napkins. Things you can't change when deciding you want to identify as a boy. "You're still a girl" was what Amanda was thinking as she watched her go by.

The drugs many of them are using to change over their normal body chemistry is causing severe consequences for their bodies and already the medical field has to explain the increase of cancer and infertility in these young 'neutrals', as well as violent outbursts of emotions although no one really seems to care. It saddens her that there is a whole generation of kids that are so lost and mixed up. If only they knew God. How will they know? How could they know? She knows that little 's' is working overtime, putting in extra hours and time into his plan to destroy the next generation. He never gives up and honestly, he attacks everyone, he doesn't care who you are, whether you are a Christian or not, he just wants to win.

Amanda wished she could have been bolder and actually say something to this poor mixed up girl in the women's section. Maybe she could just say, "Jesus loves you" and hand the girl a card to the church. But those words would not come out of her mouth because the fear held them back. Christians get beat up for less than that. Instead, she just prayed for her. How sad it would be for her to leave this world without Jesus, and in the wrong body. There's a whole generation that just doesn't want to listen.

Amanda thought about Paul in the Bible. He was bold in a world that hated Christians. Persecution was coming from all sides during the first century and Christians were hunted down and killed. Amanda wasn't sure if the world was actually killing Christians yet or just trying to tear down their lives and destroy everything in the world that pointed to God.

"It's getting worse with every passing year Lord. The people are so hateful and so evil that it seems like there is no way to reach them." She declared to God.

Amanda decided a while ago, that reaching them needs to be done by someone braver who could stand and speak with boldness and confidence. She was not today's 'Paul'. She decided that she would serve those that are already His. But why was she feeling so disconnected from them too lately? Why was she feeling confused and foggy in her thoughts?

She knows this way of thinking is wrong. God will give her the courage. Maybe there is a reason that God is showing her, her own fears. Maybe if she just trusted that the words that came from her mouth were from Him. She feels like Moses sometimes, unable to speak.

A majority of Christians in her town watch the one station left on TV with the TV Preacher Man. Amanda has watched it a few times and he is pretty good, but he's always telling his viewers to just forgive the world and those in it. Just forgive everything. Forgive them when they wrong you.

It's been very hard for people to do this in the crazy world we are in. Amanda herself has researched the Bible about this subject, and did a lesson for her Bible study as well. She read that Jesus said in Luke 17:3-4.... "If another believer sins, rebuke that person; then *if* there is repentance, forgive. Even if that person wrongs you seven times a day and each time turns again and *asks* forgiveness, you must forgive."

'Well, there you go', they say....just forgive, and do it seven times if needed. But is that what the Bible actually said? Amanda is sure that Jesus said that *'IF'* a person *asks* for forgiveness, you are to forgive them....but what if they don't ask for that forgiveness? What if they are never sorry for the wrong that they have done to you?

God's Word says, 'If they ask'.......He doesn't say to 'just always forgive' even if they don't ask. People have a hard enough time 'just' forgiving bad things done to them. So, if there is no repentance or gesture of remorse or asking for forgiveness afterwards then we are just forgiving a bad behavior or action and it really messes us up when we are told to 'just forgive' them, no matter what.

How is it even done, this 'just forgive' everything no matter what? What about the consequences for wrong behavior, if we just forgive for no reason?

If we are to forgive like God forgives, which He does when we repent and we ask for that forgiveness then we need to be asking 'how' does and 'when' does God forgive us. Logically, does God 'just' forgive us? Does He just forgive everybody, no matter what? Is everybody going to Heaven even though they did not repent and ask for forgiveness and accept Jesus? Amanda answers these questions with a definite "No."

We have to *ask* for forgiveness with a repentant heart and then He will forgive us. He doesn't expect us to do something that He doesn't do. He loves everyone, yes He does. Jesus died for everyone. Correct, even while we were sinners. How do we get right with Him? We believe, we confess, we repent and we *ask* for the forgiveness of our sins and as an adult, baptism. An adult decision as in Acts 2:38. Then we receive the gift of the Holy Spirit.

Amanda has found over the many years, that she must let God handle the grievances she has if someone wrongs her and if the person who wronged her doesn't ask for her forgiveness. She can't hold on to it and be bitter, mad or upset. She releases it, as best as possible to God so that her heart can be healed. She feels lighter when she does. She realized that she cannot WILL someone to be sorry and she cannot change their heart or actions or even force them to be sorry and ask for forgiveness. She can only pray about it and move forward. It's more of a release to God about whatever it was. Because if she doesn't than the weight will pull her down, she will stay mad, hurt, or bitter and that will or could destroy her, just as bad as 'just' forgiving. She mustn't let her own sins or others weigh her down, it just builds a wall between her and God, and that is not ok.

It has taken her many years to figure this out. The bad things that happened to her that were never fixed by a person who never asked for that forgiveness are now at Gods feet and He has cleared her mind of them and has helped her to let go and move forward and even restore a few relationships.

It's amazing what God can do when we release and turn these things over to Him. He heals us in ways that we cannot do ourselves. We can't change the past, but we can move forward with God's peace. Not the world's peace, which is quite different. God's peace, that is calming in the storm. She smiles as she thinks of the picture hanging in the bathroom at church, the one with the raging ocean around the lighthouse. If you look close at it there is a man standing in the doorway of the lighthouse. That's how she pictures the peace of God.......calm in the middle of the storm, protected by Him.

"Please let me have a mind for wisdom and look to You for knowledge and understanding. Amen."

Amanda realized that even though there are many evil people, there are many good ones too. Her life as a Christian is so different, but she must try to reach those that just don't know about God, Jesus and the Bible. She realizes that just because they may not know, they aren't all evil. There are many people out there that are awesome human beings, who just don't know about our awesome God. "How will they know?" Enters her mind.

Proverbs 3:5-6 (NLT) Trust in the LORD with all your heart; do not depend on your own understanding. Seek his will in all you do, and he will show you which path to take.

1 John 2:6 (NLT) Those who say they live in God should live their lives as Jesus did.

Matthew 7:13-14 (NLT) "You can enter God's Kingdom only through the narrow gate. The highway to hell is broad, and its gate is wide for the many who choose that way. But the gateway to life is very narrow and the road is difficult, and only a few ever find it.

Chapter Twenty

July 13 2027, Carrie

Carrie didn't want to stop reading her mom's binder, but her eyes were getting so tired and watery. *Just a few minutes is all I need.* She closed them and was quickly asleep. When she finally opened her eyes, fifty minutes had passed. Still no one was home so she picked another reading from her mom's social page. It was a letter to the Tucson Council Members:

This is on my mind......ladies on my Real Time Post page, it's time to start standing up for the unborn....this is my letter to our Council..... please feel free to copy and paste it and send copies to your state Senators, Governors, Mayors, Council Members etc.....it was in response to me sending a letter from Family American Times and they responded back to me, of course not the way I had hoped....so I wrote this second letter....it may be helpful for any of you who would like to try and get some common sense values into the heads of the people we put in office. We the people need to speak up if we want to turn our world BACK to God!! God Bless You and God Bless America.

To all the City Council Members,

This letter is in response to the reply you sent to me a few days ago.

I am very concerned that some women and some men are fighting for the right to KILL their unwanted, un-born babies on an "ALTER OF CONVEINENCE". Who is going to fight for that baby that is so easily disposed of? Are you? It doesn't sound like it.....maybe you are in such a position for such a time as this.... Every vote matters and this does matter. The way that you vote matters, not only on this subject, but many others. I do agree with you that there should be a good health care system; but there already is good health care system in place for women.

All this mumbo jumbo of a response from you is just a long way of saying you support abortion because you feel it is a "CHOICE" that a woman, her family and her doctor should be able to make, no matter what.

Maybe there should be new options on the plate.......Like.... if you don't want a baby, use protection!! Heck, you give out free drugs to drug addicts, bought with our tax money. Why not free condoms? Or maybe we should be funding a woman's choice to have her tubes tied at whatever age she would like it done or a man having a vasectomy, instead of either of them having to wait until they are 35. Tubes tied or vasectomy instead of funding the KILLING an un-born child in the womb, thru abortion.

Or how about we fund a hysterectomy *beforehand* instead of an abortion *after* a woman is pregnant? Pro-choice? How about if you don't want a baby living in your body then have the hysterectomy, that way no one dies. How about instead of pushing abortions, we push the hysterectomies. Sorry I'm repeating myself, but it is a much better choice.

July 13 2027, Carrie

I know, you're gonna say....welll they may change their mind later in life. To that, I say....wellll they may be mentally and emotionally messed up for the rest of their life for choosing abortion (KILLING their un-born baby) too. If a woman CHOOSES to have a hysterectomy, or her tubes tied, how about the government funds that instead of funding abortions. At least one option is not MURDERING another human being.

Or maybe we should make ADOPTION easier for parents who do want children instead of it costing every bit of their savings. In addition, how about we teach our children to VALUE life...all life..... at a young age in school? There has to be better options available than KILLing an un-born baby, at any stage.

You ALL are in a position that can do something good and meaningful. You can side on the RIGHT side in history and can get others to do the same. You are all supposedly, smart people who were not aborted by your mother's and all of you have had a chance at life. Why can't the babies who are being killed in large numbers live their lives as well? It's ok to have a conscience and change your mind to FIGHTING FOR life... all life, which starts at conception of a growing un-born baby.

These precious babies have a God-given right to their life. Life, liberty and the pursuit of happiness BEGINS with life. We should be DEFENDING life from conception to natural death. It is a scientific fact that life begins at conception, its common sense that nothing grows unless it is living. With all the technology, we now have with 3D ultra sounds, we KNOW the baby is developing and breathing and has its own set of fingerprints very early. To say that the fetus is a person ONLY IF the mother wants it and it is NOT if the mother doesn't want it ...IS NOT SCIENCE. And it is not health care either.

Pro-choice isn't helping women and it certainly isn't helping the un-born baby. You say women should have a choice with their body....giving MURDER a nice name like "CHOICE" doesn't make it ok..... Saying abortion is healthcare is wrong.... that is opposite of healthcare. .... Why would you support this practice....this "ALTER of convenience"? The fact is that 98% of abortions are due to the fact that, the mother just does not want the baby. This is so unthinkable. What happened to our society, where women think it is ok to MURDER a growing baby. Why would you support this? Where does your soul live? Babies should never be thought of as disposable.

All Babies Matter.....Thank you, Amanda

Carrie was surprised her mom took such a stand and spoke out to these people in high positions. Or maybe she is just brave behind her pen as she writes, Carrie smiled. There was so much of her mom that she did not know. She only knows of the loving moments she has had all these years. Carrie has no doubt that her mom has loved being a mom. She knows that her mom has felt blessed by God. No wonder she speaks out about this.

"There's no greater joy than being a mom, every stage of your life Carrie and your brother's has been a blessing to me." Carrie again smiled at how much her mom has always told her what a blessing she is and how proud she was of her, throughout her years.

July 13 2027, Carrie

Behind the Scenes

Debbie left the room and walked slowly to the drinking fountain deep in thought with many questions, took a drink and stood back up just in time to see Dr. Prong enter the room she had just left. "Wow that was close."

The doctor did a quick sweep of the room, his chair seemed to have been moved and the desk drawer was slightly open. He pulled his keys from his pocket, locked the drawer and made a call.

Proverbs 6:16-19 (NLT) There are six things the LORD hates— no, seven things he detests: haughty eyes, a lying tongue, hands that kill the innocent, a heart that plots evil, feet that race to do wrong, a false witness who pours out lies, a person who sows discord in a family.

Chapter Twenty-One

Silvia and Ruth

Silvia was the only one today at the prayer meeting that didn't have much to say. Or I should say; she like me didn't have a chance to say.

Her adopted daughter seventeen year old Ruth, who usually comes with her to class, was in the hospital. She didn't elaborate she just said, "Please pray for Ruth, she's not feeling well."

Silvia, being a foster mom, has many situations in her home. One of the boys, the twelve year old, has been dabbling with drugs, hanging out with the wrong kids and she had caught him stealing money from her purse the night before. But all she could think about was her Ruth. She hasn't had the strength needed to deal with the other kids for a while now. All her energy was spent on Ruth, her sweet adopted daughter, who was lying in a hospital bed with cancer, waiting for a miracle. Hospice was right around the corner and she felt it.

Silvia didn't plan to say anything about Ruth's cancer which had been in remission but now has come back full force. They need a miracle. She asked for prayers for Ruth in her soft-spoken voice almost ready to burst into tears, but they didn't seem to notice today.

She needed the prayers probably more than anyone else there she thought, but instead focused on the others as she asked Mary Jane, "Why do they hate you?" Even that seemed to go unnoticed, except for the rude look by Mary Jane, as she repeated that she did not know.

She wanted to be heard, but didn't dare speak up. Mary Jane could be over bearing at times and she seemed to be striving for attention over the newest lady, Susie. Too bad Old lady Nell wasn't there; her stare can put anyone in their place. For a moment, she laughed to herself as she pictured that in her mind. It took her thoughts off Ruth for a moment.

When she bounced back to reality, Mary Jane was saying the closing prayer from the top of her chair and everyone was getting up, grabbing cookies and heading out the door. After excusing herself to the restroom, she started to leave and decided to drive home first, get some food and check on the boys before visiting with Ruth for the rest of the day.

As she walked thru the parking lot, she saw that Mary Jane and Susie were still talking to each other near their cars that were parked under the shading solar panels. She was so hot that she hurried to her own car and quickly turned on the AC full blast as well as her radio.

Thinking about Ruth and the fact that Ruth didn't want anyone to worry or to let anyone else know how bad she had gotten, she quickly waved goodbye and headed home. Maybe she should have shared her worries of maybe losing Ruth to cancer crept into her thoughts as she drove away.

Ruth was again in the hospital and Silvia wanted to hurry to check on things at home and hurry back to Ruth's side and share the new stories with her. Ruth loved people and she was such a great listener, she really cared about the stories that went along with the prayer requests.

Driving faster than normal, Silvia continued to feel uneasy about Ruth's condition. She knows it will kill her someday and she is afraid it will be soon. She cleared her mind, and spent her ten-minute drive back home in prayer for Ruth as well as for each of the ladies that were there today and a quick prayer for those who missed this important time together. She prayed that God would brighten the darkness of uncertainty for each lady with His light. She knew in her heart they all loved and cared for each other. They all had stuff going on, just like everyone else in the world. The one thing they all had in common was God. And she knows that God hears the prayers for His kids, from His kids, which is why she prays so often.

Silvia's own journey had taken her down that road of uncertainty. Her walk with God through her life has hit a few roadblocks and potholes that's for sure, but she knows that laying her worries at the feet of Jesus, as she pictures it in her mind, is the only way to get through each day, one at a time. Each day is a precious gift, and each minute she is able to be with Ruth becomes another most treasured moment.

Ruth had gotten right with God a few years ago before she started coming to class with her mom, around the time she had found out about the cancer. Silvia has done everything for Ruth over the years to help her and now Ruth has begged her to help her find her real mom.

Silvia felt sad about the search, but she does understand why Ruth feels like she needs to know why her real mom gave her up for adoption before she dies. Silvia tries to be supportive about this as she does what she can to help with the search.

Ruth

In Ruth's short time on earth, she has known the love of a family that shows her how much they care and love her. She is so thankful. Silvia has always been honest with her and has given her a full time mom and lots of love. Silvia and her husband Grant have been truthful and straightforward about the adoption as far back as Ruth can remember. She has never felt unloved or uncared for. But since the cancer has come back, she feels she has very little time left and wants to have some sort of a relationship with her real mom, the one that she has never known.

Ruth's favorite line from a song she heard about a year ago, popped into Silvia's head as she drove and prayed….. "We must walk with Him every day, every minute….oh yea that's the way, and always know He is with us….oh yea it's the ticket." She smiled as she pictured Ruth in her joyful voice singing those words almost daily, since hearing the song. "We must walk with Him every day, every minute ….oh yea that's the way, and always know He is with us…….oh yea it's the ticket." She felt joyful and at peace, as she turned from prayer into song as she pulled into her driveway.

Isaiah 40:31 (NLT) But those who trust in the LORD will find new strength. They will soar high on wings like eagles. They will run and not grow weary. They will walk and not faint.

Chapter Twenty-Two

July 13 2027, Carrie

Carrie continued to flip pages and read more stories. She particularly liked the RTP (Real Time Posts) that her mom posted for her friends on social media as she started to read another:

The sun is still not out....it's a crazy rainy day.....I am home today, took a vacation day. Spending time with God in the quietness of my home wondering as I read my Bible.....who will lead the people back? Back to God. Our Nation, our world seems to not care. Yet God tells us we are to live for Him......He is our leader.

But why do they not see....the gloom in the day, the thunder in the sky, the cold wet tears from above, washing out the path ahead........ "YOU are the light of the world.......when our world, our Nation dishonors You..... when they reject and look away from You......I WILL HONOR YOU" .....Words of a song, from my church enters my mind.

My family, friends and RTP people....join me in praying for America and for leaders who will lead the people back....back to God. Honor God in everything you do and in everything you say…….we the people, God's people, will play a part in leading them back….each of us needs to stand and say….. "Jesus, lead me, so I may lead others to You"…….There is a reason and it starts with us caring about Him and our Nation ….everyone matters to Him.

So go dance in the rain, shout from the rooftops, and make a splash in the puddles, because He is the light of the world, the light in you….now go shine in the rain!!!!

Ya I know, sometimes ya gotta put up with some rain in order to see His rainbow. What's even more awesome……the light from the sun as it shines through the clouds and onto the land with the rainbow in the sky….just watch, God's rainbow, His promise, it will come, it will light up the path, the road for you to follow…….God Bless You and God Bless America.

Behind the Scenes

Debbie had a pile of printouts all thrown into her sock drawer that she had collected over the last few months. She decided she had better sort them by dates and put the ones with names at the top in their own piles. She went to the garage to grab an empty box to carry them to the table to work on them before heading to work. The more she looked, the more she noticed a pattern. She grabbed a calendar. She feels she may have overlooked something. Could the brain of the machine really print the thoughts of her most precious patient?

Chapter Twenty-Three

Amanda and Mary Jane

This particular meeting everyone was more chatty than usual. In their pursuit to speak, they seemed to only tell half of their actual stories to the group. I know this for fact, but I'm not sure how. Those personal stories all had more details to tell.

It wasn't that long ago that Mary Jane had told me more about her situation with her family in private.

As usual, she only tells us that her family hates her but never tells us why. For two years now, she has asked for prayers about this, but always changes the subject when questioned about it. And lately she says she will be homeless if they didn't help her. She has been very clear that they will not help her and says that she didn't know why.

But I know there is more to her story. I know that three years ago her family had disowned her. I know because she told me, she had confessed to me for some reason. But why did she tell me, I always thought that Nell was her best friend?

Her drug abuse mixed with her drinking was too much for them to bear. I was surprised by that because I had known her for a very long time and had no idea she abused drugs. She said it had started about ten years earlier. Although she did have to admit that it really started back when her own children were little. It was just a little in the beginning to help her get through the hard work that was needed on the ranch.

She just recently decided to get rid of the horses and cows because she could no longer care for them. It was just too much for her to handle. She confessed that even though she has lightened her load, she still has her whiskey to help her through her days, and forget her pain, loneliness and betrayal.

Mary Jane

Mary Jane is a tall stout woman with long black hair. She always wears her pink cowgirl hat and pink cowgirl boots as if to try to soften her appearance, or to maybe take away the fact that, she can be such a bossy, controlling, pushy thing. She is visibly a tough lady on the outside with tanned thick skin and a thick tough character as well to match. Most of the time, Mary Jane is not happy unless she get her way. Plus, bonus I might add, no one was going to get *in* her way either.

At sixty-five years old, she is still a tough rancher even if she did abuse drugs to help her through her painful day. With the cows and horses gone and with only chickens to tend to she spends most of her time looking at pictures of her family. Her lost family was gone and they probably wanted her gone too.

The Will she had written up a few years ago was sitting on the table. She left everything to Darleen, her granddaughter, who at this time was only ten years old.

Looking down at the picture of Darleen in her rodeo outfit at age five made her feel sad and lonely. "I need to hang in there for a few more years." Eight years she thought as she swallowed her pain pills with a shot of whiskey. Oh how she loves her whiskey.

She was thinking of the day her daughter caught her driving with whiskey on her breath as she drove up to her house to drop off Darleen. Her daughter went crazy and banned her from the family.

After being pulled over by her police officer friend John, she had gone home, flushed all her pain pills down the toilet and dumped all the whiskey down the drain. However, it didn't help and over the years, it slowly crept back into her life.

The pain of losing her family was heartbreaking. Her daughter Cindy flat out said she would never forgive her and never wanted to see her again. The last fight reminded her everyday how far she had fallen, as she reached up to touch the deep scar on her cheek.

Her journey, since becoming a Christian has definitely been a rocky one and she herself was the one throwing rocks into the path she walks. The boulders that block her way are the very ones that crush her dreams.

"GET OUT AND NEVER COME BACK, AS A MATTER OF FACT, JUST DIE!!" Cindy yelled at the top of her lungs. Hate filled every bone of her body. This was the last straw and she was not going to budge. "ARE YOU CRAZY, DRIVING MY DAUGHTER IN YOUR CONDITION….NEVER AGAIN AND I MEAN IT MOM, NEVER AGAIN….NOW GO!!"

"NOW YOU LISTEN HERE CINDY…..I'M FINE!" Mary Jane yelled back as she stumbled over the small cactus statue near the mailbox.

"YOU MAKE ME SICK, HOW DARE YOU DRIVE LIKE THAT." Then glaring at her daughter, she yelled, "DARLEEN GET IN THE HOUSE."

Mary Jane gave Darleen a *'don't you dare tell your mom'* look about the sidewalk she ran over on the way there. The look Mary Jane gave little seven year old Darleen made her lower her eyes to the ground scared as she rushed inside.

"Darleen says you're moving, where you going?" She asked with a slight slur and smile.

"None of your business, you will never see us again, now get out of here." Cindy said with a lower voice so that she would not bring any attention from the neighbors.

"I'M NOT GOING ANYWHERE UNTIL YOU TELL ME." Mary Jane took a step forward and grabbed Cindy's arm. Cindy picked up a decorative rock she had sitting on top of the mailbox and smacked Mary Jane on the cheek without hesitation or even thinking about stopping herself. It cut her cheek and blood started to fall from her face. Mary Jane's first thought was *'good thing this whiskey is working'* as she reached up to put pressure on the deep two inch long cut.

Again Cindy began to yell, "YOU'RE PULLING THE SAME CRAP YOU DID WHEN I WAS HER AGE…..YOU'RE NOT GONNA DO IT TO HER, AS FAR AS I'M CONCERNED YOU ARE DEAD TO US, AS YOU ARE TO DAD…..I'll never forgive you for pushing him away….NOW GO!!!!" Cindy was so angry, as she dropped the rock and pointed for her mom to leave. She then turned and went inside and locked her door.

"YOU CAN'T DO THIS CINDY SUE, I'LL BE BACK AND I WILL SEE DARLEEN." Mary Jane yelled at the top of her lungs. Cindy watched her get into her truck and drive away. She looked around at all the packed boxes and then called the police. She was done with her mom, done forever. She couldn't wait to move and switch Darleen to a new school.

Mary Jane found an old towel on the floor of her pickup to soak up the blood from the cut as she drove away. "Help me get home God, I really need a drink." She muttered.

Amanda

I was literally shocked by the confession from Mary Jane. I remained quiet as MJ said she was better for a short while, but was again a mess and needed to get it together. She really didn't want any help doing so, just wanted to confess for some reason. Maybe she needed that in order to move forward.

Maybe we all need closure on things in our life to move forward. Some people blurt out all the bad, some write it down and some just pray to God about it, trust, and know that He will forgive them so they can move forward. Our past has a way of showing up when we don't want it to. Little 's' man makes sure of that. I know that the past is the past and we cannot change it. I also know that we must leave that baggage of wrongs behind us. The bag of sins must be thrown away like garbage. But we also must replace the bad with some good.

I felt I should give council to Mary Jane about this, but as usual, Mary Jane spoke it and she was done and gone before I could even form the words that might be helpful. Thanking God in my mind, I was able to form the prayers for Mary Jane, and I prayed them.

1 John 1:9 (NLT) But if we confess our sins to him, he is faithful and just to forgive us our sins and to cleanse us from all wickedness.

Romans 12:2 (NLT) Don't copy the behavior and customs of this world, but let God transform you into a new person by changing the way you think. Then you will learn to know God's will for you, which is good and pleasing and perfect.

Chapter Twenty-Four

July 13 2027, Carrie

Carrie decided to go to the backyard and sit in the gazebo. Oh how she loved her moms backyard. Full of cactus gardens and fake sunflowers in pots, and if you looked closely, you can find little fairy gardens here and there. She smiled at how her mom made it all work. It was comforting and a wonderful place to sit and relax. The table and chairs were very soft and inviting. Her next read was: On My Way to Work, dated July 9th 2009:

On my way to work today with the clouds seeping in through the mountains, reminded me how it is when sin seeps into our life. Into our space. It had rained all night and many of the roads to work were flooded, many of the routes had 'do not enter' signs posted. Turn around and take another route. It made it hard to get to where I needed to be. As I looked ahead, the clouds were now covering the beauty of the mountain. It was hard to see that the mountains were even there. I must admit, I did think it looked pretty with the clouds so low, but just like sin in our lives, it may look appealing at first, but then sin can cloud our life, our mind and eventually cloud out God.

Later as I drove home, the clouds were dark and low, blocking out the whole mountain and the sun for most of my drive. As I turned and drove away from the mountain, I looked through the rearview mirror and couldn't even see where I had been. There was no mountain to be seen.

Just then, the rain came pouring down and I couldn't even see the road in front of me. Like sin, it blocks out our path, blocks out our view. Sin does that ya know. It blocks God from our sight. If left unchecked we would be blinded to God's love, care, protection and beauty. We won't be able to see Him. Knowing this makes me grateful for life's lessons, they have made me stronger.

Sometimes I take these mountains for granted knowing they are there. I see them every day on my way to work. These mountains always change and by that I mean, depending on the time of day, the weather, whether it's sunny or cloudy, they change in their appearance. Their colors, their shadows and their ridges are all unique and different. Just like how our days are always different. The beauty of each day and the blessings of the day are things we should always be thankful for. And whether I can see the mountains or not, they are still there, just like God is still there for us. He never changes. God is always great.

I have come to the conclusion that with You God, walking side by side we can overcome temptations and sin....I know temptations are not sin....sin is when we give in to the wrongful temptation and disobey God, that is sin. We must turn from temptations, when they arise.

"Ya know God, I thank You for the beauty of this day. I will enjoy it and draw closer to You. The gifts You offer me, the uniqueness of today that You bring into my surroundings, the clarity of Your path is all here, even when I can't see it. You will guide me to You, because that is where I want to be, with You, leading me home to You. Leading me by Your truths. Thank you. Amen"

Behind the Scenes

The printout simply read: *MJ turn back. Stop. Ask and receive forgiveness. Move forward. 1 John 1:5-2:6.*

Galatians 5:1 (NLT) So Christ has truly set us free. Now make sure that you stay free, and don't get tied up again in slavery to the law.

James 5:19-20 (NLT) My dear brothers and sisters, if someone among you wanders away from the truth and is brought back, you can be sure that whoever brings the sinner back will save that person from death and bring about the forgiveness of many sins.

Chapter Twenty-Five

A Cliff is in Sight

Amanda had quit her part time job about two years ago. The circumstances still bothered her to this day, and she still speaks about it to anyone who would listen. She was being harassed and bullied by her manager. She had taken on the job about four years ago, in 2022, a part time job in the cafeteria at the school in her neighborhood. The kitchen manager hated her for no reason, other than Amanda was a Christian. Boss-lady did everything to belittle and bully her. Amanda recalled the first time she realized this Boss-lady hated her and hated God. It was about seven months after she started. The day with a warm April breeze was a nice change from the bad winter weather that they were experiencing for most of the New Year.

Amanda was working on cutting up six watermelons around the backside of the kitchen. The radio was usually off most days and sat on the shelf above her. She decided that she would turn it on to the Christian station and listen to it quietly, just enough volume that only she could hear the words. No one could hear it unless they came around the corner and stood to listen. Her day had been challenging so far and she moved forward with caution. "This is the day the Lord has made, I will rejoice and be glad in it." Psalm 118:24 was the verse of the day that Amanda had chosen. She even had it written in sharpie on her hand that was under the gloves she wore.

The Boss-lady was a master of deception; dishonesty, anger and rage were her favorite moods. Amanda wondered if she was actually the bride of satan himself. Her look was evil and calculating, always hating everyone and everything with just a glare of her squinted eyes. She was a petite lady with short black and grey hair, and meaner than a seven foot three hundred pound football player.

She wore a red shirt this particular day and out of the corner of Amanda's eye, she could see that she was standing about three feet from her. Amanda kept working with her head down, but could see she wasn't moving for like four minutes. Amanda was on her fifth watermelon getting ready to cut into it when the Boss-lady stepped right up to Amanda's work area and reached for the radio above her. Amanda jumped out of the way, thinking she was about to be hit.

Boss-lady grabbed the radio and threw it to the ground breaking the knob off the side of it. "YOU WILL NEVER LISTEN TO THIS KIND OF MUSIC AGAIN IN MY KITCHEN, DO YOU UNDERSTAND ME? NEVER!!!! IT IS OFF LIMITS, UNDERSTAND? …….NOW GET BACK TO WORK." She said through her teeth, as they stayed closed, with a deep accent of hate.

Amanda still holding the chef knife stared at her without speaking almost picturing herself taking a swing at her with the knife. Amanda just stood there, remained silent and was armed in her mind with her favorite Bible verse Psalm 51:10. She stepped forward to the table with her back to the monster and started cutting the watermelon almost in tears. "Create a clean heart in me oh Lord, renew a right spirit within me………. Create a clean heart in me oh Lord; renew a right spirit within me." She repeated it over-and-over a few times in her head, then a few times out-loud almost wanting the monster lady to hear her, almost begging for her to come back and take her on, even though Amanda knew she wouldn't say a thing. Maybe she should nickname her boss, Karen.

Amanda's spirit was troubled and joyful at the same time. She finished cutting the watermelon and then picked up the radio and the knob and placed it back up on the shelf wondering if she should just throw it away since it seemed to be broke.

She stared at it for a moment knowing her husband could easily fix it. He was a big Mr. Fix-It guy. She thought about the toaster he found thrown away in the dumpster at his work about ten years ago. He fixed it and cleaned it up real good and they still used it to this day. The thought made her laugh inside. She took another look at the radio, knowing she probably will never try to turn it on ever again. And she didn't for the remaining time she worked there.

The day she finally had enough of satan's bride was the day she almost lost her mind for good. She had been starting to slip back into the depression she had fought so hard to overcome all those years ago. It actually was one of the determining reasons she was where she was today, the events leading up to the disaster still troubled her years later. The fact that no one has even called her from the school office startles her even more. Weird how a single or several events can alter your thinking if you let them. And for some reason Amanda let it get to her. The fact it was little 's' man in the flesh has scared her the most.

Amanda was in a constant spiritual battle with this Boss-lady who Amanda named satan's bride monster, SBM for short. Amanda never used her real name in her mind. Two weeks before was not the beginning but it was the focal point of the end where the cliff was in sight. It was for sure a push toward it.

"Father Lord, you know I really hate to bad mouth people. I do work on that right? I hate to say the wrong things. Situations, well that's another story. God, you know that this situation I am in at work is not good. I can't do or say anything right and when I do, it is twisted against me. My anger burns at all the lies and untruths that have been said about me, written in Emails against me by my boss, SBM. You know who she is………. Is little 's' man just working through her? Is he waging war? A spiritual war against me? Oh Lord, where are you?" Amanda asked through the tears.

Ephesians 6:13 (NLT) Therefore, put on every piece of God's armor so you will be able to resist the enemy in the time of evil. Then after the battle you will still be standing firm.

Chapter Twenty-Six

July 13 2027, Carrie

Carrie was enjoying all the stories, poems, letters that were not yet published but full of great words from her mom's life. The story she started to read about her mom's part time job disturbed her:

We are adult women. I am in my forties and I am being bullied at the school where I work. Crazy right? I feel like this Bosslady is the leader of the gang, the head honcho of the mean girls. Remember those girls in middle school who wanted to start a fight with you for no reason? Yea, those girls. I always thought that words cannot hurt you, but I soon found out that they could. They can actually destroy you if you let them.

Carrie stopped for a moment, she totally understood, same girls different generation, seems like that never ends. She continued reading:

The last few weeks have not been fun. I have been angry at the outcome of this job. Even though, I have been looking for a new job for months now, I feel angry over it. The work itself is fine. I'm not afraid of working hard. My integrity and work ethics have always shown in my performance, and I have always been efficient and successful.

I really do feel I work for You, Lord. You are my ultimate boss. Because of You, I am able to do my job even as my health is slipping and the pain is sometimes hard to bear. You are always giving me the power to move ahead, to move and accomplish the task at hand.

However, I have been using the word 'hate' to describe this job lately. I have been focused on the stuff I do not like about it for the last few months. Things like: it is so hot, there is no airflow and no AC and my hair is up in a baseball hat, and I'm so sweaty within a half an hour after getting here. Things like: I don't like the way we have to work, right on top of each other, doing the same thing at the same time, waste of time and use of time that seems unproductive. Then there are things like this one co-worker Britina, she is nice one day and horrible the next and I don't know if she likes me or hates me from one minute to the next. And the Boss-lady, is a wolf, a snake and a bear all wrapped in one small but mighty package, the SBM (satan's bride monster) does not like me, so there is a lot of tension all day in that kitchen. I know I'm complaining, but I have reason to do so. It really is not a great place to work. No wonder they go through so many people. I really need to put in more effort to find a new job.

Our personalities just don't match at all. I am a bad fit in this scenario. I always thought I could do anything for a few months then, I get a week off to regroup and start over. Not

July 13 2027, Carrie

with this group of women. Working for the school, you get a lot of time off; it's the only real good thing about this job.

Things in the kitchen started out bad, the day SBM arrived as the new boss. She was very different from the old one. SBM was controlling without explaining what she wanted done, quiet with her words at first but angry in her actions. She did not seem to like Britina or me. I really didn't communicate with her much as it seemed like I needed to walk softly, as to not step on a loud eggshell. You know what I mean, to walk on eggshells is to be afraid to go anywhere near a person or say anything to them in fear of being stepped on and smashed.

My instincts turned out to be correct. Over the next year SBM seemed to twist anything that was said and even change what was said. Trying to figure her out was super hard. It was as if yes meant no and no meant yes. The words "we don't need you" rang loud and clear, as she would say those words outloud at least two times a week. (Maybe she knew I was looking for a new job). Who knows? She had a very sarcastic, short, mean tone in her voice when she spoke to me. Was she ever nice to me? I really don't remember. I do know that I did not trust her or respect her. I know I have to respect her position as my boss, because as a Christian it is something we are told to do, but I did not respect or trust this lady. I did not go out of my way to talk with her, as it went both ways. Maybe I should have tried harder to be a friend, to be a better co-worker. She made it very hard and I didn't put in much effort either.

SBM would start a job and do it for maybe five minutes, and then leave it for someone else to finish. Britina treated SBM the same way she treated me, one-day friendly the next day hateful. However, I did notice that Britina was not going to finish anything SBM started. She would just walk around it and not touch it. Surprisingly, I actually had gotten used to Britina's mood swings. How? I have no idea. I guess, by just ignoring them.

SBM would disappear into her office quite often. Which I didn't really mind, it was much better with her gone. However, it would drive me crazy that she would leave her prep stuff unfinished, half cut up oranges or a few fries out in the boats, just unfinished and I would go work on it. It happened several times a day, those first few weeks she was there. Come to find out she was off e-mailing the office that I was ignoring her. Crazy, I know. I never intentionally ignored her when she spoke. I did however intentionally try to ignore the nastiness when I could. I will get back to those e-mails soon.

One day, I was working on filling the breakfast totes with food for the classrooms. I asked if we had any more blank, 'breakfast classroom forms' and she said she had them in the office and turned and left the cafeteria, not another word was said.

I continued working on filling the breakfast totes and she came back a few minutes later empty handed. In my head, I was like, 'Oh darn, now I have to ask again, she must have forgot.' So I hurried what I was working on and then I was to the point that all I had left was to put in the new forms. So I asked her again, she said in a most angry snotty, mean tone, "I told you to come to the office to get them and you ignored me, so I didn't get them for you."

I was shocked because I know she only said, "They are in the office", and then turned and left. So I told her, "I didn't ignore you, I wouldn't do that, I didn't hear you *say* to go to the office with you. I thought you went to get them yourself because I was still filling the bags. I wouldn't just ignore you." I defended myself.

I was actually a little annoyed at this point, because truthfully I *KNOW* that she did not say to go with her, but she played it off that I ignored her command. Things from that point on started getting worse. Stupid things. I swear I am working with a bunch of third graders. No wait, my children were much better than this in third grade. (Carrie started laughing at that.) I swear she is trying to provoke me. To anger me. I feel it in my soul. At this point, I had not yet realized I was in a spiritual battle. A real spiritual war. The fact is that little 's' man was using this mean lady to slap me down had not yet occurred to me.

Every day, all day….all day, every day stupid things, I almost want to scream and cry, and as I write this……months later…. maybe even laugh at how I have let this get to me.

I should have stood there every time something immature and stupid happened and just laugh. I should have laughed and called her out, "What are you, ten years old?" Those are the words I should have said.

But I didn't. I let it build up in me. Build up to hate. I hate my job attitude. Take this job and shove it attitude. It was the hardest thing to do every morning after sitting and praying in my car, to get out of my car and walk into work, to work for the day. It exhausted me.

Angel came in one day (She is the woman from the main office.) We all had a meeting. She says there is a lot of tension in the kitchen and things are being said to the manager like "I don't know why you have this job; you don't know what you are doing."

I sat there thinking, wow, Britina said that. At least I thought it was Britina, because I knew I didn't say it (But in my head I did agree with it....SBM is not much of a leader, or a boss who wants things to be smooth.)

I didn't have anything to really say at this meeting, this first meeting. Yeah we end up having another one, but I will get to that one soon. I wasn't gonna throw anyone under the bus. (There were tons of stuff, safety wise and cleanliness wise and attitude wise, I wanted to say about SBM and Britina.) But Angel said we were all there to get things off our chest and start over, with trust and respect for each other. So I didn't feel drumming up past stuff would be the right thing to do and satan bride monster *is* my boss and we all did need to get along. I was good with that....I didn't feel a need to bad mouth anyone......I was on board and I was gonna try.

I thought we all were going to try better. It didn't occur to me that it was NOT going to get better. It NEVER got better. It actually got worse. SBM got away with something that day; lies in e-mails that she wrote. Angel never pointed out that what she was talking about were things that I supposedly said and did. I had no idea at this point.

Funny how nothing that Angel said in the meeting about getting along, being kind and respectful was happening.

The Thursday and Friday of the following week, were only half days so that the teachers could do report card stuff. So we were only going to be serving breakfast. No lunches.

All day on Wednesday SBM kept saying, "We don't need you." She continued to say she did not need me there on the Thursday or the Friday because we were only going to serve breakfast.

July 13 2027, Carrie

"Ok, I'll save you some hours, and I'll stay home." After all, I was not feeling well anyway.

She then says, "WELL YOU NEED TO CALL Angel first." Her attitude took me by surprise.

So, on my lunch hour I texted Angel what SBM had said and Angel said it was ok to be off if they didn't need me. "COOL" was all I could think.... "Thank you Jesus."

So I told SBM and right away Britina and SBM started with this.... "OH, you just don't want to clean, cause that's what we are going to be doing after breakfast for the rest of the day, and you are just trying to get out of it."

I was like... "No, I wasn't....... It wasn't even my idea to be off. I planned on being here, but SBM said she did not need me on those two days." Okay, so I didn't say 'SBM', I did call her by her real name. I honestly wanted to just turn my back on them and walk out at that moment. Maybe I should have.

"You're the one saying you didn't need me." I said, as I looked SBM in the eyes. I felt myself backing up. I swear the eye stare pushed me back in a wild wind blow, almost like facing a harsh winter's storm.

I fell for the crazy trap she laid. I had no idea what they were gonna do the rest of those two days. I assumed they were gonna leave after breakfast on the two half days, the Thursday and the Friday.

So I showed up the next day to their shock and dismay.

Neither of them had no intention or wanted to clean, but because I came in anyway, they had to. Two can play this game! I did have to laugh inside, even though I would rather have stayed home because I really wasn't feeling well.

Too much tension, but I ignored it. I stayed and cleaned everything she wanted me to do. I did the same on Friday. I really wish I would have written notes of every little thing and attitude ….It is quite entertaining now, although at the time it was not, not really.

At the time, the stress was more than I could take. My blood pressure was on the rise and I felt like I could explode due to her harassment and bulling.

Oh and she had me clean the bathrooms, which by the way didn't bother me at all, because I actually love cleaning and organizing and that seemed to make her mad.

So the next week, thank God we were off for fall break. "Thank you Jesus." I needed the time away. I needed the rest.

First Monday back, neither of the ladies (and I use that term loosely) are talking to me. You would think that after a week off, they would have cooled off about having to clean, but not these ladies.

I go in with a good attitude, and I say "Good morning" in a chipper voice ………..Nothing! Really! Grow up! My mind wanted to shout aloud.

All morning….Britina nice, Britina mean, Britina nice, Britina mean. I laugh as I write this, because honestly how can someone be nice and mean at the same time. Yet Britina is a master at it. I actually feel sorry for her. Then, when I think of SBM, I feel sorry for myself, she is another whole dimension and level of nastiness, heartless, cruel human being.

Carrie again stops reading and is horrified. Her mom is too soft and too nice. She was pretty sure she herself would not have been, and she would have been outspoken to these two evil women. Carrie glances through a couple of pages, all meanness and evil directed at her mom. She picks up the story a few pages later:

About an hour after getting here, so like 730 am, right before the substitute helper, Martha arrives, I was cutting up oranges......and Britina walks by me and yells, "YOU CAN WRITE THIS IN YOUR NOTES!!!!!"

I'm like, "What are you talking about, what notes?" She continues walking and goes into the bathroom. She is in there for like ten minutes. When she came out I walked over to her, "I'm sorry, what did you need written down? I didn't hear what you needed."

"I DON'T WANT TO TALK ABOUT IT....JUST WRITE IT IN YOUR BOOK."

"What book, what are you talking about? Notes or book, what is it?" She kept saying "your" book, "your" notes. We did have a logbook for everything we did and the times and temperatures that needed to be written, but I believe she totally was meaning something else. Maybe she knew I might use her in a future story, but how did she even know I love to write.

"I DON'T WANT TO TALK ABOUT IT." She was yelling at me. I turned and went back to work. I laugh again as I write the words for my real book as it makes for a real good story. Although I wish, it was made up.

It was then time to go and pick up the breakfast totes from the classrooms. Martha, the sub is here now and we all start to pick up the bags. Britina says "Don't touch my bags or my clipboard ....they are mine, you can switch off with SBM"... (Okay she did not say SBM; it is only a name I use in my head.)

It actually was funny and I started to laugh as I grabbed a garbage can, "Is it ok for me to go get all the garbage?" I ask her sarcastically, because there is no reason for her to be acting this way, she was just putting on a show for Martha I was assuming.

She at this point is acting extremely angry. "I DON'T CARE WHAT YOU DO!!!"

So, I go right up to her and say "Britina, I don't know why you are so angry with me today, what book, what notes are you talking about? I have no idea what's going on." My voice sounded exhausted.

As I say that, she opens the door to the school office and screams, "I TOLD YOU I DON'T WANT TO TALK ABOUT THIS....OH MY...I NEED TO GET MY BLOOD PRESSURE CHECKED!!!!!!" she puts her hand up to her forehead as she walks into the office.

I kid you not, such drama....drama queen all the way. She wins the prize!! Really? She acted as if I was attacking her. She had been attacking me all morning and I'm trying to get to the bottom of it, and wham turned on me. Maybe I should name *her*, Karen. (Carrie paused for a moment as she laughed.)

I continued walking. I get the garbage and go back to the kitchen. SBM is there and as much as I did not want to approach this woman, I did. I asked if we could have a meeting, because I want to know what Britina is accusing of me.

SBM was just as evil. "NO! You need to call Angel. I'm not having a meeting for you!" At this point, I was like "What the heck is going on????" It honestly felt like evil was all around me. I felt like I was fighting something I couldn't even see. It was closing in on me.

So, I went to the office, shut the door, although it did not latch and I called Angel to ask if she could come by and she said she was going to be coming in anyway and would be there the next day. I said thank you, and turned around and SBM was in the room videotaping me talking to Angel. I looked right at the phone she was videotaping from and told her I was leaving *now*. I was leaving early this day for a doctor appointment, which is why Martha was there. I was supposed to be working until 9:30.

I was super exhausted by the two of them and a bit angry, but held it in as she was videotaping my conversation and response. It was only 9:10 am. But I punched out anyway. I walked to my car and re-called Angel to fill her in as to why I needed her to come in to talk with me. She again said she was gonna be there that next day.

Come to find out Angel and Ruby (Angel's boss) was coming in to confront me over some e-mails that the Boss-lady had sent in. They got down to that right away and I was shocked.

We sat in the break room with the door shut, yet everyone knows you can hear right through these walls. So many lies! So many exaggerated stories. Total lies!!! Things that never happened and things I never said or did were brought to my attention.

Several e-mails of lies written over the past several months:

E-mail one: SBM said that I know the superintendent personally and I was going to complain to him about her....I was like "I don't even know who the superintendent is, let alone go and complain to him about anything."

E-mail two: She said that I said, "I don't know why you have this job; you don't know what you are doing". I *NEVER* said that. A total lie!

Angel at that point said, "Why didn't you say that at our last meeting?"

I was like "Because you didn't say the e-mail said that *I* said that!!!! I thought Britina had said it, because I *KNEW* I didn't say it"......but here in this e-mail sent by this evil lying Boss-lady, it said that *I* said it. Wow.

"Well, you should have said something, you said nothing." Again, I say to her, directly looking her in the eyes, "I didn't say anything because I NEVER said that...... and *you* never said that I said it....I thought Britina said it, because I KNOW I did not." I was actually starting to get mad at this point. I never thought I had anger issues until I started working with this group of women. I could feel my blood pressure furnace turned up to high. I feel I'm in the principal's office and I'm in second grade.

E-mail three: The next e-mail they wanted to address, as Ruby is taking notes of my responses said I refused to take and read the e-mail from Angel a few weeks ago that SBM tried to give me about time off. She said I would not take it from her or read it.

That again was a lie. Why would I not take an e-mail that was addressed to me and refuse to read it? Such lies. Luckily, I still had the e-mail that she handed to me weeks ago, it was in my car, and a few minutes later, they let me go to my car to get the e-mail I supposedly didn't take. While I was at my car, I also grabbed the notebook of notes I had been taking after work in my car since the first meeting.

Those were the only notes I was taking. I wish they had been more detailed. I only wrote some of the things I could remember from the day, as there were so many. As I think about that, I wonder if Britina knew about those notes in my car. Maybe that is what she was referring to as '*Write it in your book*'? I don't know how she could have. I had only started writing things down after the first meeting because things didn't get any better. However, I only wrote stuff in my notebook after work in the parking lot before leaving and driving home. I never did find out what Britina was talking about, and why she was so angry with me.

E-mail four: This e-mail said I get mad and I take pictures of things that I don't like in the kitchen...........another total lie.........trust me.......I am very against people having their phones on them while working and I NEVER carry my phone on me at work when I'm on the clock.

I then got up and went to my locked cabinet, opened it and took out my purse. Then I took out my phone and said, "You are welcome to look at my pictures, you will not find any pictures in there of this kitchen and if you would like to take my phone and have experts look to see if anything has been deleted, you are welcome to do that." At this point the lies were too much, I was breaking and I was getting madder and madder. It was hard to contain my composure. Of course, they did not look at it or take it with them.

E-mail five: This one was about how I refuse to listen and was a half-truth. She said I wouldn't listen to her and cook some hotdogs. I told them I did question it and she threw the tray into the refrigerator after trying to hand it to me.

What happened was; it was nine o'clock in the morning. We had put the hotdogs on the trays to be cooked at lunchtime into the refrigerator so that they were ready when we needed to cook them. They take no more than ten minutes to cook and then are put into the warmers. The first lunch starts at ten-thirty. When she told me to start cooking them, I asked her, "Are you sure? It's only nine o'clock."

I said it in a nice way. I honestly thought maybe she looked at the clock wrong and thought it was ten. She had a cow, that

I would not cook them. She threw them into the refrigerator and some fell off on the floor and in the fridge. There was no reason to cook them one and a half hours before lunch began. That is just gross. She threw the tray back into the refrigerator and walked to her office. I'm assuming that's when she sent the e-mail saying I would not listen to her or do what she wanted me to do at that point.

There were e-mails of things that didn't happen. She said I ignored her all the time.

Angel and Ruby shortly listened to my complaints and explanations. It was as if Ruby especially did not want to hear my side of the story.

I did tell them about the lunchmeat that SBM leaves laying on the counter all day long and how mad she gets when I put it in the refrigerator or under cold running water.

I get there at six in the morning and the lunchmeat and the cheese slices would already be sitting on the counter. We didn't even start making sandwiches until after everything else was done. Sandwiches are supposed to be made fresh about one hour before lunchtime. So having the meat sitting out from six in the morning until nine or nine thirty before we even make sandwiches is crazy and I'm sure it is a safety issue.

Plus for months SBM would make us make them the day before, after the lunch hour and sitting on the counter all day long, so that we did not have to rush making them the day of. That always grossed me out. Sandwiches *should* be made fresh period! But hey who am I? These women from the office did not care what I had to say.

Angel wanted to see my notes, she at least acted like she wanted to get to the bottom of this but Ruby her boss said they didn't have time to go though *MY* notes. Meeting was over....

the whole thing with Britina that I wanted to discuss from the day before barely addressed. They were here for satan's bride....not me and that was clear.

They left the building to have a meeting with SBM. She came back laughing and smug about two hours later and even meaner to me, if you can believe that! What a very EVIL woman. They didn't have a meeting with Britina until the next day.

It was very hard to be in that kitchen with that liar the rest of the day. EVERY E-MAIL WAS A LIE! How can she get away with this?

Carrie shook her head and she skips over a few more pages, a few more days of pure evil. She stops at the title saying....The Day I Walked Away:

I made the final decision to quit my job at the school. Or I should say the more proper term is *'resigned from my position'*. What brought me to this point? Well a ton of turmoil and chaos, that's for sure and too much uneasiness in my soul. Was it the job? Was it the people? Was it just satan messing with me, a spiritual warfare? Maybe a little bit of everything.

I do believe I saw the face of satan. The evil was definitely and defiantly lurking in that kitchen and it has been ever since I walked through those doors to begin a job there. Little 's' man messed up though and showed his ugly face. I saw it in the eyes and smirk on this SBM co-workers face. I literally saw it, the demon and it scared me. I saw his face in hers.

She was like a giant in her petite frame. She made me feel so small. She doesn't seem to even care to listen to anyone. She draws you in like a fisherman reeling in a catch and then rips out the hook with such force you cannot swim again. You go with the flow, but once you're out of the water, you are fried. The satan bride monster is toxic to me. My soul cannot handle being around her. Anxiety, stress, and turmoil are all part of the spit that she sends out. My soul cannot work side by side with hers.

I backed away, I backed down, and I ran. I don't expect anyone to understand this, this is my own war. Have I gone full circle here? I'm back in the very place I found Christ in 1999 when I walked through the doors of Arizona Desert Elementary School to a church that was meeting there, a Community Church. I was in bad shape in 1999, and haven't thought much about it over the last twenty-seven plus years. But Tuesday August the 19th 2024, I saw satan and he tried to throw all the hurt, pain, and worthlessness back at me using a willing co-worker. I saw his work, his bully tactics, his meanness, and his evilness as he used this woman to torment me.

My eyes were opened. It says in the Bible, we do not fight against flesh and blood, but against the rulers, authorities, and powers of this dark world and against the spiritual forces of evil in the heavenly realms.

Why hadn't I recognized this place? Why did I allow it to push me back to the cliff? I knew where the school was, because of coming here in 1999, but didn't recognize it. Now as I think about it, I remember walking through those gates in the front of the school into the cafeteria for a church service. Sitting in the back row and crying as God spoke to me. He spoke through the words of the songs, through the teaching, through the people who were there, through smiles and through my tears. This place had led me to Him, the one true God.

But this same place just tried to destroy me. Oh, the thoughts on that Tuesday that hit me were the very ones I had when I walked through the doors the first time. Stupid small stuff, lots of stuff hitting me. All of it flooding my mind with doubts and worthlessness and feeling of emptiness and thoughts that no one can understand or even should understand. It was a spiritual war that was going on and the cliff was in sight.

Oh my, why didn't I see it? Satan was not happy the day I walked into that school, to church the day I did. The church has moved to a different location where we can learn and serve and worship, although we can do that anywhere at any time. But all of a sudden, I saw it was the battle I was in. I went back to the place that battle began. I was there and had not even realized the enemy was there too. No wonder this place seems against me. Satan is against me, he uses every chance and every circumstance to attack me, even people. "Take every thought captive Amanda, take every thought captive to the obedience of Christ." These words should have been on my mind every single day I walked through the back door of the kitchen. The spiritual warfare that took place was not against the flesh and blood. Although that is what little 's' man used.

Satan never gives up, does he? It was a long time ago that I walked through those doors. And he still remembers. He remembers that I found You waiting for me. He remembers I kept coming back and kept being fed Your truth. He is angry that I was able to let my baggage drop, let my sins be forgiven, let my life begin to reflect You. My chains broken. My armor on. My thoughts captive only to You. Your fire in me.

Can he destroy what's been built? Can he smash my hope and future? He sure tried to. He did what he could. But I saw him lurking. I saw him out to destroy. Weird how you can sometimes get a glimpse of the battle, in someone else's face. The words "Not today little s, not today" are in my thoughts right now. I believe there is a reason God allowed me to see that battle, that real enemy. He allowed me to see the edge of the mountain, the cliff of uncertainty and despair. He allowed me to see satan himself.

So I have been looking for a new job. I have sent a few job applications and resumes out. I really didn't want to quit without first having another job waiting. But this particular day, I could not wait any longer and I left, running with my tail between my legs. It was the right thing to do, the best thing to do. Flee from satan, flee from his workers, and flee from SBM.

Psalm 120:1-2 was the Bible verse I read the next day. It said, "I took my troubles to the Lord; I cried out to Him and He answered my prayer. Rescue me, O Lord, from liars and from all deceitful people."

Carrie stopped reading for a moment to absorb what she just read. She opened the Bible to the verse her mom had written on the paper. She took her highlighter and highlighted it.

Amanda had felt broken and defeated as she fled the scene. This woman seemed to have a power of hate for no reason other than to attack a child of God; it was her superpower for sure. Her friend, Valarie had warned her not to tell anyone she was a Christian at the school. Every school Valarie had ever worked at were bullies to believers on purpose, every single state and Arizona wasn't the worst, but it was close.

"They don't want Christians in the school system, because they can't teach their ungodly agendas with them there, and the word would get out to the parents who don't really pay attention to what their kids are learning."

Valarie says she has learned to just keep her head down and doesn't talk to anyone and never tells them she is a Christian.

"I've seen it happen over and over. They preach no bullying and then do nothing about it when it's done, especially to a person who loves God. Even the children from good Christian homes are bullied by the teachers and staff, and some of the teachers go out of their way to teach worldly things to them and spew their hate of God on them."

Valarie says she always prays for the children and she hopes they make it through school without being harmed much. Valarie knows full well, there are no guarantees of being treated fairly in life. God's view was the only one that counts.

"Keep your head low and learn from the situations, just stay on the down low." Valarie had warned her over-and-over. "Truth is overthrown. They don't care about truth anymore, they hate truth."

Amanda

Later, as it turned out satan's demon monster did me a favor. I hadn't seen it at first and I didn't see it for a long time, in fact just recently, I have been able to put it behind me, for the most part. Writing about it is very helpful. But to be honest, I will still talk about it anytime someone asks about it.

I try not to think about the demon woman much, but her evilness does still linger in my thoughts, and her very being still triggers me. I catch myself focusing on the bad and pray for God to take those thoughts and erase them. I must admit, I still am angry about the whole thing, if I let myself think about it. I know it is time to completely release it to God. The anger and bitterness have no place in my mind, it weighs me down and depresses me. Plus, God loves her even if I don't, He still would love for her to turn to Him.

The Bible tells me that God hears the prayers of the righteous in James 5:16-17.

"I feel righteous sometimes, and sometimes I don't. Sometimes I feel I am clothed in Your majesty and sometimes I am just in rags. I'm not worthy of anything, yet You give me and bless me in everything. I thank you Father Lord, please help me to fight this fight in my own mind, help me to remember that You gave me a new beginning when I thought it was the end, help me to close the door to satan and repair the damage he tried to do. Please turn the bad into good, give me a reason to carry on, thank you, Amen."

Carrie remembered the story she read hours before. Her mom's story that was written by her twenty-six years ago titled: The End. With a deep sigh, she shook her head. This story was just a great reminder that bullies are bad and that kindness is the way we should treat each other, it is so much better. No one knows what another person is going through because we don't walk in their shoes. Maybe, just maybe she has a reason to act the way she does.

Behind the Scenes

Debbie looked around before she entered the room. No one was paying attention so she moved quickly as she checked the brain machine. She noticed there were more wires connected to her patient and could almost feel an electrical current coming from them. Paper with thoughts began to spit out, Bible verses and notes. It seemed to be spitting out the notes with urgency.

Should she be taking these? What if it was messing up the tests? She can't worry about that now; she isn't supposed to be in here. For some reason she was assigned to a different area of the hospital today, one that was on the same floor, but at the other end and around the corner of the hall.

2 Corinthians 6:14 (NLT) Don't team up with those who are unbelievers. How can righteousness be a partner with wickedness? How can light live with darkness?

Ephesians 5:11 (NLT) Take no part in the worthless deeds of evil and darkness; instead, expose them.

3 John 1:11 (NLT) Dear friend, don't let this bad example influence you. Follow only what is good. Remember that those who do good prove that they are God's children, and those who do evil prove that they do not know God.

Chapter Twenty-Seven

Roxie

Roxie, feeling guilty about not going to see Amanda and the ladies on Saturday went right after school on Monday. She felt Amanda would hear her out and would not repeat anything. She wanted to reveal her secrets she kept hidden about her life. She has kept so much hidden and has never even tried to reveal any of it in class all these years. She knew she had many secrets, but she had lacked self-confidence most of her life, so exposing them was something she didn't feel comfortable doing. Being involved in other people's lives was easier then letting them into hers.

The fact that she was great at connecting with people and keeping the peace was her only joy besides teaching the children. She knew deep down that God had gifted her with the ability to reach and teach.

Her home life was far from joyful. Her husband Kevin was not a Christian and he was very demanding and controlling. He would lash out and hit her from time to time, especially when she cringed from his loud degrading voice. No one knew what she went through at home. She was afraid to tell anyone in fear that it would get worse.

She grabbed her arm, rubbed the bruise slightly and moaned as she walked quickly to expose her secrets to Amanda. Remembering the burnt toast that made him so mad and made her feel so alone, she bravely decided it was time to talk to someone. She needed the help and this particular day she felt it was exactly what she should do. She desperately needed to talk to someone, and now was the time to acknowledge it all to Amanda, who she knows and trusts would listen and not repeat.

Things in her life hadn't always been this bad. There were many good times with Kevin but many just as bad. She really didn't know what to do. Ignoring the punched holes in the walls was one thing but the verbal abuse as well as the physical, was wearing on her. She wasn't sure how much more she could take.

Even though Roxie had been baptized as a baby, she had always believed that there were many ways to get to Heaven. She knows that John 14:6 tells her that her thinking is NOT true and lately that verse has been on her mind a lot. *"Jesus said, I am the way, the truth and the life. No one goes to the father except through me."* She said it out-loud, it was one of the first verses she had memorized from Bible study.

She repeats it as she sits in the small room waiting to voice her secrets and picks up the pamphlet 'How to Get Right with God' sitting on top of the Bible that is on the small table beside her.

Roxie glanced at it, knowing she has seen it many times, but had never opened it. Just like her life, never really opening it up to anyone. She almost set the pamphlet back down but something stopped her. Her thoughts wrestled with her heart and she decided to give in and read it before talking to anyone. At the same time, she hesitates that maybe she shouldn't talk about Kevin after all. She has time, and she is not sure when Amanda would be ready to listen. Honestly, she wasn't sure she herself was really ready to talk.

Roxie decided she would make herself comfortable as she sat and read the whole pamphlet. It was easy to read and she had heard all this before in the lessons at church and Bible study but for some reason she had always pushed the truth from her mind and heart, accepting the lie that she was already fine with God. Looking down at the bruise on her arm again as it was quite darker today she sat and prayed a deep heartfelt prayer for herself and then said one for her friend Amanda.

She then started reading out-loud in a whisper and about half way through, it was titled 'How Do I Accept Jesus?' She continued to read it out-loud almost questioning it to herself. It gave four steps on how she personally can accept Jesus.

First, she must believe in Jesus.

She thought about this for a moment, and immediately said, "Yes, I believe, I have always believed.....Yes God, I do believe, I believe in Jesus." She smiled as she said the words, knowing that she did believe and was happy to say so. She thought some more about it and decided that she didn't have blind faith, but she really did have a faith that was based on facts, facts that she had learned about at her church.

She looked up to the ceiling and said, "I don't have to have blind faith do I? I go to a church that shows us fact after fact that is true and provable." She said directly to the ceiling, as if she expected to hear it confirm her beliefs.

"Oh God, I do know, I do know the Bible is true and provable, not only in my mind but I know in my heart and soul...... plus there are all those facts that prove it." She chocked back the tears. "Thank you, thank you so much." Roxie sat up a little taller. "Thank you Jesus for the gift of Salvation. Thank you for dying for me. I do totally believe You died for me."

The next step was to repent of her sins.

"Oh Lord, my sins are many, maybe too much. I've tried to live a good life, yet I know it's not enough. I know that just living a good life is not enough to get me to You. I know all this, but sometimes I push that truth away because I'm afraid. I know You love me and will forgive me. The words *'I'm not enough'* ring through me all the time and God sometimes I believe them. I know I need You and I do *ask* for Your forgiveness." She took a deep breath "What Jesus has done for me is enough and You think I'm worth it, right?" She knows full well that the answer to that is "YES." She knows that Jesus died for her sins. She knows that He loves her. She knows that she wants to live an obedient life and not a rebellious one. "Oh God, I do want to be Your girl, please forgive my sins. Please forgive all of them."

She sat there in the quietness for almost ten minutes before moving on to the next step. "Confess."

Again, she was talking aloud. Her mind was open to confession, after all, she was here to confess some things today, and she knows how she feels when she confesses small things, like a weight lifted off her. The confession today is big, and it seems even bigger confessing to God.

The pamphlet said to confess Jesus as Lord of your life.

"Can I confess to Amanda? A moment later, "Do I need to confess my sins or just repent of them and confess Jesus as my Lord and Savior, I want to do it right, I really do." She said with her heart full with desire, as she said the words out-loud, "Jesus I accept You as my Lord and Savior." She couldn't wait to say those words, even though no one was there to hear them. She was so excited and she repeated them over-and-over. "Jesus is my Lord and Savior." She felt like she wanted to shout it from the rooftops. She sat and confessed Him as her Lord and Savior over-and-over for the next few minutes. It made her very happy to say it and now there was no holding back the tears.

She knew the next step was baptism as an adult.

She has heard this every weekend at church. Why hasn't she done it yet? She had always been told that her parents already baptized her as a baby, and that it was enough. But deep down, she knows the Bible points to baptism as an adult, making a decision as an adult that only she can make. She has never wanted to go against her parents but she knows that she is not right with God because of a sprinkling that was done to her as a baby. She didn't make that choice and she definitely didn't know what it meant, nor could she even say the words, 'I accept Jesus as my Lord and Savior'. Will her parents understand? Will Kevin?

She knows that Kevin would not understand, but he is not going to hold her back any longer. She looked at the bruise and then feeling brave for a moment she sat up straight, but just as quick, she started to sulk back into her chair. Her life felt too heavy. "I'm sorry God, I'm so sorry, please God lift me up."

As quickly as she said the words, Roxie stood up and walked around the room, knowing she must remain faithful to the end. To travel to Jesus wasn't enough, she needed to travel WITH Jesus and so she decided that the first step in fixing her life was to get right with God, the right way for all the right reasons. She can't just live with Jesus without first having her sins forgiven in the right way. She knows the Bible is true and she knows it totally lays out the process on how to get right with God. She wants a relationship with Jesus, a good honest relationship.

"As a baby I didn't make that decision, did I God? Someone else made that decision for me, and had me sprinkled as a baby. By the way, where did that sprinkling come from anyway? It is not in the Bible. Every example in the Bible shows complete emersion. I didn't personally make the decision as a baby, I didn't even know what that meant but it is all clear to me now. I *need* Jesus. And I *want* Jesus." She said it again a little louder "I need Jesus! And He died for me!"

She needed to ask for forgiveness, repent and accept Jesus as her Lord and Savior and live right for Him. She believed He died for her on that cross, she saw it all so clear, maybe for the first time in her life. Her eyes and her heart felt open and responsive. She was separated from God because of sin. It's a life-long commitment to have a relationship with God through Jesus and she was ready. She felt fired up. She wants the relationship, a real relationship with Him. She put the pamphlet in her purse, and immediately dialed the church to schedule a time to be baptized the next day.

Maybe, just maybe her husband will also want to get right with God too. She will show him the pamphlet as soon as she gets home. She was feeling brave and confident. He needs Jesus, we need Jesus. As she thought good thoughts about that, she started to feel crippled with fear. Her mind flooded with flashbacks to all the bruises over the past. She had been married for almost twenty years to this man, most of it was good, but the bad times, those were the ones that frightened her the most.

Kevin had had a very hard life with alcohol and drugs when she first met him. He was in AA and was actually working on making a good life for them. He was a hard worker and loved taking care of her. He even would go to church with her at first. It wasn't until about fifteen years into their marriage that he started slacking and started drinking again. Over the past five years, he had gotten worse and worse. She herself stopped going to church for a while. Then she saw the cool commercials, "CCCCCC you at church" and decided to go hoping he would go with her again. Will God forgive him? Will she be able to forgive him? Can God fix what's broken? Can He take her brokenness, repair it and make her new? Will Kevin be willing to change? Roxie had seen God do amazing things in other people's lives, will He help her?

Acts 2:38-39 (NLT) Peter replied, "Each of you must repent of your sins, turn to God, and be baptized in the name of Jesus Christ to show that you have received forgiveness for your sins. Then you will receive the gift of the Holy Spirit. This promise is to you, and to your children, and even to the Gentiles—all who have been called by the Lord our God."

Chapter Twenty-Eight

July 13 2027, Carrie

Carrie flipped through a few more pages, still lingering on her thoughts about what her mom went through at her last job. She stopped at one that had been written before she was born, twenty-six years ago. "Wow mom, you have been writing forever haven't you?" She said out-loud to the air. Then, "Oh boy, I'm talking to myself again like you do mom." She laughed. This poem was typed in all capital letters and she smiled at the caps. It was titled:

WHAT'S LIFE ALL ABOUT?

YES, GOD HAS MADE ME STRONGER IN SOME WAYS........
YET I STILL FEEL WEAK
I FEEL REAL.......YET FAKE
AM I HAPPY? OR DO I PRETEND TO BE HAPPY?
I FEEL EMPTY ....YET I KNOW GOD IS WITH ME.
I FEEL LIKE I'M ON THE RIGHT ROAD.......
YET I FEEL LOST SOMETIMES.

There Is A Reason

GOD GIVES ME PEACE AND COMFORT…….
YET I FEEL ANXIOUS.
I CAN'T DIE……..YET I CAN'T LIVE EITHER.
I'M A LIGHT FOR OTHERS TO SEE…….
GOD IS THE LIGHT IN ME
I'M A LIGHTHOUSE………. YET I FEEL SO DARK.
WHERE IS THE FIRE, THE PASSION FOR LIFE?
LIFE FEELS LIKE A GAME….WE ARE ALL THE PLAYERS.
DO GOOD AND NOT DO WRONG…….
YET I FALL SHORT IN THIS GAME.
GOD MADE THE WORLD FOR US TO ENJOY
YET NOT ENJOY THE WORLD……IT IS NOT OUR HOME.
I DON'T WANT TO THINK THIS DEEP……
I DON'T HAVE THE ANSWERS.
I WANT TO WIN……BUT I FEEL I'LL LOSE.
GOD SAYS HE HAS A PLAN, A HOPE AND A PURPOSE FOR ME
YET DAY BY DAY, I FEEL INCOMPLETE.
A LIFE SO SIMPLE…….YET SO HARD.
GOD HAS PROVIDED…..SO WHERE IS MY JOY?
IT'S ALL THE SAME…..YET DIFFERENT….
IT'S ALL NEW……YET OLD.
WHAT HAVE I DONE…..HAVE I DONE ANYTHING RIGHT?
THE ROAD SEEMS TOO LONG……TOO FAR TO REACH THE END.
WILL I REALLY FIND WHAT I'M LOOKING FOR?
HOW WILL I KNOW?
I CHOOSE GOD…YET I HAD CHOSEN DEATH……..
BACK IN TIME.
DID HE KNOW I WAS SERIOUS? I CAN'T HAVE BOTH.
HE LIVES IN ME…HE SHINES IN ME….I AM NOT LOST.
I WONDER IN CONFUSION ABOUT THIS LIFE.

July 13 2027, Carrie

I MUST SURVIVE ON THIS ROAD....
HE WILL MAKE SURE THAT I DO.
THE ROAD LESS TRAVELED....HE PULLS ME ALONG,
AND MAKES ME NEW.

"Why haven't you told me these things mom, you have always seemed happy and strong, why did you have so many doubts? You never let on as you taught me about God, Jesus and the Bible all these years." Carrie talked as if her mom was sitting right there with her. She realized her mom was so lost back before she was born. She felt so thankful that in spite of all that, her mom gave her and her brother a good God filled life.

Behind the Scenes

Debbie had just checked on Ruth, today was a bad day for her. It saddened Debbie and she prayed for her and all her other patients. Her rounds today had been somewhat depressing, so many of her patients seemed fragile and unresponsive. She decided to pull her phone out and click on her Bible app. She looked for a passage in Psalms to read to them next time she made her rounds, something that would be uplifting and positive for them.

As she started to leave room 236, she could hear Nurse Shady and the doctor talking outside the room and she knew they would be coming in so she hid in the bathroom that was in the room. She didn't want to cross their path today. She kept the door cracked praying they would not open it as they entered the room. What are they up to? Another man entered with them, he says he has made the adjustments and a power shot for the patient hooked to the brain machine. Debbie could not believe what she was hearing. What is a power shot? Who is in on this, and how many more? She could not trust any of them. She needed a plan.

She froze as she heard them walk in, they went to bed two and shut the curtain. It was her chance to get out of there, before being spotted. She stopped at the doorway to listen. The man was quite mad as he spoke, "I told you to stop turning up the current. It's too much, you're gonna fry the brain and this power shot mixed with the high current may just kill her. I thought you wanted this one alive???" Debbie backed out of the doorway in shock.

Psalm 119:105...Your word is a lamp to guide my feet and a light for my path.

Chapter Twenty-Nine
Nell and Valerie

Everyone had a story to tell as they walked with Jesus. Amanda realized that not one lady from her Bible study was perfect. They sometimes seem that way and most of them think she is too. But she is far from perfect. Every one walked their own part of the path. We all struggled with real life things. Yet, it is only with Jesus that we can walk daily with our head held high and not with eyes that are looking down. There is a reason. There is always a reason. Will she get a chance to talk to them one on one? She prayed that she would.

The day that Nell came to talk with Amanda was no different from the other women. She had her own stuff and real life struggles.

Nell came to talk with Amanda a few weeks later than most of the women. She, like Amanda, doesn't like to leave home too often. She too, has a fear of the world, and her second excuse was the heat of the summer, which she can honestly say she hated. She sat there and stared at Amanda for almost twenty minutes before she decided to open up. She was here, and had all the time she needed. She bowed her head, and said a prayer to God with her whole heart, mind and soul. Then looking at Amanda she began.

"Amanda, I know you won't say anything to anyone. I know I can trust you, above anyone else." She sat there picking her words carefully, as Amanda wondered, what could be so important that she didn't trust anyone.

Nell felt a renewed peace inside knowing her life has been tough, a tough life that she herself had paved. But at the same time, she finally knows that God forgave her. She knows she wants her life to be happy. She wants to *really* live life for the rest of her life, and she knows without a doubt that God will fill the voids. He has shown her so much over the last few weeks as she spent much of her time reading her Bible and talking with Him. She wanted to share her thoughts about the baby out-loud so maybe she would be able to move forward and live her life.

"I would have told Mary Jane instead of you, but I tested her first and she failed. You see, I told her about the phone call from the hospital and asked her not to tell anyone, and well, I saw Silvia at the store and she said she was sorry about my beanie hats, so I know Mary Jane had said something, because she was the only one who knew."

She stopped for a moment and was almost ready to cry. She had wanted to trust her friend MJ, Mary Jane. She really did consider her a friend. But she knew she couldn't trust her with this. She couldn't trust her with the guilt she felt or her story. Although deep down, she knew MJ would understand. MJ had shared many times over the last few years with her, things that the others didn't know. The secrets that she shared were just as bad.

She sat for another five minutes with a far off look as she went deep into her past memories. If only she could push the erase button. Maybe she should just keep them lost in her brain, hidden from everyone. At least they would be safe there. Although they never stayed hidden from her, they reared their ugly head more than she wished. Maybe if she exposed them, they would stop haunting her. She wasn't sure but she continued on.

"There is much shame in what I am going to tell you, but I need to say it. I need to tell someone…….. I need to know what I should do, and well, saying it out loud may help me." She sadly said in a low voice, bending over to speak into my ear. "Do you know why I make those baby beanie hats?" She whispered, almost like she was telling me a secret and not really expecting to get an answer. "Well…….well I ……well it's a way, I guess, a way of giving back."

Then she stopped as if to rethink what she was about to say. She sat up then quickly said, "I gave my baby girl away when she was born…….." Silence for what seemed like hours, as she sat and sobbed staring at Amanda. Then she continued on almost regretting what she just said and was about to say.

She tried to compose herself and sat straight up. "I gave my baby girl away when she was born ………..well, I really didn't……I really didn't……didn't…….I really didn't give her away………. I……..I……..I left her. I left my baby girl."

There she said it, the first time out loud to someone, someone who might not have heard her, who won't remember or say anything to anyone. A weight lifted from her at that moment. She smiled and stared toward the window, thinking of that day. For her the choice was the right choice back then. But was it? Now that she is older and pictures it moment by moment again-and-again, was it right?

Valarie

Valarie stopped by the hospital to find out about the job she applied for in the cafeteria. She texted all the ladies from Bible study to pray about it, then went in to the Human Resource Department to find out if she was chosen for the job. Even though it was still open for another week she was hoping they had already made a decision to hire her.

Walking away, feeling down and upset because they had already filled the position, which was supposed to still be open, she decided to go up to the second floor and see if she could talk to Debbie, whom she hoped was working today.

Debbie was always available to everyone and always listened to her when she had a problem with her health, which hardly ever happened, as she was pretty healthy and in pretty good shape. Her migraines though were another story and Debbie always understood. Not only was she a nurse, but she too suffered from migraines.

Debbie looked somewhat upset as she spoke softly to some doctor. Valarie decided that maybe she should come back later, but before she could turn she noticed Debbie seemed to be nervous as well as upset, so she stood and watched her for a few minutes more, observing that she seemed to be fidgeting about as well, almost with a chip on her shoulder or something. It didn't fit well for the Debbie she knew. Something was off with her friend. Unfortunately, Debbie spoke too low, and she couldn't hear what was being said.

Valarie felt a little impatient as she watched, wanting to just talk to Debbie about her own problems, knowing she would have to ask why Debbie was so moody herself. Without even realizing it, she said a quick prayer for whatever it was.

Debbie

Dr. Prong was always so sneaky. Even though the machine seemed to work whenever Debbie went into the room, she was afraid for her friend who should have come out of her coma by now. It had been a little over three months and she heard that Dr. Prong was going to talk with the family to have her declared brain dead and Debbie decided that it was time to confront him.

"Excuse me Dr. Prong," she said in a low voice at first, "Has the coma machine been authorized as a proper medical device to be used?" She tried not to sound accusing but she knew full well it had not. Dr. Prong did not know the woman that was hooked to his machine was her friend and she did not intend to tell him.

"I noticed it was hooked up to the lady in bed #2 in room 236?"

"Mind your own business nurse, it works and I will prove it to everyone, it's just taking some time." His voice was monotone. He looked her dead in the eyes with daggers instantly flying from them. He was immediately on edge and wanted to swat her away like a fly, a dead fly.

"Now if you will excuse me....."

Debbie continued with her questioning as she walked back and forth nervously.

"But, but they say it can cause more damage, and even tumors in the brain. It may even cause her to never wake up." Debbie questioned him knowing this could cost her, her job. Trembling she cleared her mind and throat again. The world around her has gone mad and Dr. Prong was not someone to mess with.

"I told you to mind your own business, and if I were you, I would listen." He said sternly, and quickly dismissed her with a swift harsh wave of his hand.

Debbie debated with herself whether she should continue questioning him or say something to someone else. She quickly felt annoyed and upset, as she paced the floor for a few more seconds back and forth as he walked away with no other words for her. She didn't know that as he walked away he was making a mental note to himself to be careful around her.

Debbie looked down the hall and noticed Valarie standing a few doors away staring at her. She felt too upset to have a conversation, but Valarie almost looked as rattled as she was. Debbie needed time to sort out what she knew, but stopped to talk with Valerie anyway, thinking she was there to visit their mutual friend.

"Hi Valarie, how are you?" She tried to sound light and caring as she exhaled.

"Not good, I didn't get the job I applied for in the cafeteria. I'm pretty bummed. I don't know what to do; they said it was supposed to be open for another week, but I can reapply if I want." She said, already forgetting that Debbie had something going on too.

"Oh, I'm so sorry. Maybe I can talk to the manager in HR, her and I are pretty good friends." Debbie offered quickly.

"Really, that would be great thank you, do you think you can do it soon?"

"No problem. Hey look I'm pretty busy right now can I text you when I find out what's going on." She smiled as she tried to brush her off.

Almost ignoring what Debbie just said, she continued on, "Thanks again, yea I was here to check on it and it was supposed to be open for one more week, but she said it had been filled, so I came looking for you. I knew you would know what to do. My son, he is here somewhere, in radiology ya know, I'm gonna go look for him too. Maybe he knows the manager too and can talk with her as well…and……" Valarie tried telling Debbie the whole story, but Debbie cut her off.

"Oh, I thought you were here to see our friend? You know she is just up the hall in room 236 if you want to go visit with her." Debbie quickly spoke and then hurried off, back down the hall into the room that was on her right. It wasn't one of her patients but she needed to step away and figure out what she needed to do with the situation, and with Dr. Prong. She will have to worry about Valerie's problem a bit later. She could hear Valerie still talking as she disappeared into the room.

"Oh yea, I should see her since I'm here, how is she doing?" She asked but Debbie continued to walk and then went into a room. Valarie waited for a few more moments for Debbie to come out so she could talk some more.

Room 236 was just a few rooms down the other way so she decided she would just pop in since she was there, even though she had seen her weeks ago, when they all met for prayer time in the room. As she walked down the hall, she was saddened that she might not be working here after all. She was certain she would find her son before she left for the day.

Valarie had been on the run for so long that it has become part of her normal way of life. She was getting anxious again, the need to move felt like a high priority. It was a normal feeling for her when she had been somewhere for too long. But since her son was not planning on moving out of Arizona, maybe it was time to stop and put some real roots down. Maybe she could relax a little. She loved her church and the prayer warriors. She had made some real friends here in Arizona and the sunshine was growing on her. Plus she really loved the pool and exercise room at her apartment complex. She had many extra bonuses here in Arizona and a lot to be thankful for. "Lord please guide my steps," she whispered aloud.

As Valarie walked into the room, she noticed the curtain was pulled around the second bed and she could hear someone talking and possibly even crying. There was no patient in the first bed so she sat down on the chair beside it with her back facing the curtain and her face to the door she just walked through to wait it out.

The voice sounded familiar but she quickly ignored it, as she thought about her own problems. Why *was* the position filled already? And why does she need to reapply?

She was hoping she would have been picked first before anyone else, and it was upsetting that she wasn't. She debated and questioned with herself as to why it wasn't still open for another week, and why had the Human Resource lady been so quick to dismiss her?

Valerie

Valarie is a black belt in karate. She started taking lessons when she was nineteen years old and her son was only four. When he turned seven, she started him with lessons too. She was on the run for so long she almost couldn't remember why she was running. That's not true; she knew exactly why she was running.

The day she left was the day she had had enough. The baby was gone and she feared for her son. Always looking over her shoulder turned out to be the way of life for her and her son. Even though she knew he wasn't smart enough to find her, she still feared her ex-boyfriend Kevin who was the father of her son immensely.

Life was hard but she did okay. She was able to find work in the school cafeteria every time she moved and changed schools for her son. And when he was seven she found work during the summers at the karate studios and bonus……..she was able to have him there with her. Most of the time she was paid with karate lessons for her and her son for the work she would do as the receptionist. It was a win/win. Although, she had to learn to budget her money during the school year, she became an expert at living with little.

She sat and thanked God for keeping His eye on her. Everything always worked out. She silently prayed. "Thank you Lord. I was blessed with such a great kid. Smart and loving and we are okay. Lord, maybe I will stay put. Even if I don't get this job, I'll be fine, right God?" Prayer always helps and she knows without a doubt that God hears them.

She has been to many churches over the past but none like the one she attends now. She loves her church and the friends she has made. The Pastor teaches in a simple way, always understandable. He uses props to help you learn and even though he talks fast, she is able to comprehend God's truths. She loves that he teaches from the Bible and doesn't sugar coat anything. She has always leaned on God for her true happiness.

She was pretty sure that she would stay here in Arizona, not just because her son says he will not move again, but because she really does love her church.

She didn't mean to eavesdrop but when she tuned out of her own head and tuned into the voice she now recognized as Old Lady Nell's she froze in her seat. Nell was sobbing, barely able to talk.

"Well, I really didn't ……I really didn't……didn't…….I really didn't give her away ………. I………I………I left her, I left my baby girl". Then a pause that lasted for almost for a minute.

Valarie sat up straight and leaned in to hear better.

"I left my girl…my baby, my baby girl on the doorstep of my neighbor. They already had a son, and ….and….and……well, they were young like me, so I just left her…..I left my new baby girl on the door step……oh God, how do I say it……I just left her!" Nell sobbed, and her voice became a little louder as she spoke. "……. there's no excuse for what I did….I just left her there with a note on their doorstep…….I just left her, I left her, oh my, Amanda do you understand……? I walked away and

I left her!" She stopped crying for a moment and stared out the window.

Whew, she said it out-loud. It was out and there was no taking it back. Thinking and focusing on that day, she became startled when she heard something on the other side of the curtain.

"Oh my, no, no, no, no, NO" was all Valarie could say for at least ten minutes after Nell pushed the curtain to the side. Valerie was freaking out and she held her head in her hands in disbelief with her leg shaking uncontrollably.

"Valarie, are you okay…..did you hear me talking to Amanda?...........Valarie, talk to me now." Nell kept asking her, and shaking her shoulders as well. "Wake up, Valarie, talk to me, stop, stop all this." Nell started getting mad as she continued to try to stop Valerie from freaking out.

"Oh God, oh God, no, no, no, NO" was all she could say.

Valerie lifted her head and with tears in her eyes, she stared at Nell in disbelief. "Nell….. *you*……. It was you ……*you*…… left your baby…… girl???....*You* ……are the one……who, who left her…… on *my* ………on my, my……….my doorstep?" Valerie stood up and backed away from Nell.

Nell was floored as she too backed away from Valerie. Shock was displayed on both of their faces. They stood and stared at each other for many moments in time. How many? Neither of them knew, nor were they counting. Both of them were seeking and reliving the memory of those days.

Valarie had finally started to feel safe, at least talking herself into it, although she was always ready to run. She had started coming to the church because life was too crazy not to believe. She learned to trust God and now her secret was out as she discovers that Nell was the one that left the little baby girl on her doorstep forty-six years ago.

She could clearly see the baby as if it just happened as she too acknowledges it. She hasn't told anyone all these years. Only her and her son knew and of course the ex-boyfriend Kevin, and well, the mother of the little girl she had named Susan after her own mom and now Amanda of course, if she could hear them.

Valerie starts to do the math, and then starts to freak out again.

"Too many people know, too many......no, no....no, too many, too many, too many...." Her mind is already running, packing and leaving.

She should not have ease dropped. Her entire life might well be unraveling this very moment. She was so strong physically but so weak mentally and emotionally. She moved the chair out of the way and moved closer to Nell. She looked straight at her. "Why did you leave her at *my* house?"

Nell with the normal distant far off look in her eyes turned and stared out the window as she explained that she was only sixteen years old.

"I got pregnant and as soon as I knew, I broke it off with my boyfriend, he never knew I had a baby. No one did."

Valarie in a soft almost whispers of a voice asked, "What about your parents?"

"No, they were hardly ever home, I had her in the bathroom. I cut the cord with scissors and cleaned her up, before I even cried."

Nell started shaking her head from side to side and couldn't talk for what seemed like eternity, sobbing the entire time. "I didn't know what to do, I didn't know what I was going to do…….I thought it would just go away." Then the crying stopped as quick as it started recalling that day.

"I heard my neighbors come home with their little boy." She turned and looked at Valarie, examining her and looking at her for what seemed like the first time, asking herself if it could really be her? "*You* were my neighbor?" She asked in a puzzled voice.

Valerie nodded her head up and down as she too was looking for signs that Nell was her neighbor back then. Valarie lived in Texas in a small duplex at the time with her loser boyfriend. She hardly knew the people who lived next door. All she remembered was two adults and a teen girl her own age, but she never did know her and she barely said hi to her, she was too absorbed in her own life.

"Valarie, please understand, I…..I….I *didn't* know what to do……….the girl next door had a small boy and she, I mean you, seemed like a good mom……. I left her at your home in hopes you would keep her, so that I could ……… could watch her grow………. It probably was a poor choice ….I didn't know what to do, I was so young….so very young." Nell trailed off.

She turned her back to Valarie again and stared out the window as her voice became more troubled with each word. "It wasn't as easy as it is now…..I was only sixteen and I think I thought…..I really thought it would just go away. ……I wished it would go away……I barely even showed, and no one knew about it…….my parents would have been so mad." She started to cry again as she thought about it and Valarie walked over to her and hugged her.

"Valarie……you were around the same age as me and had a son, you were so mature."

"I was only seventeen at the time. I was fifteen when I had my son and moved in with my boyfriend. He was a little older than me…… when you left her at our door!" Valarie said thinking back to the day she found her.

She was wearing a pink knitted beanie and wrapped in a pink knitted blanket, and she was the most beautiful baby she had ever seen. Her own son, as handsome as he was, didn't compare to the precious little girl at her door. She still remembered the short note that was placed inside her blanket.

"I knew you would love her because you loved your son so much. I left her with a note wrapped inside her blanket that said…………" Valarie and Nell both said the words at the same time. "Please keep her as your own. She is yours now, thank you."

They stared at each other for a few moments and then both began to sob uncontrollably, holding each other's hands watching each other cry, then Nell stiffened up and let go of Valarie's hands.

"What happened?!?" She said in an almost mean, questioning blaming voice.

Valarie froze….she did not want to answer. How could she tell Nell what happened, especially in front of Amanda?

Nell began to get mad and with bitterness she asked Valarie in a louder more accusing voice "VALARIE….WHAT HAPPENED TO HER?"

Nell could see that Valarie was just as upset as she was and tried to calm down her voice "Where did you go, you left when she was only two?" Nell demanded an answer.

Nell's mind remembered weeks going by and only seeing the man. The lady and the boy and her daughter were gone.

She has always wondered where she was, but had no way of finding her. She didn't know her full name or anything about her. She only knew that for two years, she was a good mom and her daughter seemed fine.

"Valarie, please tell me NOW! Where is my baby? Where is my baby girl?"

Valarie couldn't look her in the eyes so she sat back down, as she started shaking her leg with constant movement. Her voice was shaking as well when she said, "He sold her for drugs." Nell stood there speechless. Time froze for everyone there.

They both seem to realize where they were, then at the same time looked directly at me, with no expression on my face. Did I hear them? They both decide to talk more at the small coffee shop around the corner from the hospital, alone.

Romans 8:28 (NLT) And we know that God causes everything to work together for the good of those who love God and are called according to his purpose for them.

James 5:16 (NLT) Confess your sins to each other and pray for each other so that you may be healed. The earnest prayer of a righteous person has great power and produces wonderful results.

Proverbs 28:13 (NLT) People who conceal their sins will not prosper, but if they confess and turn from them, they will receive mercy.

Psalm 32:3-5 (NLT) When I refused to confess my sin, my body wasted away, and I groaned all day long. Day and night your hand of discipline was heavy on me. My strength evaporated like water in the summer heat. Finally, I confessed all my sins to you and stopped trying to hide my guilt. I said to myself, "I will confess my rebellion to the LORD." And you forgave me! All my guilt is gone.

Chapter Thirty

July 13 2027, Carrie

Carrie picked a short note scribbled on a piece of paper that was tucked in between a few pages. Random thoughts? She wondered as she read them:

**God is not like a light switch to turn on when we need Him and off when we don't.

**We all lived a different walk. We haven't walked in the shoes of the others and they have not walked in ours.

**The message You have written in my heart will save my soul. James 1:21

**Help me see through Your eyes Lord. Love like You do.

**My life, Your way

**Prayers are our lifeline to God.

**Immeasurable peace comes from God

**Complete surrender to God. Be open and honest.

**Painful truth is better than lies.

Carrie wondered if there were poems or stories in the binder with these titles as she got up to walk around the house to stretch her legs.

Behind the Scenes

Dr. Prong called Nurse Izzy and Joe for a meeting. They needed to plan the unfortunate death, termination of coma lady in room 236, bed 2. It was basement time for this one.

"Everybody's in?" All three nodded yes.

"Joe, I'll need a real knocker of a jab, it needs to completely make her look like she is gone, is that clear?"

"You don't need to tell me what to do, I know my job." Joe answered with a sarcastic tension in his voice. He hated when Dr. Prong questioned him and acted as if he couldn't do his job correctly without his direction.

"Now boys, settle down." Nurse Izzy said in a calm voice as she made notes into her notebook.

Joe looked intently at Dr. Prong and gritting his teeth he said, "You need to leave the machine alone….no more current." He growled at the doctor. Dr. Prong nodded his head okay but in his mind he quickly dismissed the words from Joe. If he needed to fry her brain to get the machine to work, he was willing to do so.

Chapter Thirty-One

Amanda

My mind feels like it is sorting through so many files, transporting them in the small room of my brain with so many secrets and so many truths. I tried to organize my thoughts.

Why were they confessing to me? I have to figure this out. My mind was packed full of truths, and I know more than I am allowed to say or can say. The whole prayer was inside my mind. The whole story traveled through my brain. Each story was told to me in secret. Where am I? Why am I in disconnect from all of this? I need to scream. "Disconnect....Disconnect!" Some days I can almost do it. I can feel the electric current traveling through my many ports. It's so hot and tingly.

Most days, I don't even know what day, month or year it even is. Past memories, traveling in chaos floods the files. Conversations that seem far away yet are close. Bible verses that I've memorized, which I don't mind come in front and center as I lay here. Why can't I speak? The day feels foggy like a dream.

There is evil lurking about. He comes every day to check on me. The drugs make me so tired. I can't concentrate and I can't wake myself enough to open my eyes. I don't know how to get started, or where I will end up, but You do, right Lord? I cling to You and to Your truth's.

As I rummage through the files in my mind, all the random stuff thrown into folders here and there with no names, just random junk mail mixed with important files. Poking through them, I find bits and pieces of the book I'm writing and bits of lessons I have taught and will teach. How strange that one person can have so many random thoughts and memories in one tiny brain.

My brain feels like a computer with so many files and folders, just shoved into different drawers. Random thoughts, verses and prayers mixed with experiences and secrets all jumbled together, needing a place to go. How do I organize it or file into the correct folders? The computer room of my brain is composed of light and darkness, in every inch, at every turn. I can almost wake my brain enough to pay attention on most days, but I can't convince my eyes to open and can't move my body to alert them.

The one they call Doctor Prong is not my friend. This I know as a fact. Plus the other guy who pokes me with the needle is not my friend either, and he seems to be a bit of a hothead.

I tried to wake up for just a moment but fell back asleep as Nell and Valerie talked. The same dream replayed in my mind, the one I had many years before. 2001, yes that's when it first occurred, as well as a few more times through the years. I wrote about it and now here it was again replaying in my head, as I fall back into La La land with many Bible verses dancing around to direct it too.

Behind the Scenes

Debbie came in as Valarie and Nell were leaving. They looked so serious.

Did they know? No, there is no way they knew. Debbie herself shouldn't know, but she searched the original medical records. She couldn't share the information with anyone. Not that she would. Amanda was her best friend and she had no idea why she was in this state of mind. She knows there was no way that Amanda could have done this. Debbie did however suspiciously know, who was to blame.

Debbie turned on the brain machine and it started to print. So many secrets known by Amanda began to spit out written in her own handwriting, advice, prayers and Bible verses for each of the women. Again, as many times over the last few months Debbie tore them off to take with her.

She glanced down and her name was at the top of one of them, the first line said: "Look for me……. I'm in here ………I'm here…….. I know….. You're here…… Debbie. Please stop him."

Debbie gasped. "Amanda, Amanda, I am here. But I need to go the doctor will be in soon. I'm shutting the machine down, so he doesn't know okay. I'll be back later and we can talk."

Debbie quickly shut down the printer part of the machine. This was the first indication that she has had that Amanda really knew what was going on, or at least knew that she was there. She couldn't catch her breath as she hurried to the bathroom and shut the door rattled in her thoughts.

The hand printed notes only seemed to happen when she was there, but they have always been somewhat jumbled up one-liner notes, Bible verses and every once in a while, what appeared to be initials would emerge, as well as some names. She had dozens of the printouts stored safely at home and decided that she would read all them on her next day off. She had noticed a few patterns to them the last time she read them over and organized them.

Debbie had started turning off the machine after the first note appeared, the first week Amanda was admitted back in March. She didn't trust Dr. Prong and she suspected he would experiment with Amanda's brain if he knew his machine was working. From her research she knew the machine should not even be in Amanda's room, it had not been authorized.

As Debbie rushed out, it hit her that he must be the one who was keeping Amanda in the coma. He has to be. She knows, or at least has a feeling that Amanda could possibly come out of it, if Dr. Prong was not there. Debbie didn't know what to do. Who can she tell? Who can she trust?

She needed to be here to watch over her friend, and this, this note, changes things. Amanda knows, and she just communicated directly to her.

Debbie has suspected the last few weeks that Amanda was really conscience in her mind, but didn't think it was possible. At least not by what she can decipher from the coded notes in the chart, although she did pick up on the fact that the brain machine seems to only click on when she is there alone in the room.

Debbie quickly left the bathroom, ducked into room 236 for a final look at Amanda and said a prayer over her dear friend. "I'll think of something Amanda, I promise." And then, she quickly left the room.

She started down the hall, when Dr. Prong came around the corner, almost knocking her over. She grabbed a hold of him to stop from slipping and he glared at her. "Sorry, I wasn't watching where I was going" she said as to take all the blame onto herself for the collision. He grumbled something under his breath and continued down the hall to Amanda's room.

As he went in, Debbie turned around and followed him many feet behind. She glanced into the room but the curtain was drawn. Praise God he didn't find her in there. She sure wished she could see what he was doing.

2 Timothy 2:19 (NLT) But God's truth stands firm like a foundation stone with this inscription: "The LORD knows those who are his," and "All who belong to the LORD must turn away from evil."

Chapter Thirty-Two

July 13 2027, Carrie

Carrie found a dream written down from 2001. She never put much thought into dreams as some do. She chuckled, as she didn't think her mom did either. Why would she write down a dream? You can always make a dream into something, but should you?

STRANGE DREAM INDEED...BUT I THINK IT'S TELLING ME SOMETHING:

I'm at a church, my church or is it "the church"....the church in general?

    Up the cement stairs to a covered deck, away from the bright sunlight

    "Come on come on....I'm excited to show you....follow me....up the stairs" said the tall man

    I notice the chain link fence around the deck

    Oh no, it's falling apart, it's held together by watches...it's leaning in toward me, the watches are so heavy

    There's a pool far below. I must be careful not to fall

July 13 2027, Carrie

The watches do not seem to be a good way to fix the brokenness

Weird, for a split second, it seems like the watches all stopped on different times

My attention is pulled to the building........I'm told to wait here....the tall man goes into the building, I'm on a back porch....high in the air

I can't remember how I got up there...stairs right? But how long ago did I climb them? I cannot remember

Sliding door....I could see inside, through the sheer drapes, but it's somewhat distorted

It looks deserted in there, yet I decide I need to go in, I feel somewhat afraid

I'm supposed to wait

Then someone, (the neighbor?) appears inside with two oval dishes with strange looking food to try

I step inside, but as I do, I trip over the track for the sliding door, I fall, and the dishes smash to the ground

I begin to cry and start to gather the pieces....they hear me, who I don't know, but they do

Where's the food, where did it go? Did the food disappear?

How do I replace these oval dishes? Do I replace them with new and better dishes?

It needs to be the same I think, I am pretty sure

I'm so confused and I don't know what to do.....broken dishes, I look around and begin to cry again

"One was already cracked, I remember seeing it, as it fell," I said aloud and then I sobbed almost trying to justify my clumsiness

Did someone already fix it? Someone before me? Had someone else dropped the dish?

I notice that everything inside around me was torn up, replaced with something different

I'm not sure why I know, but I do

I go back outside with the broken pieces in my hand

The neighbor is gone. No one knows where he went. I look around, I'm standing there alone

I stand there in disbelief, where do I go from here? How do I fix this?

The pieces, the dish, the fence, the protection, the watches

Where do I begin? Where is the food?

Everything was in decay all around me

I remember about the food, when it hit the ground, it disappeared, and it was strange looking all right

I wasn't sure about it anyway

When I accidentally tripped, fell, and broke the dishes, the food disappeared when it hit the floor, yet the pieces remained

The pieces were clean breaks with no soiled food on them, how could that be?

God's Kingdom, the church needs repair

Was I careless? Clumsy? Not paying attention? How did I drop it?

Was it broke....was it my fault or the conditions? The watches tick, all in different times

So many questions, but then the dream was over

Wow Lord.......lead me in Your truth....I need Your food. Let me pass Your truth to the next generation....time is running out. Countdown begins....help me to fix what is broken. Fix it before time stops again.

We need to start with Your rainbow. You gave it to us as a promise, I saw the colors.

July 13 2027, Carrie

Carrie could picture the whole dream as it was written; wondering if there was any meaning to it. She reread it and tried to see it as truth from an unknown source. If anything, it would make for a good story. She had always loved reading fantasies, as well as who-done-it's, and suspense and romance…..actually she loved reading everything. So much imagination goes into writing. After reading these writings of her mom's, she considered maybe doing some writing of her own. It could be fun.

Behind the Scenes

"Ya know little lady, you're not going to win….the test showed brain waves. It's time to go!" Dr. Prong glared down at Amanda. "I'm done playing games." He tapped her forehead. "I told you if you don't respond, I will….." he bent down to her ear and whispered, "I will cut your brain open and get the answers my way, little lady, and you're not going to like that." He laughed as he stood back up.

Chapter Thirty-Three

Mary Jane and Susie

Mary Jane and Susie were still talking in the parking lot long after everyone else left. They decided to go for coffee in a few days and talk some more. Susie was not thrilled, but she wanted the money that Mary Jane had promised her.

Mary Jane walked into the coffee shop and ordered a large coffee but had it put into the larger cup she brought in with her. Mary Jane loves to be in everyone's business, and she wanted to know more about this newbie, Susie. Plus, she really did have some good intentions for wanting to talk with her. She wanted to talk to Susie some more about getting baptized before she left for Texas to find her real family. All night long, their talk a few days before rumbled through her mind. She was hoping to convince Susie that God was on her side, she just needed to want Him on her side.

As Susie walked into the coffee shop, she too thought about the conversation from the other day. She knows she needs to decide about God, but when she comes back from her trip and not before. For now, she believes but has a need to test God. Will she find her real mom? Will He help her? Seeds had been planted in her life about a relationship with God through Jesus but she has never tried to do anything about those seeds. They have never taken root. She has never felt a need to seek Him out, at least not wholeheartedly.

Susie nodded to Mary Jane, as she ordered a cup of coffee, walked over and sat down with her.

Mary Jane stood about three feet taller than Susie. Her long black hair hung loosely around her head. It almost looked like a wild stallion's mane as a fan blew on it. Mary Jane's manner was almost as wild too.

Mary Jane wasn't gonna mess around with small talk and got right down to it. She barked out, "Look Susie, I know you don't know me well, but I'm telling you, you need to make things right with God now and not wait." She was happy with herself for starting out so boldly. She always felt more in control when she mixed a little of her whiskey with her coffee.

"I appreciate what you're saying Mary Jane, but honestly I have had no need for His help all these years and He has let me down." Susie said in a low voice as if she didn't want anyone else to hear her, or even God himself.

"What are you expecting, talking like that, why *should* He help you?"

"I don't need to listen to you and your lectures about God. He let me live on the streets for most of my life, even though it was my decision to run away but even when I cried out to Him, and I did sometimes, He let me live on the streets. So if He helps me now, maybe I will accept Him. But only if I find my real mom."

Susie was getting madder and madder at Mary Jane with every word spoken. All she wanted was the money Mary Jane said she had for her, and get on her way. However, Mary Jane wouldn't let up.

"We all have it bad Susie you're not the only one." She said gruffly. Susie sat at the table looking toward the door wanting to make a mad dash for it. She really thought a lecture was not worth it. No amount of money was worth listening to this overpowering woman.

"Listen, bad things happen because we live in a fallen world, bad things happen to everyone." Mary Jane noticed she was being a bit intense but she didn't care as she continued.

"My family hates me and I'm all alone with no family so in a way I have nothing, nothing at all except God, at least you have a husband." Mary Jane glared. "And you aren't homeless anymore. I'm old and I'm probably going to be without a home or a family very soon."

As Susie started to get up from the tall bistro table, she bumped her coffee and it spilled on the napkins that lay beside it. "I really need to get going, we are leaving in a few days or weeks and I have a lot to do, if God leads me to my real mom, then maybe I will come back and get right with Him and accept this Jesus as a savior" she said sarcastically again.

Mary Jane grabbed her arm and spilled more of the coffee. "You're not leaving yet, I'm not done." Mary Jane insisted.

Susie sat back down and dried the table with the slightly wet napkins not looking at Mary Jane. Again, she wondered if she should just leave without the money, but at this point she was afraid to do so and she didn't want to cause a scene. She never did like dealing with aggressive people.

Hal, her husband had dropped her off and went to get a haircut and to the store to get some food and wouldn't be back for at least forty-five more minutes.

"If you want this money, you will need to hear me out." Mary Jane demanded.

Susie looked annoyed but decided to hear what she had to say, even though she knew she wasn't gonna let this woman beat Jesus into her. She started to mumble but caught herself.

She stared at the scar on Mary Jane's cheek and wondered how she had gotten it. Probably in a bar fight she chuckled to herself as she mumbled again under her breath, not stopping herself this time. "Don't make me smack you." Lucky for her, Mary Jane didn't hear her.

"I have no purpose in telling you this, but I have made a mess of my life, but the one thing I have done is fix things with God. I tried to fix things with my family years ago, but they can't see how I have changed, and I have no idea where they are anymore."

Mary Jane was still feeling upset over the phone call with her daughter that very morning and was feeling sorry for herself, and wanted some sympathy.

Susie not knowing why reached out and touched Mary Jane's hand, "Okay, I'm listening." As she withdrew her hand, she put both of them into her lap, and tried to act concerned.

Mary Jane continued. "I don't want to be homeless, I'm too old to be on the streets but I may be losing my ranch any day now and my daughter won't take me in. I know God will take care of me like He has taken care of you, at least I see that. I have changed. I'm not the person that my daughter makes me out to be."

She stopped for a moment at the lie she just told. She almost believed it herself as she sipped the secret whiskey spiked coffee. She justified the whiskey with herself and with God. She needed it as much as she needed Him. At least that is what she tells Him. But even as she says it, she knows that it is not true, some days she still needs the whiskey more. For a moment she stopped, she felt like a hypocrite. She's good at talking the talk, but right now, she felt a twinge of conviction, she surely was not walking the walk at least not for the last year or so. MJ stared out the window, and apologized to God for messing up, yet again. And for a moment, she felt almost defeated and lost and wanted to just get in her truck and drive away.

Susie began speaking in a hurry this along voice. "I'm sorry Mary Jane, but what does this have to do with me?" She tried to speak softly but in her hurried push, she was a little louder than she wanted to be and the couple at the next table both looked over at them.

Susie's voice startled her back to reality and Mary Jane glared at the people next to them, and then said, "Nothing, none of this has anything to do with you." She continued to glare at the next table, "I just wanted to tell you about Jesus."

Mary Jane could see that Susie was not interested as she rolled her eyes at her. She sat there for another two minutes not saying a thing. Susie also decided to remain quiet.

"Here is the money I promised." Mary Jane said as she let out a deep mouthful of air. She looked at Susie and put a hundred dollar bill down on the table, grabbed her pink cowgirl hat and stood up and walked out the door.

Susie sat nervously at the table looking out the window as she watched Mary Jane drive away in her full sized four wheeled, four door black Ford Bronco and thought, how fitting that truck was for her.

Susie couldn't wait for Hal to get there so she could share the wild conversation she had with Mary Jane. She had just met a crazier lady than herself and she couldn't contain the laugh and people began to stare, which made her laugh even harder. She continued to laugh and mumble and chuckle to herself as she drank what was left of her coffee.

It was around 11:00 when Silvia walked into the coffee shop. Her attention was immediately drawn to a woman at a table ahead of her that was laughing aloud but no one sat with her, she was completely alone. As she got closer, she noticed it was the new lady from their Bible study group. Silvia quickly turned her back towards her hoping she didn't see her or even recognize her.

"May I help you?"

"Yes, I will have two caramel lattes to go please." Silvia stood still and never did turn around as Susie behind her laughed and talked to herself in a mumbling voice. She grabbed her lattes and quickly exited the coffee shop.

Susie waited for about thirty more minutes before Hal arrived and felt a huge tugging to go see their teacher Amanda again before she left town. She had just seen her a few days before at the prayer meeting, and she was still asleep, but she was hoping that this time she would be awake. For some reason she felt it was easy to talk to Amanda. She really enjoyed talking to her months ago when Amanda gave her some money. Amanda really seemed to care. Ya, she will have Hal drop her off so she can see her one more time.

2 Corinthians 6:2 (NLT) For God says, "At just the right time, I heard you. On the day of salvation, I helped you." Indeed, the "right time" is now. Today is the day of salvation.

Chapter Thirty Four
Silvia, Ruth and Susie

"I'm so glad they let you come down here to the cafeteria. This cinnamon roll should be great with our favorite lattes, right?" Silvia nudged Ruth, to try some. "They're so warm and gooey, please try some." She nudged some more.

Ruth forced up a smile, "Okay," but didn't try it. She was so tired and dizzy. She wanted to go back to her room and sleep some more but she knew her mom needed this time with her.

Silvia looked at Ruth and noticed how much color Ruth had lost in her face. She was so pale and thin just like her beautiful blond hair. With more and more hair gone each day, Silvia felt like crying. Ruth was so weak from her loss of weight and had dark rings below her sunken eyes. It was heart wrenching to see her this way. So much weakness, she looked so fragile. Silvia forced a smile as her eyes began to water. Ruth was always such a sweet and beautiful girl.

Silvia was worried the time was near and Ruth would be gone. She couldn't bear it. She needed to spend as much time as she could with Ruth. She hoped that Ruth would eat a little and enjoy the latte. Ruth looked so tired. Maybe she shouldn't have brought her down to the cafeteria today. Ruth was a trooper, but she could see she was wearing out very fast.

"Let's pray first." They bowed their heads and closed their eyes, praying to God. He has always given both of them strength to keep moving forward. As they opened their eyes, there stood Susie just standing there staring at them.

Startled, Silvia said "Oh hi……. It's Susie, right?"

Susie nodding her head yes continued standing there staring at them. She looked a little rattled herself as she started to mumble a little.

Ruth tried to laugh and asked almost in a whisper, "Ya wanna join us?" Silvia quickly turned her head to Ruth as she said "No shhhhhh, she prob….." but was interrupted with a "Yes, of course," from Susie as she sat down in the chair next to Ruth, who was sitting in her wheel chair.

"Ruth this is one of the new ladies at our Bible study, her name is Susie….Susie, this is my daughter Ruth."

Susie nodded and then started telling them about how she was coming to see Amanda and saw Silvia over here so she thought she would come over. "Are you visiting her too?" Susie asked, ignoring the wheelchair, and the hospital gown that was draped around Ruth.

Ruth slowly lifted up her arm with the I.V. tubes. "No, I practically live here now." She started to feel even more nauseous as she started to regret asking Susie to sit down; the smell of cigarettes was so strong. She put her head down for a moment on the table.

"We really should be going Ruth." Silvia suggested as Susie began talking quickly about many different things.

"Hal and I are leaving to go find out about my birth mom but we need more money, and well I was wondering if you had any you can spare? I was hoping that Amanda could put us in touch with someone at the church. I asked everyone at the prayer meeting. I could still use some more help and I need another pack of cigarettes too. Texas is where I'm going to find my real mom." She took a huge breath and continued.

"We are going to Texas and we have to pay to get the information." She was talking non-stop and almost without taking a breath of air. The tone in her voice was almost direct and planned. "Like I said we need money for our trip to find out about my birth mom."

Silvia felt ill herself as the air filled with a deep stench of menthol or something, she couldn't quite place it. She tried to sip her latte but the smell was making her nauseous and her own taste buds tasting the air of cigarettes could not be covered with the latte.

Ruth popped her head up, she felt so drained. "I'm searching for my mom too."

Accusingly Susie questioned Silvia, "I thought this was your daughter." She looked at Silvia as if she had lied to her.

"She is my daughter, I adopted her when she was a baby, and she is my daughter in every way." Silvia smiled at Ruth.

Ruth mustered up some strength and in her excitement blurted out, "I'm searching for my birth mom on the internet. The records are all open and you just need to know where to look. There is a lady on the web site that is helping me. She seems real nice. I can give her your information when she is done with me, maybe she can help you too." Ruth was now a little more awake and enthusiastically offered to help Susie. She felt as if God was giving her an assignment, and she was to keep moving forward eagerly.

"I will need your full name and date of birth and where you were born. Oh and any info you may have or already found yourself." Ruth said in a hopeful encouraging voice. She turned back to Silvia and asked for a pen and paper. The simple motion reminded her of her massive headache. Her head was going to explode any moment. She really needed to rest, but she stayed as upbeat as she could.

"I'll see what I can do after I read to Amanda. I'm hoping to feel better after some rest. I love reading the Bible to her, and I'm hoping I'll be able to go to her room today." She looked hopeful at Silvia knowing she needed to lie down and rest soon if she was going to have enough energy to read later. Her head was spinning and she laid it down into her hands as she tried to hold it up.

Then with a little mumbling Susie sarcastically said, "I've looked at the Bible and I know all about it, there is nothing *I* need from it."

Silvia was shocked by her comment and stared at her without saying anything but thinking that she didn't strike her as someone who reads. And if she did, it was obvious she didn't comprehend. Silvia felt annoyed with her and didn't want to share what precious time she had with Ruth. She had never heard someone say out-loud they didn't need God or His Word.

Silvia didn't want to be judgmental of her, but her words made no sense. How can anyone expect God to be in his or hers corner and help them out if they rejected Him and His Word? Her stubbornness and rejection seemed almost planned, overly aggressive, attacking, mocking and deliberate. Even as Christians, we sometimes find it hard to read the Bible consistently. But the Bible is the Word of God and it speaks to us like a living breathing voice. It is our sword against the enemy. It is more precious than any treasure.

The fact that someone can rebel against and defy God was alarming. Susie's thinking was distorted and her pride had overcome any intelligence. Silvia wanted to let her know that the battle was already won, Jesus died for us all and He rose on the third day defeating death. How could this lady not need God and His Word? She wanted to share, but didn't know where to start to make it as simple as possible. How could she find any common ground with her now, so she could explain?

Silvia started to get up as Ruth let the words go unnoticed and again asked for pen and paper to take Susie's information.

It was a crazy couple of months for Amanda. It seemed as though everyone was coming by and talking to her, telling her their deep secrets from their past and present. She was having a hard time keeping a time line in her head. Everything was jumbled; her thoughts, the pages of the book she was writing as well as everyone else's secret stories, situations and prayers. The weight of the prayers felt so heavy on her shoulders. They all needed to be heard. They all had a reason to be prayed.

"Can we all grab and comprehend what it means to be in Your presence? Walking with you? The journey to the end? Fight the fight? Why is it so mixed up in my brain? What day is it, what month? How long have I laid here? How long has it been?"

As she talked with God she thought of Ruth and of her reading the Bible to her and added a prayer, "Thank you God, for Ruth, I love hearing Your Word. Please let her be whole and well. Let her be completely healed. Amen."

She then thought of how much the world seems to be much like it was in Bible times. The same battle against the same enemy……then she drifted into a deep sleep.

Philippians 4:19-20 (NLT) And this same God who takes care of me will supply all your needs from his glorious riches, which have been given to us in Christ Jesus. Now all glory to God our Father forever and ever! Amen.

1 Peter 1:6-7 (NLT) So be truly glad. There is wonderful joy ahead, even though you have to endure many trials for a little while. These trials will show that your faith is genuine. It is being tested as fire tests and purifies gold—though your faith is far more precious than mere gold. So when your faith remains strong through many trials, it will bring you much praise and glory and honor on the day when Jesus Christ is revealed to the whole world.

Psalm 55:22 (NLT) Give your burdens to the LORD, and he will take care of you. He will not permit the godly to slip and fall.

Chapter Thirty-Five

July 13 2027, Carrie

Carrie reads another short note toward the back of the binder:

    I wonder sometimes what my purpose is and today I've been reminded of Your love. I have purpose because of You and for You. I am Your girl and there is nothing more beautiful than that. You will produce fruit of love, joy, peace, gentleness, and patience in me. I must stay connected to You. My purpose is to represent You in every step I take, for Your Kingdom.

    So I keep moving forward as Your girl. You will give me the ability, the courage, and the power I need to succeed. That is all that matters. I move forward in Your light and love. My purpose is fulfilled in You. Amazing grace is what You provide for me.

    My purpose does not have to be some crazy big thing. My purpose is loving You and moving forward as Your representative, shining Your light for others. Help me to do that Lord, help me to walk as Jesus walked, with purpose in every step. There is a reason. You are the reason. You are the purpose of my life.

You died for me, so I choose to live for You. You provide all I need. I just need to be obedient and follow You in every aspect of my life one hundred percent. Thank you for guiding me through the Holy Spirit. Thank you Father for Your sacrifices.

Carrie was extremely happy with this one as she let out a huge laughing sigh. Positives, now this was more like her mom. She didn't know why but she suddenly had a flash of her mom doing her robot dance.

"Oh my goodness." She laughed some more. The robot dance was such a funny memory. Her mom would do the robot dance quite often just to try and embarrass her as she was growing up, along with her loud opera singing in the morning to wake her. Carrie loved these memories that she would always treasure. She laughed again, almost tempted to stand up and do her mama's robot dance. She knew she couldn't do it as well and again laughed at the thought.

Behind the Scenes

The machine again popped on as soon as Debbie walked in the door. It was quite long, with many names on the sheet and many words. Sentences that made a little more sense, and they looked urgent, with Bible verse under one-line statements.

"You have been busy, Miss beautiful Amanda." Debbie sat on the side of the bed and touched Amanda's cheek. "Oh sweet friend, I need you to wake up. I'm not sure what to do, please try to wake up." She genteelly coaxed Amanda.

Chapter Thirty-Six

A Look Back, March 2027

Debbie was working the evening shift. She was supposed to be off at five in the morning. She planned to go home, get a nap, and then go to the women's Bible study. But as she started doing her last rounds, taking vitals and checking on the six patients she was in charge of, she noticed that a new patient was on their way up. Amanda G. Garrison, her best friend and leader of their Bible study class.

It was a little before five a.m. when she sent out a group text. "Amanda is here in the hospital. Please everyone pray for her." Debbie then called her husband and told him she would be late getting home, she wanted to stay at the hospital a while longer to sit with Amanda and her family. She then sat down next to Amanda and prayed.

She knew she should get Amanda's paperwork done, finish up the rest of her other paperwork, and punch out, but she couldn't move. Something was keeping her there. So she continued to sit there and pray.

Two of the ladies texted back right away as she was praying.

Mary Jane's text came first, "I'll be there at nine to see her I have a few things to go over with her anyway." Next was Silvia, "Oh no does she need anything? I can bring it. I'll be at the hospital at nine too."

Debbie considered whether she should text, them back and let them know that Amanda was not in good shape. She appeared to be in a coma and her family was here in the waiting room. She decided that she would just pray and leave it in God's hands.

She felt a little concerned and troubled as to why Amanda was here on the second floor as she stood up and turned off the alarm on the IV drip. It was low. The oncoming nurse should be in soon to do her vitals. Worriedly she looked down at Amanda again and began to pray, when suddenly Dr. Prong came in seemingly excited. He jumped when he saw her standing there. He expected the room to be empty, except for his coma patient. The machine he was pushing into the room almost fell off the cart. He caught it just in time. He composed himself and not looking directly at her he walked past her to check the IV that had started to beep again.

This was the first time Debbie had seen Dr. Prong this early in the day. Normally she worked the day shift with him, and he never showed up until like ten in the morning. She has never seen him work the five p.m. to five a.m. shift she had to work, once a week.

Weird that he was there, and just where had he been all night or did he just get there? She speculated this to herself. She was not a big fan of his. He was always so secretive in his manner and his note taking on patients almost seemed to be written in code.

She decided it was time to get her paperwork done then go to the cafeteria for some food before coming back up to Amanda's room. It was going to be a long day. She left the room without saying a word.

Dr. Prong was glad the nurse didn't say anything. She just left with no words spoken. He looked at his watch, her night shift was over and he should have a few minutes to get things hooked up before the next shift started their rounds. The alarm sounded again, and he quickly silenced it. He had to hurry to get it right. Most of the nurses never questioned anything he did which usually was the bare minimum for their patients. "They won't even notice the extra machine hooked up to this one." He mumbled.

He glanced at the wrist bracelet:

Amanda G. Garrison, July 14th, 1977, age 49. Blood type: B+. Doctor in charge: Dr. L. Prong.

He was feeling a bit proud of himself for getting there late last night to test a few of his experimental drugs on his unknowing patients when he became aware of this slightly comatose lady as he was leaving through the ER department. He had overheard the nurse talking with the paramedic and he quickly went over to the computer and changed his name to the doctor on call. He knew no one would question it. The skeleton night crew in the emergency room barely noticed when Joe took her away. It was perfect timing.

He scanned her admitting chart for possible reasons that were given to the paramedics by the husband. It had seemed that she had taken to many sleeping pills and had fallen and hit her head. He truthfully didn't even know if that was true. He just knew that the woman in the cubical was out cold.

He called Joe and told him to move the woman to the second floor and give her a heavy sedative and he would then take it from there. He quickly went back to the computer to change a few more things. When he finished he went to talk to the family, which were sitting in the ER waiting room.

"Mr. Garrison, it seems that your wife is in a coma, she should wake up in time. We will need to do some tests due to the fall. A CT and possibly an MRI of her head will tell us what we need to know." He lied to the man and his daughter quite easily and told them she was going to be okay. He was going to have her moved to a room where he could keep a closer eye on her.

"Okay, thank you." Was all Chris could say as he held on to Carrie's hand. Christopher walked up as the doctor turned to leave.

"Please stay here, we'll call you once we have her settled." Dr. Prong said as he turned and walked away grinning and happy with the perfect timing.

He then told the nurse on duty that his assistant would be down to take her for the CT. She seemed relieved that she didn't have to take the time to call for it and that the doctor was there and taking the initiative. It was almost time for her to be off and she was relieved and didn't even give the patient another thought when she went back to her other charts.

Dr. Prong walked away and into the elevator. He wanted to get her settled into a room away from the trauma unit before doing too much. He'll have the CT and MRI done on another day. Right now, he needed to get his machine hooked and running. Then he can go back to the computer in his office and fudge a few things.

"YES!!! SCORE!" He almost yelled out-loud. It was time to test his machine. He was almost giddy and anxious and excited to test it out. He hadn't been this happy in years.

Debbie left quickly down the hall and stopped at the nurse's station. She felt a twisting in her gut as she hurried to type in her notes before punching out of her shift and heading to get herself some food. She glanced at her watch, knowing she was on overtime. She just couldn't shrug off the weird encounter with Dr. Prong.

She went to the cafeteria and purchased a granola bar and a coffee. She sat down at a table feeling just sick to her stomach. Again, she closed her eyes and prayed. She knew she needed to eat something if she was to remain strong so she sipped on the coffee and ate a few bites of the bar.

She sat longer than she had intended lost in her thoughts. As she got up from the table, she noticed Dr. Prong going out the front door. She walked to the door and watched him go around the building. She decided to follow him and peeked around the hospital building. He went around the next corner to the back, toward the employee parking lot. She watched as he drove away in his silver Cadillac. She leaned against the building feeling the soft wind. She took a few minutes to enjoy the early morning quietness and she wondered why he was there and where was he all night?

Debbie loved to invest her time in people knowing that when she does, she is serving God. She began to go back inside and back to Amanda's room when Valerie texted.

"Hey, I'll be driving right by the church, would you like me to put up a sign on the door that the Bible study is cancelled today and that Amanda is in hospital?"

Debbie reached the room and looked down at Amanda with tears in her eyes and texted back "Yes, please, thank you." She bowed her head for the tenth time and said another prayer for Amanda, begging God for His complete recovery for her best friend.

The machine hooked to Amanda spit out a small printout, *"God is the shelter…. For the righteous…. But evil…. Is lurking….. Battle has begun…… Players are in place…. Prayers."* She felt spooked by that as she tore off the printout and put it into her pocket. Why was this brain machine hooked up to Amanda? And what do those words mean?

Debbie couldn't stop trembling as she cleared her mind. Again, Dr. Prong's actions seemed off as she tried to figure out why he was there. She decided to walk to the nurse's station and look at the printed schedule she had printed out and kept in her personal drawer. She hadn't noticed his name on there. Picking it up and glancing at it, she noticed she was right; his name was not on there. As a matter-of-fact, he was listed as off for the Friday, Saturday and Sunday, which was a surprise. The doctor on call was Dr. R. Rolland. She checked the log on the computer and noticed he never checked in all night, but neither did Dr. L Prong. Yet, he was listed as Amanda's attending doctor.

She then went into the computer feeling like an investigator and found that the schedule on-line listed Dr. L. Prong on

A Look Back, March 2027

call. Maybe they switched? She questioned no one but herself as she printed another copy.

She never questioned Dr. Prong and if she did point out anything wrong, she was sure she would be out the door. Dr. Prong was not one to be messed with. Debbie was pretty good at avoiding him for the most part. Maybe she was just tired and reading more into it than what was there. Yet…….. she had a strange feeling that she needed to be here to protect Amanda. She hurried back to her room.

Another printout spit out from the machine. *"God's word…. Our standard…We are blameless …..In his sight…… Avoid evil."* Again, she tore it off. Looking over the machine and the wires connected to Amanda's head, made her wonder who had approved this machine. She was sure that it was not yet authorized for use. She was pretty sure it hadn't been made available yet for experimentation. So she turned it off for the time being.

Just then, Amanda's family walked in somewhat rattled and scared for Amanda.

"She'll be okay." Debbie reassured them as she hugged each of them. "I'll make sure I'm her attending nurse okay?" She nodded then asked what happened.

Chris answered. "She fell somehow, in the bathroom…. about two or three this morning….I heard a loud noise and went to see what it was and she was on the floor, her head was bleeding. I think she hit it on the sink."

Carrie started to cry. And sat on the bed and held her mom's hand. Her brother Christopher just stood there in silence.

"She was conscience for about a minute. She said she took sleeping pills……I asked her how many she took and she said she thinks she took three……..oh my God, why would she take that many?" He started to freak out as he looked at Debbie wanting her to answer.

1 Corinthians 16:13 (NLT) Be on guard. Stand firm in the faith. Be courageous. Be strong.

Chapter Thirty-Seven

July 13 2027, Carrie

Carrie couldn't wait to read some more. The Buzzzzzzing Fly peeked her interest:

That buzzzzzzing fly………………………….That pestering fly
The fly that won't stop his hours of buzzing,
he was persistent
He was at my work, in my car, at church and now at my home
Was he sent by You Lord? Are you trying to get my attention?
I was busy……..Yes, busy doing Your work……..Stuff for You
Yet I do know
Busy with my hands and feet……….
Can rob me of time with You
Our time together……………..Just You and me
I'm so sorry……………..Please forgive me
Time alone with You is what I need
I looked at my opened Bible on the table….I started to read
The fly landed and then was gone….the buzzing stopped
Thank you for the reminder

Thank you for the buzz……..That buzzzzzzzing fly
that wouldn't quit

Carrie had to laugh as she set the book down and watched a fly land on the table next to her drink. "Ya I know God; we are to walk daily in our lives with You by our side. We are like a walking Bible to the world. Everything in the scriptures is lived out in our lives as You direct us. The words of the Bible have not changed. Many generations have gone by and the Bible has stood the test of time. God, I thank You for the words of scripture and I delight in them. My mom, she delights in Your Word too. We can read Your Word for hours, days and years and still be uplifted with Your wisdom. I just want to thank You. Amen." Carrie loved just talking with God. Carrie put the binder down, picked up the Bible, turned to Psalm 116 and read.

Behind the Scenes

Dr Prong quickly exited the hospital through the front door, hoping that he wasn't seen by any of his staff. The nurse barely looked at him as he pushed the brain machine into the room. He doubts she even noticed it.

As for the lady in the bed, he couldn't wait to start having fun with the experiments. He will prove his machine works with no complications. It might even be fun to inject her with Joe's experimental medication as well as shut down sections of her brain. That is, after he maps it all out.

He loved how he is able to use the experimental shots in his unsuspecting patients and close down the morality thought processing portion of their brains. He may even go as far as inserting the CHIPS into this woman's forehead while he is at it. Too bad, she wasn't a real comatose subject. But she will do! It will be quite easy to keep her that way. He had to admit, Joe's cocktail shots were amazing.

Dr. Prong called the husband on his cell phone from his car and told him his wife was getting settled in on the second floor room 236 and he could go up to her room but to let her rest and not try to wake her. He told him he would keep him updated daily and asked what time was a good time to call him.

Dr. Prong knows from experience he must appear to be caring and friendly with the subjects family if he was to get away with…..murder. Once he kills them off, he is able to get them to the basement for his tests. First, he must play the game of trustworthy doctor.

And this one, this woman, this subject is special. She is hooked to his brain machine. He'll have to try to keep this one alive.

How was he ever gonna rest with all this on his mind?

Chapter Thirty-Eight

Late June 2027, Amanda

Most of the ladies have been coming in to talk with me. They all think it's a good time to get things off their chests and expose their secrets. They don't know whether I can hear them or even think about what they are saying. They just want to talk. Oh and yes, pray as well. I love when they pray.

It's nice to have visitors. It's nice to hear them pray for me and for each other. Most days I can comprehend and pay attention if they come early enough in the morning. At least I think it's morning. That is when they seem to come clean the room and change the bedding. The strong smell of bleach wakens my brain. I finally have figured out, I am not at home. I am not at church teaching my class. I'm here at the hospital. 'Squirrel' "Hey Toto, I have a feeling were not in Kansas anymore." Oh good I still have some humor left. Well at least I think it's funny.

Debbie is here several times on most days and I am able to release some thoughts from my brain to that brain machine.

Dr. Prong is here most days and nights as well and the drugs that flow into my veins confuse me and make me very sleepy. I try to fight it, I try to open my eyes, but I can't. I feel like I'm paralyzed. How long has it been? Are the sleeping pills still working? Am I dreaming all of this? I didn't mean to take so many. I just needed the rest. I want to wake up, I really do.

The blood in my veins moves so very slow and my breathing feels just as slow. My lungs barely fill with air. Everything feels like it's in slow motion. I can almost feel my blood move throughout my body, thick and sluggish, like old motor oil.

Chris is here every day as well. I really wish he would get some rest. He is so worried and sad. I want to send him a message but what if he doesn't notice it come out. I can't take that chance, not yet. The stuff the doctor says when he is here scares me, and I'm sure he is drugging me to keep me still and asleep. I can only release my thoughts to Debbie.

My kids, Carrie and Christopher come every few days, usually when Chris is here. Carrie cries a lot and holds my hand. Christopher doesn't say much, but I can tell he is very worried.

The doctor hasn't come in this morning yet, did he forget about me? Maybe he has other plans for me? My mind feels talkative today and I can't wait for Debbie to come in. I need the one on one with everyone while I can think. I need to say thanks and I need to help them. Will today be the day I wake up? Gosh, I sure hope so. I feel like I almost can.

Debbie

Debbie had the day off and decided to start laminating and organizing all the printouts, she had collected. She loved how they came out each time she entered the room, even though she turned off the machine every time she left for the day. She was sure that Dr. Prong turned it on to check it, probably mad that it was off again. She made a mental note to herself to check the roll of printing paper in the brain machine. It would be a dead giveaway if he were to notice it getting low with nothing to show for it.

She was amazed at how the printout writings looked like Amanda's own handwriting. It really was awesome. The technology was superb, but not approved due to the electrical current being administered to the brain which could cause more damage in the long run. Overall, she was stunned that the machine worked and it did allow for a two-way communication. Although if she really thought about it, maybe the only reason it's working is because Amanda is not in a real coma ….she is just in the one, that they have created. Debbie had suspected for a while now that Dr. Prong was keeping her in a drug-induced coma, she just couldn't prove it.

She felt a little exhausted and needed this day off at home to regroup and get these printouts organized. Depending on how long it takes, she was hoping to still make it up to the hospital to check on Amanda, even though she knows Chris will be there at some point. He stops by every day. Different times. Sometimes before work or at lunch time and sometimes he comes after work and stays for hours.

She started with all the printouts with Ruth's name on them. She decided to put all of Ruth's printouts on pink paper with flowers around the edges. Colorful flowers. It was perfect for Ruth, who was so colorful and happy the whole time she has known her.

Debbie wanted to reach out to her and tell her about the printouts but wasn't sure she should reveal them to anyone yet. Soon, it would have to be soon. Ruth was in no shape to be waiting. Each day she is declining quickly.

Late June 2027, Amanda

She decided that she would at least tell Ruth that she knows the gift of her reading the Bible is appreciated and is truly loved by Amanda. It was the best gift she could give. Although she is sure that Ruth already knows, because Silvia reads to Ruth when she can't do it for herself and she is so thankful. Debbie loves that about Ruth; even though Ruth is barely moving some days, she always is so thankful for everything. She truly is grateful. Debbie has never met anyone as appreciative as Ruth. She is such a great example and inspiration to Debbie.

Ruth ….Thank you. You read to me. It fills my heart. God's word is what I need. 2 Tim 3:16, Rom 15:4, 2 Peter 1:19-21, Psalm 19:7-11

Ruth ….Fear not sweet girl. 2 Cor 5:8. Forever home. I'm grateful to you. Your time, your Bible reading to me. I know. Deut 31:8-9

Next, she chose purple paper for Silvia. She used small handprints around the edges that were pink in color and found it to be very relaxing.

Silvia….. Seek His peace. Hold on to His promises. Matt 5:4, Rom 12:15, 2 Cor 1:3-4, Rev 21:4

She chose a blue paper with white clouds for Nell and used some cute pictures of pink and blue yarn around the edges of the paper. She was quite impressed with it as she glued the print out paper to the blue with clouds and then laminated it like the others. She then put the laminated sheet into her folder labeled 'NELL'.

Nell......Ask Him for forgiveness. Believe. You are forgiven. Matt 11:28-30, Rom 8:26-28, 39, Psalm 34:18, Prov 28:13

For Mary Jane she chose a light brown paper and used the stickers she had with cute pink cowgirl boots and lasso rope and put them around the edges.

Mary Jane....Tough girl. Thank you for your prayers. Don't harbor secret sins. Don't tolerate that sin in your heart. Make a clean break. Phil 4:13, Prov 17:3, Prov 17:9, Prov 20:1

She decided to work on Carries next. Florescent green paper with books around the edges was her choice. Brilliant she thought, because everyone knows that Carrie loves to read. She finished and put hers in a folder and labeled it with her name.

Carrie....Don't be sad. Help brother, understand. 1 Thess 4:13-18, Prov 16:17

There were a few printouts that were addressed to Pickles. She didn't know any Pickles but made the scrapbook pages dark green and placed photos of pickle jars in the corners.

Pickles......It's not too late. Seek. Rom 12:2, Prov 15:2, Prov 16:7, Prov 19:23

There was one printout for Susie. She laminated the printout on red paper with roses in one of the corners of the page.

Susie......Prov 19:3 Seek Him. Don't blame Him.

Roxie was next. ABC paper with colors of red, blue, green and yellow, was a perfect choice for her.

Roxie.... Today, get right with God. Josh 1:9, Rom 8:28, Acts 2:38

Then Valerie, with a mustard yellow paper with swirly lines around the edges was her choice.

Valerie....Stay put. Col 3:13, Prov 16:1

She then did her own. Labeled Best Friend Debbie in bright yellow, which is Amanda's favorite color and sunflowers throughout, Amanda's favorite flower.

Debbie.....Prov 16:3

She had several more with no name, and some that looked like prayers. And there were many with random Bible verses. She made copies of those, one for each folder, as they were appropriate for any of the girls. She placed those on plain white paper to laminate.

James 5:16....Pray for each other. He hears.

Luke 6:37....Do not judge.

Eph....4:31-32

She had one more pile and labeled it Chris for Amanda's husband. Much of them labeled as apologies and prayers.

It had taken her almost seven hours to complete them all. But they were now all laminated and into their own yellow folders. She hand printed the Bible study verse for their class on the front. Proverbs 27:17 As iron sharpens iron, so one woman sharpens another, for all the women.

She placed all the folders into an empty computer paper box and cleaned up her mess.

She glanced at the clock and realized she hadn't eaten all day and it was almost dinnertime. Her husband would be home soon. She then started dinner. She finished just in time for her husband to walk through the door.

Chapter Thirty-Nine

July 13 2027, Carrie

Carrie flipped back to her mom's RTP rambles that she posted to social media:

The last few weeks have been challenging to me....to speak the truth of God when it's unpopular and might offend someone.......it is and can be a hard thing to do.......I have been faced with several different scenarios lately.........to give people Biblical truths and then pray that a seed was planted..... My Christian friends, I pray that you all will stand strong on ONLY God's foundation.......anything that does NOT line up with what God says in the Bible or contradicts what God says in the Bible ....is false...period!!! If it offends someone to speak the truth, so be it......we can NOT give in to the world's demands, we must stick with God's truth....period.......we must however treat people with respect, dignity and kindness....the golden rule, that Jesus teaches us in Matthew 7:12........every single person was created by God, each one was given freewill..... freewill to either accept or reject a relationship with Him....... every person has a life to live....choices to make....good and bad……no one is perfect……and we are not here on this earth to judge anyone….that will be the task at hand for Jesus…….. so many do not believe in eternal life….they live for the here and now….but that is their life….their freewill, their choice….I CHOOSE GOD and I choose a life with Him….it is MY choice ……..my freewill to do so……..weird how that offends some people…..but I will say…I will not back down….I will speak the truth in love when God places it on my heart to do so……..I will not pressure anyone….I will provide truth….God's truth……and then I will pray……..I write today to encourage all of you who are Christians, those of you who belong to God…….if something is spoken that is not correct……replace it with truth…….. you can't make people accept the truth…… so far in America we can still speak about our Almighty Father, who loves us so much……we need to LEARN, LIVE and GIVE……so, don't be afraid to speak God's truth….don't miss an opportunity to GIVE a gift of Gods truth to those around you….LEARN it and LIVE it….. God Bless You and God Bless America.

Behind the Scenes

Joe entered the room, it was very early. The skeleton crew was busy doing their various jobs and they wouldn't notice him. Three-thirty in the morning was the perfect time to come. Dr. Prong insisted that he continued to keep her heavily sedated.

"She has too many visitors, I don't want her to wake up or move in any way."

He didn't care what was in the I.V. or the injection as long as it mixed with his many experimental medications. He checked the brain machine, turned it on and made sure the wires were

July 13 2027, Carrie

all connected, correctly. It appeared to be fine, even with the extra wires and high current which surprised him.

After injecting the drug into the I.V. port, he quickly went to Dr. Prong's office and left a full syringe for the doctor to inject later in the day. He then hurried down to the basement to work on his many other subjects.

Chapter Forty

Nell

Oh how Nell hated the monsoon. This season was not her favorite time. In case you're wondering, monsoon is a singular word that describes all the storms that form during the summer here in southern Arizona.

The day was hot and muggy. Even in her home, the sweat trickled down the back of her neck. On most days, she just stayed indoors because going outside felt like sitting in a sauna in the middle of the desert, miserable to say the least. It was hell itself outside of her small two-bedroom duplex. Nell had lived in duplexes her whole life. She liked the feeling of knowing someone else, anyone else was close by, even though she was not social with any of them.

She had all six of her fans running along with the swamp cooler, which did nothing due to the humidity. It still felt like 120 degrees. She laughed to herself, "Dry Heat??" They say that it's a dry heat but she has never believed it for even a second. The mugginess and humidity during monsoon can last anywhere from two to three months and is almost unbearable. Her tolerance for the heat has all but left her these last few years. She has hated this time of year for years now but moving seemed even worse, so she complained to herself and somehow she always made it though year after year.

Nell had started storing water and food back in April in hopes that she only needed to leave her home for church and to deliver the hats she made for the hospital every month. Luckily, her old beat up Ford had AC and both the church and the hospital weren't far away.

Nell chuckled to herself as she looked around the spare bedroom full of water and supplies. She even had tons of different yarn for knitting her baby hats. She was feeling so proud of herself for this brilliant idea of stockpiling stuff for the summer. She grabbed some water to put in the refrigerator and remembered how her parents used to do the same thing in their home when she was young, for when the snow came. They had taught her well even though they were not around much.

Nell was a tall woman and even taller when she wore her mama's heels. They made her feel domineering and even strong at times. Both her parents have passed on, and she felt very alone in life especially when the weather was wet and gloomy, like today. She had moved to Arizona to avoid this kind of weather.

She took one last look at her stockpile and thought about the young lady that lived next door. Her name is Holly and she is in her twenties and lived alone. Nell again chucked at the thought that Holly must have a room or at least a closet full of scarves. Nell watches her from her window as she leaves for work each day, wearing a different scarf, even on the hot days. Again, she chuckled to herself, as she knew she was not exaggerating that thought. Holly had a different scarf for every day, all year long, even though this was Arizona.

She laughed again, as her eye caught the pile of yarn, "Well I may have her beat. I have enough yarn to make thousands of hats." She smiled and decided she would make Holly a hat with a matching scarf for Christmas this year. She felt happy and content right then, knowing Holly would love it.

Even though she was asked not to bring any more beanies to the hospital, she decided that she would still make them and some larger hats and scarves for all the ladies in her Bible study too. She felt good about that decision. Maybe she can even give them away to the Veterans at the VA hospital.

As she walked back to her living room, she decided to lie down and rest for a bit. Even though it was late to be napping and even if she did manage to sleep with the fan blowing on her, she probably would be up all night. But regardless, she felt like a short nap would do her good.

As she lied down, she thought about her grandmother. So many memories danced in her head. She remembered how her grandmother would sit in her big orange recliner knitting the most beautiful blankets. Nell still had the one her grandmother made for her when she was five years old. She still remembers that day. Her family was still a family at that time and she was so excited because grandma had made a matching even bigger blanket for mom and dad's bed too. Grandma passed away when Nell was only nine years old and all she remembered was that her family was never the same. They all just survived. Nell felt so ignored after grandma was gone. She was left alone most of the time. She definitely raised herself from that point on.

Nell

Nell started knitting at around six years old. Her grandma sat her down and patiently taught her. She wasn't very good at it, but kept practicing especially after her grandma had passed away and she fought with her mom to keep all the yarn and needles in her bedroom, instead of giving them away.

Now lying on the couch she reached for that knitted blanket, knowing no one would ever appreciate the blanket like she does. She wrapped herself up and lightly cried herself to sleep. Oh how she still missed her grandma.

It was the middle of the week around 5:30 pm when Debbie called her and woke her from her dreams.

"Hey there Old Lady Nell, how are you? This is Debbie from the church, you know from Bible study?"

Nell wiped her sweaty hair out of her face as she sat up almost feeling like she was in a trance, wishing she had let the phone ring. She was so emotionally drained today.

"Oh, yes, yes, hi dear" then in her mean voice "What do you want?" She asked as she wondered why Debbie was calling her and how she even got her phone number.

She knew Debbie was always a nice lady, almost too nice and cheerful for Nell's taste. Debbie was always seeing the good in everything and everyone. Truthfully, Nell thought it was all just an act. She always said how much pain she was in all the time, from her migraines and Nell knows that pain does not make you happy. Yet, there was Debbie, the happy nice cheerful lady.

Nell never could pretend to be happy, and most of the time she didn't even try. She decided to tell everyone to call her Old Lady Nell so that she wouldn't have to explain herself. They would just pass it off to the fact that she was old. A great excuse for being unhappy, bitter and negative which is how she felt most of the time anyway.

When Debbie hesitated for a moment, Nell asked again, in an even more angry voice "Well dear what do you want? I'm trying to nap." As she said the word "dear" almost sarcastically, she caught herself at how mean she can be sometimes. But she really didn't care, not any more. She felt God's forgiveness, but here again; she was in her own pity party. It takes a lot of hard work to stay joyful she thought.

She had gone to talk with Amanda, and Valarie had interrupted her confession at the hospital. Even though she had felt some relief inside, she continued to be angry and she was no closer to knowing if her little girl was okay. Forty-six years she hadn't known, but hearing what actually happened when she was only two years old put her mind in a state of shock. She refused to believe or acknowledge the ugly truth.

She was wrong all those years ago. How will she ever be able to live with herself now? She thought about Valerie and prayed for her, and the situation she put her in forty-six years ago. Valarie was on the run and in hiding most of her life, looking over her shoulder, not wanting to be found. It was all her fault and she felt sad about that.

Nell had moved to Arizona when she was in her thirties, after her parents decided to move to Maine. She cleaned houses for a living. She didn't have much social interaction except for when she went to church or to the hospitals to bring the beanies. So many years have passed and she has been a loner for most of them.

Again, Nell asked Debbie, "Well….what is it dear?"

Nell

---※---

Nell really didn't want to be out driving right now. Not only was the sky looking like rain in several areas, but it would be dark soon.

It wasn't safe to be out at night, especially during a monsoon storm. Then unexpectedly, her worst fear materialized, the sky suddenly got darker and quickly it was above her. BOOM! The sound of thunder blasted above her. She could see the lightning strike, and she knew it was all around her. And just like that, rain drops as hard as a hammer hitting a nail hammered her car. A monsoon storm, there's nothing like it. You never know when it's gonna hit, which is why she stays home.

Nell wondered if she would get there in time. She always felt there was some sort of connection between Ruth and her, but never in her wildest dreams would it be this.

Debbie's words on the phone had her heart racing. Could it really be true? Could Ruth really be her granddaughter?

Susie

That very same day in Texas, Susie found out her birth mom's name was, Nellie R. Jones.

Psalm 66:18-20 (NLT) If I had not confessed the sin in my heart, the Lord would not have listened. But God did listen! He paid attention to my prayer. Praise God, who did not ignore my prayer or withdraw his unfailing love from me.

John 15:7 (NLT) But if you remain in me and my words remain in you, you may ask for anything you want, and it will be granted!

Philippians 4:6 (NLT) Don't worry about anything; instead, pray about everything. Tell God what you need, and thank him for all he has done.

1 Peter 3:12 (NLT) The eyes of the Lord watch over those who do right, and his ears are open to their prayers. But the Lord turns his face against those who do evil."

Chapter Forty-One

Mary Jane

It had been three years since her fight with Cindy and Mary Jane had made many changes. She even went to counseling to get help. Well, it wasn't on her own accord, but she did go.

Mary Jane sort of remembers the day. After all it was three years ago. What she really remembers is that the police stopped her on her way home afterwards. A fresh cut on her check and that darn sidewalk. That particular sidewalk always gets her, even when she's sober. She was lucky the police officer was a friend of hers and he didn't give her a ticket or throw her in jail. He followed her home and made her promise to get some help. He stood there as she made the call to turn herself in for counseling so she could get the help she needed.

She did really well for the first two years, the courts made sure of it. She tells everyone she has been clean for years now and her only drug was three pieces of dark chocolate she eats every day at noon. But with all the changes she had made, she has not been able to see her granddaughter Darleen.

Again lately, the bottle seemed to be her only friend and it was always there for her and always on her side. Her tendency to be in control got worse over the years, and every attempt to contact her daughter or granddaughter had been shoved back at her. The courts have made it clear she is not to have contact with them, not that she could. Cindy had moved them and changed Darleen's school. Her phone number however has remained the same, and Mary Jane is sure it was only to torment her.

Touching the scar on her cheek, she began to feel sorry for herself yet again. She was no longer mad but sad as she drank a second full shot of courage. She tried to call Nell but there was no answer.

Forgetting that she had already done so months ago, before all the craziness started, she figured since Amanda was the one everyone went to, she would go too. After all, she did give good advice based on God's Word. She knew she could trust in that. And Amanda would not tell anyone. So she got herself up, out the door, into her truck and off she went, hoping Amanda was finally awake.

Mary Jane wanted to tell Amanda about the conversation on the phone she had with both Roxie and Cindy. She needed prayers. And even in her condition, she knew Amanda would pray them.

There was an accident a few miles from the hospital and it helped to keep her from dozing off. She had to admit she was a little bit drunk and tired. As she drove by, the flashing lights from the fire trucks and police cars made her feel dizzy as she watched from the rearview mirror thinking that one of the crashed cars looked familiar.

It easily could have been her due to her condition, but that thought didn't even occur to her.

The rain pounded on her windshield and she loved it. BOOM, another crash of thunder. Her whole body enjoying the sound and looking at the flashes of light out every window, as the lightning danced to its own song. The wildness of the night sang deep to her soul. She has always loved monsoon time. Water was always good on the ranch and much needed in the fields. The rain makes her want to dance and sing.

How fitting it was for this night. She craved another drink even though she knew it didn't take away any of her pain. "Well just a little, a little pain can dance its way out." She wiggled a little dance and laughed as she glanced one more time in her rearview mirror.

Nell

Old Lady Nell's heart was racing, her thoughts and emotions going in five different directions. The thunderstorm was raging, almost as much as her mind was. All she could do was think of Ruth laying there on the hospital bed ready to meet her maker. Debbie's explanation left her with so many unanswered questions.

Nell was quick tempered with her so she hurried the conversation along as fast as she could. "Listen..... Nell...... are you sitting down?" Debbie said in her kindest voice.

"Ya, ya, go ahead. I told you I was napping, go on...I'm listening."

"I have some exciting news for you," she said without even listening to the response that time.

"I'm not sure how to say this, but I am calling for Ruth and I have some news for you. I know who your granddaughter is. And you know her too. It's Ruth. Ruth is your granddaughter." Debbie was so excited as she explained to Nell.

"Ya see, Ruth has been searching for her birth mom. And she has found her and to make a long story short, you are the grandmother; your daughter gave Ruth up for adoption seventeen years ago." Nell tried to process what she was hearing.

"Hello, Nell did you know that you have a granddaughter? Nell you need to get up here to the hospital. Ruth is here and may not make it much longer. Ruth is not doing well at all. Ruth wants to give you a hug." All those words and so much confusion flooded her whole body.

Ruth needs her to be there. Ruth wants a hug. Ruth is her granddaughter?.....? How could this be, when she doesn't even know who *her* own daughter is? Her daughter is missing. Valerie's boyfriend traded her for drugs. I don't even know her name. I have a family? What? Her mind was going in different directions.

Could the test she had done eight months ago to find out her genealogy locate a whole family? Was she dreaming?

"I'll be right there Debbie." She said and hung up the phone. She felt like she was in a trance, something was leading her out the door and into her car. She asked God to protect Ruth, her granddaughter. Just maybe she will find her daughter as well.

So much was on her mind as a spark of lightning flashed in front of her. Rain was pouring, hitting her car. Even though she was unable to see in front of her, Nell hit the accelerator trying to go as fast as she could. She was on the fastest route from her home to the hospital but the roads were so wet already and huge puddles were already forming all around her. If she didn't hurry she would have to turn around and go another way.

Rivers of water developed as quickly as a blink of an eye every time the monsoon hit, everyone knows this. Flash floods were nothing to joke about. Never ever should you try to make it through the areas that are flooded, but as one of those areas appeared Nell went for it. The car in front of her made it, so she went for it, ignoring the signs that read 'Do not enter when flooded'. Knowing her car could be swept away as quick as a flash she went for it as fast as she could................YES..........She made it. She made it, and her heart raced. That was kinda scary and fun and so stupid all at the same time. She never was adventurous and now she felt renewed as her heartbeat faster, she felt like anything was possible. After all, she may have a family.

She pulled over to the side of the road, she needed a minute. Her heart was beating so hard. The river was flowing so hard. How did she make that? As she tried to look back, she thought she could see the white car that was behind her bobbing down the river. The flash of lightening lit up the water, but this time she didn't see it. The white car was gone, already down the river. She needed to hurry. She reached down to grab her phone out of her purse and called 911 just in case the white car needed help. She was afraid to continue to the hospital and afraid to go back now.

She prayed about the missing white car and then asked, "Could it be possible Lord......... a family, a real family?"

The huge streams of water all around her made her think of the day she was baptized. They made her go completely under the water with her nose plugged. She didn't like getting her face wet but it had to be done. Completely under. The Bible never said anything about sprinkling with water on top of your head. So under she went.

"Has it taken this long for You to forgive me? Or has it taken this long for me to forgive myself? Have I known all along but pushed it away? Oh God, I do believe, I do believe You died for my sins, oh please forgive me, forgive me Father. Why have I been so stubborn? Thank you for this, thank you for Ruth." She sat for a few more minutes and thought about all the Bible verses she had read. She knew full well that satan causes the bad things to happen. He is relentless. She felt a sense of renewal, one she has been feeling since she spent time in God's Word going over the verses from the Pastor's wife.

Her mind was leaping with joy in the middle of a real storm. Ruth was her granddaughter. She needed to get to her. She needed the hug. And she needed it now.

She could see the green light ahead, so she pulled out and gunned it to make the light. There was no stopping her now. As she approached closer to the intersection she saw the light turn yellow ….faster, faster she thought, as her foot pressed down harder, willing her beat up old car to go through. Just as she was rushing through the intersection her eyes focused on the windshield wiper blades, "I should have replaced those weeks ago," she said aloud. Then she caught a glimpse of the red light above her and the shadow of a huge dark truck headed right toward her side of the car. She didn't even have time to release a scream as the sound of screeching tires and a blast of a horn caught her ears and flooded her mind.

Mary Jane

Mary Jane passed the accident and watched from her rear-view mirror as it disappeared into the dark sky, her good mood fading for a moment with it. BOOM, more thunder. The rain was coming down in buckets now and she instantly wanted to squeal with laughter, but again for a moment she stopped her rejoicing and prayed for the people in the accident. It saddened her that they probably were not enjoying the thunder and lightning and rain symphony that roared in the night.

She suddenly realized as she prayed, that nothing had changed in her life and again she saw she was so messed up. She knew wholeheartedly that she had better start that cleanup in her life again if it was gonna work with Cindy's demands. Another BOOM and she decided to turn around and go back home. She will have to go some other time, maybe in the next few days to talk to Amanda.

She made a U-turn and passing the accident for the second time, she slowed down to concentrate on her driving and to get a better look. She was sure that the car looked so familiar but she couldn't place it. The rain made all of it as distorted as her eyesight was. She decided she needed to get back home and sleep it off.

Then another BOOM BOOM and once again she was back in dance mode. Tomorrow was the meeting with Roxie and her daughter, Cindy. She needed to be clear-eyed and mentally sharp.

Roxie was a good person and a good friend and she went out of her way to convince Cindy, to hear her out and see if they can reconcile their relationship, maybe a little at a time.

Roxie had assured her that she would be there to mediate it, in a casual place where both of them could be comfortable and not feel threatened.

Mary Jane wanted and needed to do whatever it took to be able to be part of Darleen's life. "Father please help me do this, help me clean up my mess, please Father God help me. Help me again." She said in a slightly slurred voice as she approached her home, still wiggling and dancing to the rain.

She knew she needed to pour out every bit of whiskey she had as soon as she went inside. A new beginning was going to take place right now and she knew 'the devil made me do it' was not going to work this time. She needed to take responsibility of her life and her actions.

The call from Cindy warning her that she had conditions and that Mary Jane will have to comply when they meet or else she would be gone again for good and forever rattled through her in a shiver as she took one more swig and then poured out all the whiskey she had. She even poured out the hidden bottles for the second time in her life.

Will she really give in to all the demands, whatever they are? Can God help her through this? She did feel sincere and serious this time, and she knew God would forgive her if she turned her life around and went in the right direction. She really did feel sorry she had taken this on-ramp to sin and disobedience to God. She knelt down, asked for forgiveness, and asked for help to be His girl. She felt broken and it hurt. She knew that only God could fix this mess if she did *her* part to fix things.

She couldn't help but think about the lesson on sinful nature from Romans chapter eight. She knew her life needed to be centered on God, and she needed to do it today, right now, not tomorrow. Feeling guilty, she knew yesterday would have been the better choice to start. But here she was again apologizing to God and praying that He would forgive her, and praying that Cindy will too.

She then remembered the lesson about those controlled by the Holy Spirit and how they do things to please the Spirit. Oh, how she wanted that, she did not want to please her sinful nature any more. She was a child of God, she had made the decision to get right with Him, and she needed to start living as if she belonged to Him. She wants Him to be pleased with her. She must fix her eyes on the good, right, pure, lovely, admirable, excellent, and things that are worthy of praise.

He is the reason for living. He has already given her the best gifts of all. His Son. Forgiveness. And Eternal life.

Mary Jane continued to pray and talk with God throughout the night.

Psalm 71:20 (NLT) You have allowed me to suffer much hardship, but you will restore me to life again and lift me up from the depths of the earth.

Psalm 51:17 (NLT) The sacrifice you desire is a broken spirit. You will not reject a broken and repentant heart, O God.

Psalm 34:8-9 (NLT) Taste and see that the LORD is good. Oh, the joys of those who take refuge in him! Fear the LORD, you his godly people, for those who fear him will have all they need.

Psalm 147:3 (NLT) He heals the brokenhearted and bandages their wounds.

Chapter Forty-Two

July 13 2027, Carrie

Carrie had been reading all day. She couldn't believe how much time had passed. She thought of calling her dad, but decided to read some more instead, another random thoughts page:

Be still....listen....reveal the truth.....blessings....kindness....Jesus....eyes opened....heart full.

My mind does have room, my heart overflows, my thoughts are Your thoughts, my body responds....Your words, the writing You have put on my heart....the kindness of the pen...the key that unlocks the room.....a new room to explore.....a new room to be filled.....clear intentions....anticipation....revealing....gentleness of Your touch....my soul leaps with joy....my soul reaches for love...the exposure of my thoughts....the knowledge of a revelation....centered on Christ....the protection that surrounds me...I walk in His presence.....words cannot explain.....yet it is written so well....You look deep into my soul.....show me You are here......forever......Your words are written down….I honor You…….Your Word sustains me…..Your words never leave me….written in my heart….the beauty of the stillness…..the beauty of Your kindness…….a sliver of what is to come….peace…..thank you for Your strength when I have none….the courage when I am frightened…..the ability to serve when I feel I have nothing to give…..the calmness in the storm when I feel anxious…..the love when the world offers none…. thank you for reminding me….this is not my home…..I am undeserving yet spoiled …..there are no favorites, yet I am special…….I am part of the flock that follows so close….I sing praise yet I can't even sing….the words are beautiful….Your love fills me….so in the stillness, I listen…..You reveal Your truths and blessings are given freely……Your kindness is so sweet….Jesus, my Lord and Savior…..my eyes are opened and my heart is full. You give me reason to carry on.

Behind the Scene

Dr. Prong decided enough is enough. There is no reason the brain is not shooting out the thoughts. He again turned up the current. "This is going to fry your brain little lady, you better start talking." He waited for a few minutes longer, "That's it!" He was intensely frustrated and completely done with this portion of his experiment. He decide he better call the husband and declare her brain dead. She obviously was too stupid to respond or even know what he was capable of doing to her.

"Boohoo little lady, I'm calling your family. They need to sign you off." He smirked as if he had already won.

He couldn't wait to call the family to let them know that she was not going to make it.

Chapter Forty-Three

Late June 2027

Morning came too quick for Roxie as she jumped up and realized it had stopped raining and the sun was shining bright through her blinds. Roxie had convinced Mary Jane and her daughter Cindy to sit and talk with each other and she would be there as their mediator.

Kevin was in an unusual good mood as she rushed to get dressed for the day. Today she was on the 'light' street. She felt happy and alive. It had been awhile since she had felt this joyful and she praised God as she put on her shoes. "Shoes of Peace." She smiled.

Her thoughts then focused on how Kevin had been in a support group many many years ago. But ever since they moved to this apartment, he hadn't even tried to get connected with them. Maybe she could have a talk with him when she gets home, as long as he was sober. She took a moment and prayed about it.

Late June 2027

Kevin

Kevin had become closed off to any new ideas or friends and became overly defensive at even the mention of going to church with Roxie on the weekends. His negativity over the years has contributed to his anger. Taking responsibility for his setbacks in life was much needed, but never happened. It was always someone else's fault.

The move to an apartment had been a major setback and a downgrade for his ego. Turning to alcohol was his remedy, his fix. If only he hadn't started drinking again. The poison brought out his ugly side and his anger full throttle.

He had been given many chances by his boss, many do-over's, many fix it's, and many cover-ups until it could no longer be tolerated and he had to be let go from his job. He knew the boss had no other choice.

He knew that losing his job was only part of their many problems. The loss of finances landed them where they were now. Luckily, he was still picking up a few side jobs along the way, working for a friend's company, helping as a bricklayer. "Drinking is just part of the job" he justifies it and excuses it.

Kevin's good mood today had Roxie wishing she could stay home and enjoy it with him. But Ms. Peace Keeper needed to work her magic. The meeting today was overdue and she prayed it would be successful.

She was headed out the door when Kevin stopped her. "Hey Hun, let's go out for lunch today, I have a few things to discuss with you……." He smiled and kissed her.

The look on her face made him smile. "Don't worry it's all good." He continued to smile in an almost flirty way.

Kevin watched her get into her car and then pulled out the pamphlet he had in his pocket that his new co-worker Fred, gave to him a few days ago. He sat and read it for the second time. Then he prayed.

Roxie

Roxie decided to stop by a yard sale on her way to the meeting. She was extremely excited to check it out and she was glad she had left a few minutes early. She followed the signs that said, 'huge used book sale and lots of other stuff too'. She loved the homemade signs they put out with the paper plate eyeballs that looked in the direction she needed to turn.

Roxie loves books and as a teacher, she has been buying up all the history books she could find for the past several years. It appeared that the world around her was rejecting and/or rewriting history and she was not okay with that. The newest history book recommended by the U.S. Department of Education, 'The New New World History' was already in print for next year's classes, and it had only one small paragraph on 9/11. When she reviewed and rejected the new history book, it had barely a mention of the Holocaust as well. When she asked the supervisors about these oversights, she was told that many of the schools around her were not going to be covering it in class anyway. She was shocked to learn there was no way to stop it, so she put her mind and money into buying every old history book she could find. Many of the teachers were just throwing the old history books into the dumpsters at their schools. Upon hearing the news worthy facts, she decided that real American history would be her main focus in the coming year.

As Roxie pulled into the yard sale, she wondered if the day came when she needed to take a stand, would she? Thinking about that and her husband, she wondered and worried about the future, and what may be in store for them and their marriage, even though today seemed light and good.

She sadly concluded and was fairly positive, if it came down to it, he would probably turn her in. Word on the streets says that in the future, if someone turned in a Christian for not getting the CHIPS, they would receive free apps for their own CHIPS. It was all talk and hearsay, rumors, but would it come down to that someday? And would he turn her in? They had been married for almost twenty years and have had many ups-and-downs. However, if things didn't change for the better, she believed she would be doomed.

Today was good so far, and she was happy about that. Today would be a great day to sit and talk about their future. She was looking forward to that. There was something brighter about Kevin this morning and she thanked God for that.

How had her life become a two way street? One way was dark and the other way was light. Some days she was sure she was on the dark street with no direction and with no way to fight. Other days she was on the light street, confident and strong, walking tall, head held high.

She smiled and was at peace, for now. She had gotten right with God in private at her church. The pamphlet she had read made so much sense to her. She wanted to share it and the experience with Kevin but she had chosen not to. Not yet. She still needed more prayer time about it and allow God more time to work on Kevin's heart. So far, lately, He has softened him and Roxie was so thankful. But like most of the past, good changes to bad quite quickly.

There Is A Reason

Roxie arrived at the school before MJ and Cindy, even though she had stopped and bought a few treasures from the yard sale. She used that time to make some coffee and arrange the chairs in the teacher's lounge. She sat there feeling almost too anxious to drink her coffee when the door creaked opened. Mary Jane had arrived first.

Roxie poured MJ a cup of coffee and noticed her eyes were a little blood shot. Mary Jane noticed the look and knew her eyes gave her away even though she had poured a ton of eye drops in them.

"It's not what you think….well maybe some….but I didn't sleep all night….I prayed."

Roxie nodded then said, "MJ let me do the talking okay, at least at first, and then you can ask her for forgiveness."

"Ya okay."

"I asked Cindy to come a half hour later than you, so no worries, I'm sure she will show up…..now relax and enjoy your coffee."

Exactly a half hour later, Cindy walked through the door alone. Mary Jane felt her blood pressure rise, along with her temper. No Darleen in sight. Roxie stood up and put her hand on MJ's shoulder, with a slight squeeze, she applied pressure to help cool MJ down, and with her eyes, she told MJ to calm herself.

Cindy walked in with an air of confidence, toughness and inflexibility all wrapped together. As Mary Jane stood up, Cindy walked right over to her and grinned as she looked at the scar on her cheek.

Roxie interrupted the non-verbal exchange, "Would you like a coffee?"

"No thanks." She replied and then sat in the chair across from Mary Jane and quietly sat there waiting for someone to talk.

Roxie and MJ sat down and Roxie asked if was okay to have a prayer together before they started. Both women nodded yes and MJ and Roxie bowed their heads and closed their eyes while Cindy sat and watched them. "Amen."

Roxie began with what she had already said on the phone to Cindy. "As I discussed with you over the phone, your mom would like to try and reconcile your relationship. She feels she has made many changes over the years and she would like you to consider forgiving her. She knows it may take some time, but she is willing to put in the work." She nodded to Mary Jane.

Mary Jane felt she needed to be truthful as she looked at Cindy. "Listen Cindy, I'm not perfect, but God is. I do want to have a relationship with both you and Darleen. I miss the two of you, and I am sorry. I have made so many mistakes in my life and I know *I* have caused them myself and I know I have hurt our family and mostly you........I'm ashamed and I am so very sorry and I'm asking you if you would please forgive me?" Mary Jane bowed her head and asked again, "Will you please forgive me?" She trailed off in her words.

She wanted to say more, but felt the stare of them both as she looked down at the floor in shame. She really was sorry and she felt humbled as she asked for forgiveness from Cindy.

In the back of her mind, she knew Cindy had come with demands that would be shooting at her any moment. She said a silent prayer for God to help her hold her tongue because she felt angry that Cindy didn't bring Darleen with her to the meeting.

Her eyes still stung from the night before and she could tell they were still bloodshot. She could feel her face flushed as well. She continued to stare at the ground with her head hung low and her shoulders drooped. She was just keeping it simple like Roxie told her to do and she knew it was good advice. She knew the wisdom came from God.

Cindy smirked and again directly stared at the scar. "I have conditions, as I already told you *mom* and we'll see if you agree to them." She laid them all out, one in particular.

Mary Jane expected that she would have to be clean. No more whiskey. She was prepared for that. She was even prepared for the supervised visits. She was not prepared for what came next. As Cindy explained all MJ could do, was nod and agree as she listened. She really wanted to see Darleen and she knew full well that Cindy would not give in to her demands. Mary Jane had to quickly think of what she should say.

Roxie was shocked that Cindy already had the CHIPS. She was even more shocked that MJ appeared to be considering the CHIPS (Computer Human Injected Pairing System) so that her name would link up to her daughters in the new computer world called LINCS (Life Information Network Cataloging Storage).

Cindy made it clear that it will be the only way she will communicate with Mary Jane or allow her to see Darleen.

"Ok, I agree that everyone will have to do it anyway and I guess you're not asking too much of me." Mary Jane lifted her head and asked Cindy a direct question, "If I get the CHIPS and I pay for Darleen's CHIPS then you will allow me to have time with her, of course with supervised visits at first?"

Roxie disagreed as she blurted out "NO, not everybody will be getting the CHIPS!"

All children are to start receiving the CHIPS when they are born, starting in a few years or if they are already born, when they hit the age of fifteen unless the parent decides to bring them in to get it earlier.

The CHIPS will be free at birth. It is the one way the government was making sure everyone had it in the far off future. But any person, age fifteen or older wanting it now must pay 100.00. At some point no one will be able to shop, vote, work, travel, or even mail a letter, etc without it. The time was coming when everyone will need it, and most believe that.

"Mary Jane, your daughter is blackmailing you for the money to do Darleen's CHIPS, do you not see that?" She wanted to shake her. MJ just sat and shook her head in agreement, even though Cindy had not yet answered her question or said she forgave her.

Cindy glared at Roxie, as she spoke to Mary Jane "Listen mom, if you want to ever see her again, you will do what's right and give me the money to protect her." Cindy was determined to make Mary Jane pay as she sat there forcing her to answer.

Roxie was shaking as a chill ran down her spine and she spoke again. "Please don't do this. God is patient and wants us to live holy lives, be blameless, we cannot take the CHIPS. I really feel it is wrong, please don't give into her demands, think about this logically." Roxie didn't have the words to say but she felt rushed to say something. She quickly asked for God to help her in a silent prayer. Mary Jane sat quietly for a change, which surprised both Cindy and Roxie.

Roxie then paraphrased from Revelation as she reached across and grabbed MJ's hand to get her attention. "Satan would love for you to take the CHIPS, the mark, whatever it is, without it you will not be able to buy or sell. I know it sounds scary and crazy, but God warns us in the Bible....you know this Mary Jane! We can't give in, and we should never be forced to do it." Roxie glared at Cindy shaking her head in disbelief at her.

Then she looked Cindy straight in the eyes, "How dare you use your child to threaten your mom. You are blackmailing her! Not allowing her to see Darleen? How can you do this?" Roxie felt a surge of fearlessness and added, "No one is perfect. I don't know what your beliefs are, but the CHIPS can be seen as the first step towards the mark of the beast. I really pray you will do your research. The CHIPS will enslave us to satan, I really feel it will. Please don't do this to your mom or to Darleen."

Mary Jane knew Cindy was not going to budge. If anyone was more headstrong stubborn then her, it was Cindy. She raised her like that. A strong and stubborn girl. MJ admired that about her. Her daughter was just like her, and she loved that.

It didn't faze Cindy at all, she just smugly said, "It's a tough world out there and desperate times make for desperate measures." She shrugged. "My employer paid for mine and it is awesome. Darleen will need to have it soon enough and I really feel I am doing the best for her."

Cindy stared at Roxie who didn't have anything more to say. A few minutes passed before Cindy finally replied again in a dreadful hateful voice and an ugly smirk, "You. Won't. Stop. Me……. I will get the money no matter what. Darleen will get the CHIPS. I don't believe in your God, I will not bow down to Him." Cindy's voice sounded almost monotone and possessed, evil and scary to both MJ and Roxie, as they both turned and stared at her.

Afraid for only a moment by that voice, Roxie added "Yet you will bow down to satan. Because that is what you are doing." She sat up tall and stared directly into her eyes. Cindy blinked and then turned as she stood and directed her words to Mary Jane, smirking again at the scar, "Either you give me the money or you will never see Darleen again, and that is final!!" Then in a more casual happy tone, "That's the way it is, I will not budge." She playfully flipped her hair back and again looked at the scar on her mom's cheek, saying the exact words her mom used to say to her when she was young.

Roxie stood up and looked at the plaque on the wall that read 'Listen to advice and accept instruction and in the end, you will be wise.' Proverbs 19:20.

Cindy exited the room in the same way she came in, cool, collected and sure of herself.

Mary Jane surprisingly just sat there and watched her daughter leave the room and Roxie almost felt sorry for her as she stared down at her and said "Listen Mary Jane, don't let your past disobedience keep you from totally returning to God. Don't be half-hearted……. Listen, you may not be able to fix things with your family, but you do need to fix them with God."

Then as she turned to leave, she said, "Cindy told me about the alcohol and drugs. You talk a good talk but it's time to start to walk the walk. I'll be praying for you." Roxie felt a little bit angry and disappointed at the whole situation, especially for the hint of whiskey smell. If anyone knew the smells of alcohol, it was her.

"Roxie, you don't know anything about me, if this is the only thing I need to do to see my granddaughter, then so be it....this is my life!!" Mary Jane fired back.

Roxie looked at her in disbelief thinking she was not going to reach Mary Jane at this moment so she walked away and out of the room. She didn't even turn around when she heard

Mary Jane pick up a chair and throw it down in a fit of rage. This meeting was definitely a mistake.

Mary Jane was the maddest she had been in years. No one was gonna tell her what to do, especially Roxie. But as quick as she thought those words, she stopped and realized her own daughter Cindy *was* telling her what to do.

She grabbed another chair and threw it against the wall. The plaque fell and landed at her pink cowgirl boot. She read it aloud, "Listen to advice and accept instruction and in the end, you will be wise". Proverbs 19:20.

Mary Jane fell to her knees and started to cry real tears that she hadn't done in quite a while. She then stopped and prayed a heartfelt prayer for guidance, as she hugged the chair with her head burrowed into the cushion.

2 Timothy 2:19 (NLT) But God's truth stands firm like a foundation stone with this inscription: "The LORD knows those who are his," and "All who belong to the LORD must turn away from evil."

Chapter Forty-Four

July 13 2027, Carrie

It had already been a very long day for Carrie. She put down the binder and went to the couch to take another nap. Why was it taking so long for her dad to get home? He had told her to stay there and wait, but why was he taking so long? What happened?

She tries to ask questions all the time, but he thinks he is protecting her by not telling her the total truth. She knows it's not good.

The binder laid open to a short poem:

Only a Bible

I've come to you with only my Bible....my God's blessed book. I have His weapon, and should I be forced to defend myself or my principles or my honor, if it is a matter of life or death, of right or wrong....then this is my weapon, the Bible, the blessed book of God.

I will fight the fight....I am God's Girl.........I am God's Girl,
but I won't fight like a girl.

I will use God's mighty weapon and strength
and fight for His Truth. Today I go as His warrior.

I go as GOD'S GIRL.

Behind the Scenes

Amanda's brain felt like it was on fire....she had to fight. She needed to get her thoughts out to the ladies. She needed to do it before her brain was fried. The doctor was ruthless. The more he adjusted the machine the harder she fought against it. If she could only wake up, if she could only move, just a little, just for a moment. If only she could make the tears fall from her eyes. They flooded her thoughts. She felt she would drown. Yet the current through the wires struck like bolts of lightning jolting her conscience. The pulses traveled like electric surges of fire, burning even the simplest of prayers. Everything was a mess. The room in her brain was a complete ransack of thoughts, papers, files, folders, emotions, prayers and Bible verses.

Chapter Forty-Five
The CHIPS to LINCS

It was back in 2025 when the warnings went out across the Nation. It has been two years and most people don't believe it will actually happen. Some do and those are the ones that are saving the money to purchase their own personal CHIPS, while some are already getting them installed in their wrists and then there are others that are preparing to fight against it.

The government warnings say that the electric grid will only go down for twenty-four hours but could possibly be up to three days across the whole Nation and across the entire globe. The target date is on January 1st, 2030. The warnings are everywhere, on billboards, on every news station, every radio station and every commercial ad on TV, even on the grocery carts at the stores. They say to be prepared for a longer duration of time and to prepare for possible weeks of no power. It's all part of getting our Nation and the others prepared for the New Global Government.

Everyone will be thrown into darkness, except for the light of day. The government has warned everyone to stock up on batteries, flashlights, candles as well as water and food, and already those items were becoming harder and harder to find. Most people had gotten use to the shortages of supplies over the past several years. Simple supplies like toilet paper, paper towels, dog food, baby formula, famine hygiene products, meat, eggs, coffee and even gas in some parts to name a few. Most families have already been stock piling a few things with each grocery-shopping trip. The shrewd ones try not to draw any attention to what they are doing and everyone is already being affected in one way or another.

Amanda even started making candles out of crayons, something she learned a few years back. It was quite simple. She had a ton of old used crayons and peeled off the paper. She broke them into small pieces and shaved a few too, then melted them slowly in the microwave. She had some cute glasses she used to pour the melted crayons into and placed a wick down into the middle. She even used some essential oils in the melted wax to give them some scent. She learned a secret over the years to use beeswax or paraffin waxed crayons for the best candles, and used them mixed with the old crayons for a better burning candle. They will probably come in handy some day and it was a fun craft to do. It's amazing the things you can learn from those survival guides.

Amanda and Chris had started a survival stash of things like tarps, duct tape, rope, knives, first aid supplies and more back in 2020. Plus, Chris was secretly stashing even more stuff at The Ranch with a few other men from the church for safe-keeping and for emergencies.

The men didn't want to add to the fear that some of the wives already had as to how bad things could get. Amanda knew a little more only because Chris had shared with her the basic plan about everything back when he took out a huge amount of their savings to help purchase 'The Ranch' and the supplies to start fixing it up and adding rooms to it.

Chris along with six other men had purchased an old ranch style home on twenty-two acres of land up against the side of a mountain, which they have been fixing up for years now. They have been very busy with the home as well as with building a huge wall around the property using live trees, bushes, natural material such as rocks, mounds of dirt, grasses, weeds and building blocks.

One of the men Fred, once worked for one of those companies that travel the nation constructing those fake rock and forest sceneries in zoo's and in large hotels and casinos. The wall they are building is sturdy and strong, it stands about twenty feet tall with a ledge, and several look out posts around it. From even fifty feet away, you would have a hard time distinguishing the wall from the actual surroundings. As for the ranch home itself, you would never know of its existence, they have camouflaged it so well.

The men go every Saturday for hours, and once a month they go for a long weekend to work on things. On the full weekends, the guys even hold their own Sunday service teaching for an hour. They each take turns leading the class. Chris enjoys that time. The more they do over the years the better they become as men of God, working hard together to build a place for the future to keep their families safe. It's becoming a very spectacular homestead. Someday, possibly in the near future they will all live there with their families.

Anyway, the public has been warned of these power outages, which will happen, supposedly in the next three years. The media says there will only be a one-week warning beforehand, so you had better be ready which is why they have started the reminders so early.

It is said that once the power comes back on, the CHIPS to LINCS will be the only way you will be able to do anything. If you do not have it by then, the cost will go up to $300.00 to get it and get it hooked in.

Many stations around town are authorized to get people linked up, including tattoo shops and nail salons. I know crazy right? These shops are learning just how easy it is to install the CHIPS. So far, most people are going to the urgent cares and hospitals to have them easily installed. At this time, the only CHIPS to LINCS that are actually working are the ones that have been installed into the new first responders and military men and women.

The only way you will be able to bank, shop, send or receive mail, vote, pay taxes or do anything will be through your personal CHIPS. From the sounds of it, there are applications already installed on the CHIPS that come free. But the apps that are used for all purchasing and banking will have a built in formula that will automatically charge the person a small percentage for each transaction. The main computer and programming that holds the CHIPS to LINCS will have all your personal information, income and purchases you make, your health records, blood type and DNA, your education level, jobs you have or have had, any law infractions, military or law enforcement, all financial aspects, every family member under the age of 15, every single thing you do and where you go using a military grade GPS. There will no longer be real freedom like we have now. The government will finally have full awareness and maybe control over everyone.

They say it will start where you are. When the power grid turns back on, the CHIPS to LINCS will be on-line and you will know your status immediately, everyone at the same time on their own personal computer.

If you are receiving any government assistance, you will instantly see your government account, on the new smart phone they will give you at the time of inserting the CHIPS. Plus on day one when it turns on you will see the five hundred dollar bonus in the account the government is promising everyone just for being ready.

If you are a hard working individual who actually works for a living, your paycheck will be direct deposit to your personal LINCS account, which you can then log into using your CHIPS. However, you are not given the new smart computer phone, you must already have one, which most people do anyway, and don't even know it. You will just need to go to your settings and upgrade the new system and the LINCS program will be downloaded onto it. That's big government and Big Tech for ya!! Again, the big incentive for many people is that the government is promising a five hundred dollar bonus for anyone having the CHIPS installed in their wrists and the download to LINCS on day one.

Either way, everyone will need to have the CHIPS installed in their wrist to access their accounts. Just about, everyone has to admit they are surprised at how much information the government already has compiled for each person in their data banks. They know every app you have ever downloaded, every store you enter, what you buy there and the coupons you use. They know your political views, your religious views, what books you buy and even if you own a firearm. They have much of the population categorized and divided already into many basic groups. You will be able to see where they have you placed and in how many groups once the electric grid comes back on and you are uploaded to the program. They have surprisingly much of it already installed into the phone most people carry around. Soon real money will be a thing of the past, outdated and long gone like the telephone booths. Although it is said that the paper money will remain for five years until it is all collected. Not sure how that will all work, but they have a plan. But so do we.

According to the government, they are giving people plenty of time to get hooked up. The five-year window that started back in 2025 as mandatory CHIPS for all existing military and police officers is still in the courts, but many of the states are not allowing for any exemptions. They tell us to be ready, chaos is coming.

Many of the essential employers are giving their employees until 2029 to be in compliance. Basic hardware equipment is being purchased and put in at all the main buildings and stores, some are even getting government tax breaks to have them installed by the end of 2027. Things like scanners and time clocks that are now fingerprint activated, will soon be CHIPS activated.

Computer. Human. Injected. Pairing. System…… CHIPS to LINCS…. Life. information. Network. Cataloging. Storage.

So basically, you will have a small programmable circuit, a computer if you will, put into your body that will contain everything. The CHIPS itself is a Nano circuit, which is smaller than a Microcircuit. The entire thing is just slightly bigger than a single grain of rice. It doesn't sound like much but it is a fully programmable circuit that again will contain a person's entire identity. It's truly incredible the amount of information it will be able to hold.

It will scan like your credit card or debit card does now. Only it's in your wrist, that you scan. Of course, they say it is for your protection, but not everyone really believes that, except for the crazy ones that always trusts the government and what they do. Because they have always been so trustworthy, right???

They say you will be able to scan in to *any* computer as long as you have your special six-digit social login code and the newly six digit number combination along with your social security number to see all your personal information, a lot of numbers if you ask me. Some people are considering tattooing the numbers somewhere where they can see them instead of memorizing them.

If you want someone else to see your info then you must scan in, and put in another generated six-digit password for them to be part of your profile and likewise for you to be part of theirs. You will be able to add anyone you want, like all family members, spouses, and children for example. How it's all going to work is quite extensive and in-depth but from what everyone is told it will all work once the new green electric grid comes back on.

Many of the big businesses already are offering scholarships for early CHIPS radicals as well as many incentives to help motivate people to join in. Such as free groceries if you get it this month. Most are external incentives, but some advertise an internal satisfaction, as if the person is satisfying a sense of achievement or doing the earth and other people a favor by being positive about this. Always working on our emotions, saying how our wellbeing depends on being part of the greater good. I know it makes no sense, but they say it's for your own survival, and the emotional state you feel will outlive the life you choose. Who doesn't want that right? It's just bizarre and creepy if you ask me? Sounds like the government just wants us to feel good about what 'THEY' are doing.

Amanda is sure there is a way they are changing and altering a person's thinking through the CHIPS as well. Add in all medications they try to pass off as vaccinations, that they also say are for the survival of the people. It's really crazy. They act as if they want people to live and survive while they are killing them off. The only thing that always makes sense; is the amount of power they want over us all.

Matthew 10:28 (NLT) "Don't be afraid of those who want to kill your body; they cannot touch your soul. Fear only God, who can destroy both soul and body in hell.

John 16:33 (NLT) I have told you all this so that you may have peace in me. Here on earth you will have many trials and sorrows. But take heart, because I have overcome the world."

Chapter Forty-Six

July 13 2027, Carrie

As Carrie continued to wait, she decided to try her mom's new strawberry shake mix she had on the counter. She used the small blender, put in some crushed ice, the mix and whipped it up. Wow, she needed that, it was so refreshing. She then decided to call her brother Christopher. He was a few years younger than she was and lived a few miles in the opposite direction than her from their parent's home. He was probably working but she thought she would try anyway. He answered on the second ring, thinking she had information about mom. She didn't but it was still nice to touch base. He said that he too was called by dad to meet at the house and that he would see her when he got off the clock. As she hung up a small chill ran through her body. Carrie then continued to read:

Blessings
My cup does overflow
Today you have shown me....Your forgiveness
I must not carry around all the old

You give us new life in You
We are to watch, listen and be still
As we prepare our way....You direct our steps
Someday, they will not know who I was
But they will know what I left behind
And those blessings will be bestowed on them
Teach them now, show them now, and love them now
Pray like crazy for the next generation
Pray for the ones that are not yet here
Pray for the not yet seen
We can have the impact now......and an impact then
After all, those before us left behind their blessings
Their prayers for us
Those we did not know, those who pictures seem so long ago
Generations have gone by, praying for those to come
We too must pray for those to come
Thank you Lord, for hope, for purpose, for life
And even though we are on the enemy's turf
We still belong to You
We are blessed

Then turning again to her mom's social page, this one caught her eye:

Proverbs 14:34...Righteousness EXALTS a Nation, but sin is a disgrace to *any* people.

Are we a Nation of 'righteousness' or of 'disgrace'? It is a fair question.

Righteousness or I should say 'doing what is right' exalts (blesses, lifts up or prospers) a Nation. Does our Nation still believe in 'right and wrong' or in the 'moral code'? Or does

July 13 2027, Carrie

it just believe in whatever it wants to believe in? Truth is in the eye of the beholder they say….but it's not so. Maybe my truth is not yours but you can't argue that our Nation is stable the further it gets away from God. It is not stable at all. Look around people. The further we get from God, the more we fall. EVERY Christian in our Nation needs to PRAY daily for our Nation.

Proverbs 14:34…Righteousness EXALTS a Nation, but sin is a disgrace to *any* people.

We need to fear God, which is the beginning of wisdom for us and for our Nation. Then we need a Nation-shaking spiritual awakening that sees millions come to Christ. If we do not see such a thing, we are doomed to ashes….. A little dramatic right? NO it's not…….even our Founding Fathers saw that we need to respect and follow God and His Word.

Again, Proverbs 14:34…Righteousness EXALTS a Nation, but sin is a disgrace to *any* people.

Much of the Nation not only neglects righteousness, it despises it with scornful hatred. It not only allows sin, it promotes it…let's not be those people, let's stand for God's truth and morals.

Why is America declining? You tell me….. Is America righteous or sinful?

Many say that Christians should have no say in politics….. but my opinion is that we NEED to have a say, after all our Founding Fathers had much to say about God's morals and standards and principles that our Nation was founded on. The Proverb above challenges us ……..indicating that a nation's greatness and power are determined by its MORAL character and not by its political, military, or economic strength. When selecting public officials, our first and foremost concern should be the officials who will ADVANCE policies upholding Biblical standards of righteousness ......Biblical rights and wrongs on MORAL issues must take precedence over any other issues. Whether or not America will continue to exist into the future is completely dependent on how we the citizens embrace and apply.... Proverbs 14:34...Righteousness EXALTS a Nation, but sin is a disgrace to *any* people.

Will any of the candidates get it completely right? Probably not....but there are definitely ones that are much closer than others that is for sure....and if anything the last three years have shown us, is that we could be a Nation that is getting closer to the fire. We NEED to get back to our roots. This 'anything goes' is not ok for our Nation...... It is so important for everyone to get out there and vote......plan on it. Evil and corrupt people have tampered with this in the past...let's continue to pray for our Nation based on Godly morals....let's bring God back into our Nation in a big way....show Him that we WANT and NEED Him and live in such a way that your life speaks of God, speaks of right and wrong, speaks of family, speaks of hard work, speaks of pure integrity and Truth.

Right now today........ don't wait for righteous rulers to lead you........... start as an individual being righteous.....until it catches onto families, relatives, friends, neighbors, and eventually, our society. We need to live spiritually contagious, righteous lives that impact the world around us. It starts with Getting Right with God and then living right for Him.

If we don't then we shouldn't be surprised when we fall to another rising power ...."Here lies the United States of America in ruins for she turned from righteousness and chose sin . . .." God Bless You and God Bless America.

July 13 2027, Carrie

Behind the Scenes

    The basement of the hospital was cold and no one intentionally went down there. It was a makeshift storage area for old medical records, x-rays, notes, old outdated bookshelves and office furnishings as well as outdated medical equipment. There were aisles of shelving full of files and boxes almost like a library. Over to the left side of the door were boxes of Christmas decorations and a few other holiday items as well as old beds, mattresses, blankets and sheets.
    To the right of the entrance was a secret room behind a cleverly constructed wall made up of rolling boxes that hid the doorway.
    Dr. Prong had made a hidden doorway out of boxes that were labeled confidential on a small cart with wheels that slid to the side leading to the main locked door of his secret twelve by twelve room, his personal lab.
    There were only three people who knew about the room; Himself, Dr. Joe and Nurse Izzy who was a bit shady even for him. But, she had proven to be on his side many times. She is a great assistant and Joe seemed to like her as well.

Chapter Forty-Seven

Late June 2027, Ruth

This very morning Ruth had had some energy, and even ate some food. She had read to Amanda and was excited to have finished a whole chapter from the Bible. But as she finished, she was so drained and so very tired that she immediately needed the nurse to take her back to her room and back into bed. She could barely be of any help to the nurse as she lifted her up. She made a mental note to bring her cell phone next time, and have the phone read aloud from the Bible app to her and Amanda. Reading takes so much energy from her, energy that is fading more and more quickly, every minute of every day. She was just so very weak and so very tired.

She had come back to the hospital months ago, almost around the same time Amanda had gotten there. As the months pass, she feels she will be here in this room for the remainder of her life. She could feel her life draining away, but she was still able on some days to fight it. She knew her time on earth was ending, and soon she would be home with Jesus.

Late June 2027, Ruth

As soon as the nurse got her settled, she began to throw up so she asked the nurse for some pain medication and something for her stomach before she left her room. Her head was throbbing, and her back was achy. She couldn't concentrate or be uplifting and positive which is what she strived to be when her mom was there. She didn't want to worry her.

Silvia closed the curtain to give them some privacy as she helped Ruth. She grabbed a washcloth and poured some cool water on it from the bedside pitcher to wipe Ruth's forehead as she asked her how the search was going. After Ruth seemed to somewhat return to normal she moved to the comfy chair next to the bed, the one she has gotten very used to and has became good friends with, knowing every wrinkle, bump and soft spot.

"Nothing yet mom, I may never find out." Ruth said in her fake sad voice with an added smile, as she reached for some water to rinse out her mouth.

Ruth looked over at her moms eyes with the dark circles under them, and thought they looked almost as bad as hers did. She smiled again and tried to sound upbeat even though she felt so weak and so tired. "It's okay though, you are my mom, you have always treated me like your own kid………and that has always been good enough….. thank you for loving me." She said reassuring her as she closed her eyes.

With her eyes now closed, she added, "I shouldn't have even started this search, I know it bothers you and honestly, it really doesn't matter all that much to me…….. you're my mom and I love you." She started to mumble as she trailed off to sleep.

Silvia's eyes began to water and just when she was about to answer with 'I love you too', the computer sounded a beep. Ruth opened her eyes and looked at her mom.

Was all the hard work on the computer and web site about to pay off? She had a message waiting for her to open from Mrs. Halo, the woman from the social services, who was helping her to locate her birth mom. Silvia read the message to her. It said:

Dear Ruth,

I am very pleased to inform you, that with the information you provided me, I was able to do a more thorough search for your birth mother. Here are my findings:

The name of your birth mother is Susan De La Medley; her birth date is February 17, 1988.

It appears she gave you up for adoption the day you were born, at the Texas Community Hospital, November 20, 2010.

Her last known address is in Austin, Texas. It does not give an actual address or any other information. I am still looking for a current location for her and I will notify you as soon as I have more information.

I also have some more information for you. After further research and the results from a recent DNA test that was added to the system approximately eight months ago, it looks like your grandmother's name is Nellie R. Jones; her birth date is June 5, 1972. The most current location I have for her is there in your area, Tucson, Arizona. I am still working on getting a current address and phone number for her.

I hope this information is helpful to you in your search. Good luck and I will be back in touch with you once I get any further information.

Sincerely Mrs. R. Halo

"Mom, can you grab that paper that Susie gave to us last week, I think it was over there by the water." Ruth sat up the best she could, her head was about to explode. She hoped that the nurse would return soon with some more pain meds. She hated to take them so often, but she just couldn't get by without them lately. She knows that soon they will keep her as comfortable as they can, once she is in the Hospice care.

"Could it be? Susie is my mom?" Looking down at the paper that still had a pungent smell of cigarettes was a scribbled name and date of birth. Susan De La Medley, Feb 17, 1988, Texas.

Debbie

Debbie's shift had just started. She was on the graveyard shift, which ran from 5:00 pm until 5 am, a 12-hour shift. She didn't mind though, she actually liked it. She was one of the blessed ones that worked there. She was always scheduled four eight-hour day shifts and one twelve hour night shift then got three days off. Her schedule changed every week as far as which three days, but she always had them together after the twelve-hour night shift. Most of the nurses were not as blessed.

She had the next three days off and the day shift doctors were leaving for the day and the second shift doctors just coming on didn't really watch or question her every move, yes blessed indeed. She loved the extra freedom she had and was able to spend more time with Amanda and with Ruth during these evening shifts. It was a skeleton crew and she sorta liked that. She only had to call the doctor if needed and that hardly happened.

As she checked her charts, she noticed that Ruth's day had started out good, and that she had even left her room to go read to Amanda. However, as the afternoon turned to early evening she seemed to have gotten worse. She began throwing up about an hour ago and was not doing well. The Hospice Care representative had been in and recommended that she be moved to Hospice Care soon. She noticed another meeting was scheduled for the next day.

All her blood tests had come back abnormal and were a clear indication she was not improving. It had been noted in her chart that she was experiencing increased nausea and some blurred vision, along with the vomiting and was complaining of a severe backache, which was a new symptom. It was also noted in the chart that Ruth was experiencing severe headaches throughout the day. Debbie knows all too well about headaches. Her migraines get so bad at times that she can't function. Debbie said a quick prayer for Ruth then continued to read her chart.

It saddened Debbie for more reasons than one. Ruth had such a beautiful soul, always with a positive attitude, much like her own. She really loved being around her because she added so much life to everyone and she was such a wonderful example for all the other teen girls she hung out with. Debbie smiled as she thought about all the visitors that Ruth gets. She wins the prize.

She decided to check on Ruth first, but was redirected to few other beeps. It was almost an hour later that she was able to get to Ruth's room.

Oh, how her heart ached as she looked down at Ruth lying in the bed. Silvia was there too, asleep in the chair, a sight she was used to seeing. Normally she and Ruth would have to force Silvia to leave for the night and to go get food during the daytime. Ruth had her feet hanging out of the covers, which were pulled up to her chin. Debbie started checking her IV's to make sure they didn't need to be back-flushed or anything.

Ruth's determination to live was so encouraging and Debbie knew it is what added days to her life, followed by the price of extreme exhaustion. She did what she could do, as best as she could. Ruth didn't want to let anyone down.

The cancer at this point was throughout her entire body including her brain. Small tumors had been detected and Debbie knew it wouldn't be long before she would go home to God. There wasn't much more the doctors could do at this point, other than give her medications to soften the pain. Medications up until recently Ruth had been avoiding because they made her want to sleep on top of already being so sleepy from her battle.

Ruth looked so thin and pale, Debbie noticed her breathing seemed to be faster today, almost panting, and when she touched her forehead, it felt clammy and feverish.

The touch made Ruth slightly open her eyes and she smiled the best she could as she pointed to her computer. Debbie pushed the enter button and the Email that Ruth had received came up.

She read it out-loud and looked down at Ruth with shock and excitement in her eyes. Then she looked and relooked at the name Nellie R. Jones, Tucson Arizona. She questioned it in her mind for what seemed to be several minutes.

As she read the name out-loud again repeatedly, Ruth asked in a very weak voice, "Is everything okay?" Debbie returned to the moment at hand.

"Ruth, I believe Old lady Nell's last name is Jones." She said with her big brown eyes as wide open as they could be.

Ruth had a ray of light around her as she reached for Debbie's hand and said, "I need to give my grandma a hug..... and soon."

Silvia was now awake and sat up in her chair as she too said, "Yes, I believe you are right, Nell Jones could be Nellie R. Jones" And then added, "And Susie must be her daughter, Ruth's birth mom."

Debbie looked confused and puzzled and they explained the meeting with Susie, the new lady at Bible study. Debbie had only met her once several months ago and honestly couldn't remember what she looked like. But the puzzle pieces seemed to fit.

Ruth closed her eyes and smiled as she fell back asleep. Debbie looked at Silvia and said, "I'll go call Old Lady Nell."

Nell

Nell started to awaken in the ambulance. She could still hear the thunder and the rain. Her body hurt like never before. The paramedic working on her looked no older than twenty-five and maybe even younger than that. She wanted to ask him what happened, but he wouldn't let her talk.

Her mind screamed, "Please, please I need to see Ruth. Ruth my granddaughter needs me"................then she started to pray the words out loud the best she could, slowly she prayed "Oh please, I surrender my whole life to You God. Please forgive me and the wall I built, please God. May I please be with my granddaughter."

The paramedic wanted to stop her from talking but bowed his head with her when he realized she was praying. He watched her eyes become more alive and focused. Her words were slow but recognizable. He reached down and held her hand.

Nell could barely force the words from her mouth, but wanted to pray to God and as she did an immeasurable peace fell upon her. Sadly, those were her last thoughts and words as she closed her eyes never to reopen them. She was pronounced dead at 6:17 pm as tears of rain fell from the Heavens that very moment.

Ruth

Debbie returned to Ruth's room and lightly shook her awake. She looked so pale, so tiny and so fragile as she lay on her bed so still. "I called your grandmother Nell, she is on her way."

A weak smile from Ruth's once beautiful lips, now dry and as pale as her face almost brightened the room. Debbie saw it as a look of hope. All Ruth wanted was to give her grandma Nell a hug as her granddaughter.

Debbie turned to leave as Ruth struggled to stay awake. Silvia held her hand.

Debbie knew that Nell needed to hurry if she was going to get here in time. She prayed while walking to the nurse's station.

Ruth grew weaker and weaker as her pain grew more and more. She could no longer feel anything but the pain. A few minutes later, her blood pressure spiked to a high of 220/120 as she cried out and then went limp. It was 6:17 pm.

Silvia's shriek was heard throughout the whole floor as doctors and nurses including Debbie all rushed into the room.

Revelation 21:4 (NLT) He will wipe every tear from their eyes, and there will be no more death or sorrow or crying or pain. All these things are gone forever."

Ecclesiastes 3:1-2a (NLT) For everything there is a season, a time for every activity under heaven. A time to be born and a time to die.

Matthew 5:4 (NLT) God blesses those who mourn, for they will be comforted.

John 11:25 (NLT) Jesus told her, "I am the resurrection and the life. Anyone who believes in me will live, even after dying.

Chapter Forty-Eight

July 13 2027, Carrie

Carrie was woken up by the dog barking next door. She sat up and stretched. She decided to wait just a little longer, and then she was gonna go home. Going back to the table, she opened the binder again to read:

> And so I walk in the Lords presence
> as I live here on earth Ps 116:9
> "I am like clay in Your hands Lord.
> Mold me and shape me and sometimes rebuild me.
> I pray that I will use this vessel that
> You have given me for Your good.
> I pray that I will not harden my heart in my rebellious ways,
> for then I cannot be useful for You.
> Please continue to water me and keep shaping me and
> making me Your masterpiece
> That You have created. Let me yield to You.
> Lord, reshape me so I am valuable.
> Let me hold onto Your hand as we
> walk together through this life

And in to the next.

Behind the Scenes

"Listen Joe, you're the anesthesiologist, you need to make her look dead. The family needs to think she is gone, for however long they decide to stay with her after I shut it all down… can you do that?" Dr. Prong said sarcastically.

"You know I can….what's up with the attitude….you're really getting on my nerves."

"Ya well this all needs to go smoothly….once they leave you will need to get her down to the basement. Have Izzy help you." Then he added, "I'll take care of the computer and erase the transfer to the morgue. I'm going to go and convince them to let us use her body for medical teaching, for the new students of course….I'll promise them we'll only have her for three days and I'll make sure the family wants her cremated then I'll have Izzy send some ashes to their home." He smiled to himself, knowing it would be easy since they seemed like do-gooders and would want the woman's body to be of help even after she was gone. He had a knack for talking people into things. He was super excited to be getting a live subject and not one that was already gone.

"Oh and have your buddy Bongo, Bingo or whatever his name is pick up at least two of the other subjects so we have room for her." Dr. Prong added. Joe nodded and Izzy made notes.

Chapter Forty-Nine

Beginning of July, Amanda

I know there is a machine hooked to my head. I can feel the pulsations as they try to invade my brain. Why can't I wake up? My blood pressure feels quite low and the heart monitor feels slow. Yet I feel so nervous and anxious. I must relax these feelings and get them under control or else I will explode, and the doctor will know that I know. I can feel his presence as he lurks over me. And when he speaks, I try not to breath.

I know deep down inside I am being used as his unwilling test subject. That is the truth and I want to scream. The medication he injects into my arm, stings and feels cold as it travels thru my veins. I want to shiver but I can't. I can tell the light is on in the room, it feels warm above me, yet there is a very cold evil sensation throughout the place. Another poke and there it is again, the cold sting in my veins. It's so powerful.

Dr. Prong tells me he would have rather used an actual comatose patient for his experiment, but there wasn't one available and he was too impatient to wait. He says he is forced to keep me in this state of mind, this drug induced coma. He wasn't done with me just yet, although he says he is tired of waiting for results. The words he whispers to me, frightens me. His machine should be printing out all of my thoughts for him. All of my feelings should be on display for him to see. He was growing annoyed and irritated with me, his experimental patient. He comes in almost every day. I have to be on high alert. I will not play his game. I decided months ago that I would try not to think any thoughts when he was in the room making the adjustments on the machine and pumping me with his drug. I have to fight harder then I have ever fought in my entire life.

As Dr. Prong looked down on Amanda, he had to fight his impulse to shake her.

"If I didn't know any better, I would think you were messing with me, and lady…..you don't want to do that!" He said accusingly to her once more. "I will make you out to be some crazy suicidal gal who took too many pills and oh well, died on my watch." He glared at her once more and angrily smacked the side of the bed before leaving the room.

A tear formed, and I was so glad he turned to leave, because I couldn't contain it. Many tears were at the edges of my eyes. "Please God don't let him see them. I can't hold them back anymore. Give them boundaries like you do for the oceans." I'm so tired yet again and off I fade into the deep dark hidden room in the center of my mind. "Thank you God for protecting me...." my thoughts tenderly tucked in.

Am I complaining? Yes I am. The machine drains me and I only let my thoughts out when I know Debbie is in the room. She is the only one I can trust with the printouts. She wants what's best for me. I hear her prayers that she prays over me. It feels like she is my guardian angel and I thank God for her.

How do I get a real message to her? One that makes sense, my thoughts, they feel quite jumbled as my mind flashes from past, present and future. My next message is urgent, it needs to make sense.

The End was urgent too my brain reminds me as it flashes to that time many moons ago. "It's not anymore. I want to live. I have so much to live for." I scream, but no one hears. Why can't I get the thoughts out on paper as clear as they are in my mind? I handwrite all the notes in a secret, private peaceful small room in my brain. Some days it feels so peaceful, I just want to stay there. I love the alone time, I always have. You're here with me God, I know that You are.

I know that Debbie has read my chart, she is a nurse after-all but it never occurred to me that she would believe what was written in it. From the way she talks to me, she makes it sound like I did this to myself. Does she know that he drugs me?

A few hours went by or was it a day or two.... I wasn't sure, all I knew was that Debbie was in the room with me. I could hear her crying and I could smell her perfume. I have always loved that smell. Does she really think I did this to myself? Maybe there was a time in my past, but not now and not ever again. I love God and I live for Him. Now that I have a relationship with Him, I look at life totally different. Sure, I have struggles, just like everyone else and sometimes those struggles and challenges can get me down but I know how to let them pass.

When I feel down or depressed or sad and sorry for myself, and even cry, I focus on God Word and not my problems. He is greater than any struggle I may have. His peace warms my heart, my mind and my soul. Little 's' man wants me to be so emotional that I cannot focus on God and all the great things in my life, and all that I am thankful for and blessed with.

I choose to live, I choose to live for Him and not be pulled down by satan. I choose to fix my sights on what is true, honorable, right, pure, lovely, admirable, excellent and worthy of praise. I love those thoughts. I have learned to do my best and I have prayed continuously for His help and wisdom to think that way, especially in the down times of life. Everyone has them and everyone knows exactly what I'm saying here. But before God, I didn't know what to do, I do now.

Satan tries to throw stuff at me, and sometime a lot of small stuff that add up and it is a struggle to get through some days, but I have a very important puzzle piece and that is that God is with me. He will not allow me to be overwhelmed. He has my back.

Every single person can make that choice, to get right with God and have what I have. It's a blessing an endless blessings. "Squirrel" boy would I love to insert and smiley face right here because blessings make me so very happy deep in my heart. But let me continue these thoughts........ Or they can choose to ignore God and reject His peace and be down about this life He has given to us. (Sad face inserted here).

How long have I been babbling here, focus Amanda. Wait, where was that file?

My life wasn't working and I was a mess. I tried the anti-depression medications. The meds didn't help me, they almost made me worse. I thought that maybe I had a chemical imbalance, but what I really had, was a spiritual imbalance. All I needed was God. He says if we seek Him, we will find Him. So I did with all my heart. I made sure the soil of my heart was good, soft and ready for His Word and His leading to take root. He rewired my brain, He gave me new thoughts to process.

I must focus, come back to the here and now. Debbie is here.

I did not do this. Not on purpose. I can hear Debbie asking me why I took so many sleeping pills.

I couldn't stop my thoughts as they were being printed out. The machine was quick to grab them and print them. Like so many other times in my life, I had much to say and my mind felt like it was overflowing.

They were my thoughts, but jumbled up. I had to make Debbie understand I wasn't in here for anything that I did. It was the doctor, and I know it. Those were the thoughts that needed to come out. Darn this machine it is printing things from years ago, mixed with current.... "Oh the current, it's flashing through so fast, it's pounding on my head, so fast my mind can't keep up, turn it down, my brain is on a fast spinning wheel." Mmmm do random squirrels spin on wheels? I wanted to scream as a bunch of jumbled up thoughts printed instead, thoughts from many years ago, confused with today's thoughts.

Debbie sat there holding my hand and through her tears, she glanced over some of the words from the printout as she shoved them once again into her pocket. I could hear her almost begging me to wake up as she spoke "No Amanda, you are always there for us, you always listen to our problems, but who has been there for you? I am so sorry, I've been so busy I didn't know, oh Amanda, I didn't know how lost you felt….. oh Amanda I know you must be afraid, and so am I, please Amanda please wake up." Debbie sat there and cried as she put her hand in her pocket to feel the note. She will have to read it completely when she has more time.

"No one will ever know." Debbie said as she stood up and walked slowly out of the room.

Back at her desk, she opened Amanda's initial check-in admittance file in the database and cleared the words 'Possible Suicide Attempt'. She then went through the whole chart and erased all the notes written by Dr. Prong about her state of mind, and anything that mentioned suicide. She let out a deep sigh and then smiled. She was right about the four-digit number she saw written on the file when she was snooping in Dr. Prong's desk; it *was* his password for Amanda's file.

She sat there remembering one of Amanda lessons on this very subject about ten years ago. It was titled: Suicide is Not the Answer. She sat at her computer trying to remember some of the bullet points from the lesson.

She recalled that Amanda was very clear about how it affects so many people, the one involved of course, who is no longer here to live their life, as well as the family and friends, co-workers and acquaintances. Everyone is affected. So many lives are touched.

As a nurse, Debbie knows that any thoughts of suicide along with periods of depression should be recognized as an illness that may require treatment. She remembered Amanda saying to go see your doctor first and check for any chemical imbalance or medical treatment that is needed, because suicide is final and is not the answer. Just because you're having a few bad days, that doesn't mean you have a bad life.

Debbie knows there are signs to look for like, isolation and feeling alone, negativity, aggressiveness, and mood changes as well as avoiding people and generally having an unhappy attitude. But even all that can be explained and caused by other things as well.

Amanda had talked about how we only have this one life and God can help us through it, no matter what problems we faced. Amanda was so passionate about that lesson. It is final; there is no do-over, no mulligan. We are not reborn to start again. The fact that it is final was the main point. It just passes your pain on to others and could cause them to think *they* have failed you somehow. It was exactly how Debbie was actually feeling that moment. Had she let Amanda down? Had she missed those signs? They are best friends, but why had she taken so many sleeping pills?

Debbie felt a knot in her stomach as she tried to remember more of the lesson. It seemed so different now that it directly affected her. She has been a nurse and has seen so much in her life as a caregiver yet, she has managed to stay professional and strong. This is just too close. She felt sick. She needed to protect her best friend no matter what.

The words now erased 'Possible Suicide Attempt', flickered in her mind as she questioned herself again for the third time, were there signs she missed?

All Debbie could think about was how strong Amanda was in her faith and in God. This didn't make any sense. Amanda had passed out phone numbers of people that could help if needed, why hadn't she used them herself?

No one would have wanted Amanda to do this, and everyone would have helped her, had they known. It had been a powerful lesson and the one where Amanda had read her own story 'THE END'. But that end had been her beginning. It was the beginning…….the beginning of her life. A life she owed to God!!

There has to be another explanation. Who had done her initial check-in that early morning on March 5th 2027? It's weird that his name is the only name on Amanda's chart.

Debbie closed the file. There were too many unanswered questions from day one. Why was Amanda on the second floor in a coma and why did Dr. Prong, minutes after her getting to the room push in his brain machine? Secret notes and tests all in code. And why did the printouts only work when she is there? What is the reason and why isn't Amanda waking up? There were so many other unanswered questions. She pulled out the printout from earlier and read it quickly, and shoved it back into her pocket then stood up and stared at her computer.

'Possible Suicide Attempt'…….Well, those words were gone now. She made sure it they were deleted and no one would ever see them. As she walked back to room 236, she passed Nurse Shady and cold shivers ran down her spine. Something about that woman spooked her.

"Nope, I refuse to believe it……. Amanda I know you are communicating with me, and I'm here to help you my friend……. The machine is lying. Amanda this can't be true". She said aloud and almost angry as she reached into her pocket. She had been getting better at reading the printouts, deciphering the past stuff and the present stuff as well as future stuff jumbled together. Untangling the mess of words to make sense was getting easier but today it felt wrong.

Debbie decided to go read the whole printout slowly. Maybe she missed something. She left the room and headed to the bathroom where she could have some privacy and not be seen. Pulling out the note, she closed her eyes and prayed. She prayed for Amanda and then her thoughts went to every lady in the Bible study. She prayed for them all, asking God to give them all strength, comfort and His love. She prayed that they all felt loved and knew they were not alone in this world. She asked God to help her connect to them and encourage them. She opened her eyes and reread the note slowly, one line at a time:

How do I make it back…… to The End?
I'm depressed, lost somehow?
No one heard me? I'm stronger, but I have failed?
I didn't mean to? A down moment…… everything fell apart, years of chaos?
I took the pills…… just to sleep? Was it just to sleep?
I'm not there anymore.
That's not my life.
Sleep? To sleep? I did, I do ……a deep sleep, and I can't wake up?
I want to wake up, I try?
The reason ….in this bed, at that time
I will keep to myself? The reasons…. will never tell anyone.
The fear of the world strangles me?
I just want to get home.
But not now.
The meds …..anxiety never helped me. I quit taking them.

Was that smart? Well only if you were me .....you knew where you wanted to be and go....but no not yet?
Is it better to stay? Who goes first?
This is not intentional...listen, it's not? It's not. I try to make sense...... can't my thoughts are confused and mixed up.....help me.
The end is here...It's on me?

Debbie focused on what was good in the note. It read more like one of Amanda's stories, her thoughts, not a confession of what had actually happened. Amanda always did love to write mixed up stories, poems too.......Debbie loved to read them, they were so suspenseful, so thought provoking.

The question marks. Too many questions? It was a mistake. If she took too many sleeping pills, than why isn't she waking up? What's stopping her? It's been months. She knows what she suspects must be true, it's Dr. Prong. She noticed that Amanda questions herself in the note. She's trying to tell me something. Debbie tried to make sense of the printout. She needed to focus.

Debbie turned her thoughts over to the years behind, she has had many people come to her about depression and her first recommendation is always for them see a doctor and deal with the physical stuff. Then she has always loved directing them to a positive outlook for their life. And since the lesson, she has always given a copy of it to whoever needs help with depression. It was spot on and the suggestions worked. Debbie took a moment and wrote down all the suggestions she could think of:

* Since life always has it's up and downs, we need to be careful not to wallow in it.
* Be God's girl and think well.
* We cannot trust our emotions, they will let us down because they change all the time.
* We must think and take our thoughts captive.
* Put on the whole armor of God.
* Take one day at a time and refuse to participate in your own pity party.
* Focus on the things we are thankful for.
* Try something new, because when you do the same thing, you get the same results.
* Avoid down time. Idle hands are the devils workshop.
* Be content and most of all stay close to God. Read your Bible and pray every day.

Amanda had encouraged everyone in class that day to sign up for everything at church, and be there. She said to be careful what was entertained in our mind. And we should listen to good Christian music, positive stuff. And ask for prayers. Plus she had encouraged everyone to volunteer in some area at the church.

"Why? Why God, why is Amanda here?" Again, Debbie questioned.

Debbie sat for a moment, and then texted everyone in the Bible study group. "Everyone pray for Amanda!"

She then added, "Stop what you are doing and immediately pray for Amanda. And please don't forget to stop every day at nine am to pray specifically for her. If we all pray at the same time, I know it will be powerful. Thanks ladies." It was the only thing she could do right now for Amanda. She looked down at her watch, and she had been in the bathroom for almost an hour. She washed her hands and exited. Walking back down the hall, she passed by Nurse Shady again and she asked her, "Where have you been?" Debbie shrugged as she continued walking, "Around, checking on patients." Izzy shrugged as well and made a few more notes into her notebook then continued down the hall in the opposite direction.

Hebrews 4:16 (NLT) So let us come boldly to the throne of our gracious God. There we will receive his mercy, and we will find grace to help us when we need it most.

1 Thessalonians 5:16-18 (NLT) Always be joyful. Never stop praying. Be thankful in all circumstances, for this is God's will for you who belong to Christ Jesus.

Chapter Fifty

July 13 2027, Carrie

Carrie flipped through a few more pages. She was having trouble putting the binder down. She read another RTP, Real Time Post dated from 2/1/22. The words from her mom's RTP's inspired her and her mom's smile was etched into her thoughts.

She giggled for a moment, thinking about her mom's teeth. She has a tooth that is out of place, a little high on the left side that looks like a fang. Little kids used to ask her why her tooth was up so high and she would snicker at them, tilt her head and show the fang and say "it's to get you my little pretty" in her high squeaky voice and then run after them to tickle them. The thought made Carrie laugh aloud, as she thought about the front tooth as well. Her mom had gotten a capped tooth when she was fifteen. It was suppose to be a temporary tooth yet she still had it glued in place. She always tells the hygienist to stay away from it every time she had her teeth cleaned. Yet it was the whitest tooth in her whole mouth, right there in front. Dad called it the "chicklet". She continued laughing thinking about how it really did look like a piece of chicklet gum.

Suddenly she stopped laughing and feeling more serious, she started thinking about how young her mom was and how much she didn't want to lose her. Once more thoughts of her teeth came crowding into her other thoughts. Just like mom's crowded teeth, especially the bottom ones. Then she remembered on the right side of her mom's mouth she had a baby tooth still in place at the top. If you looked at her teeth from that side of her face the baby tooth almost looked like a small gap.

A small gap in time is all we get. We are born and we die. We live between the two. That's life. Yet Carrie knows there is more than just the little dash between the beginning and the end. There is Eternity. And depending on what you do with Jesus, during that small dash called life, you will either spend Eternity with Him or separated from Him forever.

Carrie shook off the random thoughts, knowing how blessed she was that her parents had chosen Jesus. They brought her and her brother up knowing all about God, Jesus and the Bible and as soon as they were old enough, both of them couldn't wait to get right and live right for Him.

Carrie sat and remembered the start of her own personal relationship with Jesus. She asked her mom to baptize her in the pool in their backyard. She was thirteen and she believed and was ready to confess Jesus as her Lord and Savior and repent of her sins and ask for a new life in Christ, a life only He could provide through His death on the cross. The day was glorious, sunny with a beautiful blue sky as her mom and she stepped down into the water. It felt refreshing and new. The flowers on the side of the pool seemed more alive and colorful and she knew she was making an adult decision to accept and take Jesus as her Lord and Savior. It happened so fast after she plugged her nose, "……being buried with Christ through baptism" under the water completely and "rise to live a new life." She came up from under the water, thinking about the gift of the Holy Spirit she just received.

Hugging and clapping took place as she remembers thinking about how her chalkboard of past sins had been erased. She remembers thinking, that even though she didn't feel like there were many, she knew that everything was gone. She loved that feeling.

She remembers looking at her mom's smile and how every single tooth showed in her mouth and how extremely happy she was at her decision. She was reliving her great memory when the phone rang.

She saw that it was Debbie calling, and decided not to answer. Debbie left a message. But Carrie couldn't bring herself to listen to it, "not yet…..not yet." She whispered.

"Oh mom, I sure miss you, it's not time yet, fight!" She let out a sigh, wishing she had spent more time reading her mom's writings throughout the years. She would have loved to have sat with her and gone over them all. The time she wished for, may just possibly be gone soon.

"Please God keep my mom here with us, we need her….. I need her. It's not her time, protect her from the evil one who wants to hurt her and kill her, please God, please hear my cries and my pleas." A quick popcorn prayer gave her some comfort.

Without hesitation, she began again with one of the RTP's:

Yup, you guessed it, I have something to say today. Do you ever feel so focused on the big problems of the world or the big problems in your own life? I do at times. I think we all do.

Especially when we focus on all the crazy corruption in our government…… When we focus on all the people out there who have lost jobs or businesses closing because freedoms are slowly being taken away from us….. When we focus on empty grocery shelves of our favorite foods….. When we focus on sickness, colds and diseases…..or when we focus on our feelings being hurt. Whatever it is……we tend to focus on the problem instead of focusing on our God, our problem solver.

Reading today I was reminded how the Israelites approached the promised land after having been delivered from slavery in Egypt…..Moses had chosen twelve men to go into the land to check it out, the land that God had promised to them. They all knew that God had delivered them from slavery…..and with all the evidence of God they still focused on their problems. And when the spies came back, most of them could only talk about the size of the giant people….they were so focused on the size of their problems that they couldn't see the size of their God. That generation lost the blessing that God wanted to give to them…..a land flowing with milk and honey, the Promise Land. It is a reminder to me that God is not afraid of all the problems in our world, or in our lives. And we must focus on Him, not those problems.

Did you know that there are 365 verses in the Bible that say, do not be afraid and do not fear? That's a verse a day for an entire year. Yet, we all fear, me included. I do it more than I want, that's for sure. Why is that, especially when we know? In 1 Peter 5:7 it says…… "Cast ALL your problems on Him for He cares for you."

There is so much treasure found in His Word, the Bible. It's priceless! Thank you God for helping me focus on You, Your Word and Eternity today. God Bless you and God Bless America.

July 13 2027, Carrie

Carrie finished the reading from her mom's social media and for some reason she stood up and stared into the mirror, looking at her own teeth, knowing just how unique and special each of us are. Just like our unique fingerprints. She decided to grab the phone and listen to Debbie's message. After all, the last time she called it was just to see how she was doing, nothing more.

Behind the Scenes

Chris glanced down at his cell phone. Debbie, Amanda's best friend was calling. He got a knot in his stomach as he pushed the green button to answer.

"Hello, this is Chris."

"Hi Chris, this is Debbie." A short pause and then she continued. "I need to talk with you in person, not over the phone, we need to talk. Can you meet Donald and I sometime in the next few days?"

"Is this about Amanda?"

"I would rather not say right now…..I called and left a message with Carrie as well, I didn't have Christopher's number. Maybe we can all have dinner at our house and, and, and talk?"

"Ya, that's fine, but if this has anything to do with Amanda, I would rather not involve Carrie or Christopher yet please, okay?"

Debbie let out a breath of air "Okay that might be better anyway." Then she asked, "Tomorrow at 6:30 okay? We can meet at our house. I'll make tacos….. is that okay? We can eat and then talk?" Debbie was nervous and felt like she was babbling.

"Sure, I'll see you then."

"Okay, bye."

"Ya, bye and thanks."

Chris hung up and as soon as he did, the doctor called. He had much to say.

Dr. Prong in his clever ways, knows he needs to do things correct, on paper that is and he needed the family to sign off on the paperwork to allow the hospital, and ha-ha him to put her down. Okay, so he will use a little more tact than that. He almost got a tear in his eye as he talked slowly and sadly to the husband.

"We shouldn't prolong this, I'm very sorry but she is no longer with us, she is brain dead and she will not recover." He sniffed his nose, as if he was sad and grief stricken.

"The brain monitor shows no brain activity as I told you months ago. She seems to have an anoxic brain injury with severe trauma, from her fall." He lied quite easily. "The trans cranial direct current stimulation which stimulates the regions of the brain shows nothing. I am positive she will never regain consciousness." He continued on knowing the big lie was in motion and the husband couldn't hear anything more, his mind undoubtedly was on his lost wife that would never recover.

Speaking with his sad, slow voice was fun to him.

"Sorry if I have given you any false hope over the past few months, but we have tried all we can and well sir……..she just isn't going to recover. Even if she were to wake up, which I can't see how…….she won't……….Sir, she will not have any quality of life. As you know we have given her brain time to heal, plenty of time…….month's Mr. uh, uh, Mr. Mr. uh Garrison. When she came in, she had quite a bit of sleep medication in her system along with a large hematoma with laceration on her forehead from a presumed fall. That hematoma put quite a bit of pressure on her brain and reduced the flow of blood and oxygen……." Dr. Prong stopped talking and could hear nothing but sobbing on the other end. Oh how he loved this part. He had done this very same explanation several times over the years, and he never tired of it. In fact, he fantasized of starring on one of those doctor programs on TV. He would win an Emmy for sure. He laughed inside and then continued.

"All her neurotransmitters show no activity and again there is nothing more we can do for the Reticular Activating System (RAS) and as you know, we performed a Cerebral Angiography to verify flow cessation to confirm brain death." Dr. Prong almost liked throwing in big words that he knew the patient or their family had no idea what he was talking about. He could still hear the sobbing.

"If you would sir, we explained that even if we kept your wife alive using life support systems, as we have been, her heart will eventually stop due to the issue with the RAS…..and sir, not to sound cold hearted but ……..As you can imagine this type of intensive care does and will require full life support and is…..well to be honest with you, quite costly. And for a patient who will never wake up, well, your insurance company may not pay for it." Dr. Prong paused for a moment as he thought; Why hasn't this man stopped him yet? So he continued on.

"I'm actually surprised she hasn't had a seizure or a brain aneurism yet. Her brain is in a deep state of inactivity, it is unaware, idle and unable to feel any………."

Amanda's husband finally cut him off, which was a good thing because he was starting to sound upbeat, instead of sad. Being callously blunt was so fun.

"I'll be there, and I'll sign the papers. I need to call my daughter and a few people okay, give me a few days okay?" Chris managed to say.

"Of course, today would be great, the sooner the better, or if you need some time, tomorrow is good too. I will be here both days until six. Call with a time and I will see you soon….. oh and again…I am truly sorry."

Dr. Prong smiled as he hung up the phone and did a pretend 'mic drop'. He then grabbed all the paperwork he would need for turning off all life support, and of course the paperwork to keep the body for three days for medical training and the cremation paperwork. He had it all covered and ready. He will go over all the procedures and paperwork when the husband calls back to schedule the time, that way he can hurry up the sad moment when he and his family comes in. Matter of fact he will give Nurse Izzy the clipboard with the paperwork and have her ask him to sign here and there and over here. The lady in room 236 bed 2 was almost all his.

Chapter Fifty-One

Today is the Day

Debbie was on her way to work earlier than normal, knowing today was the day. She had almost every minute planned. Everyone that would be there, had a part to play, even the ones that didn't know it. Her heart was beating so fast she could hardly contain it. This had to work. If it didn't, she surely would be fired as well as in a small jail cell.

Debbie had always played by the book, her whole life. She was a straight 'A' student, always listened to her parents, and never gave them any trouble even as a teen. She went to every church function at her church and waited until marriage to have sex with her high school sweetheart. They had gotten married right out of high school and they both worked a part-time job while going to college to make ends meet.

Early on, they had chosen not to have children of their own, because they both had such demanding careers. Instead, they decided twenty-five years ago to volunteer as mentors at their church in the 4-6th grade classroom. They have been second parents to most of the children that passed through their classes every weekend for what seemed like just minutes passing. Debbie and her husband Donald have been married for thirty-two wonderful years so far, but she knew it would all go away if today didn't go as planned.

She couldn't think about that now. It was too late and she was committed to the plan. She tried hard to shake off the feeling of danger and the annoying whisper in her head that kept reminding her of how she's had never even gotten a speeding ticket. Hearing that whisper made her think she could be making a huge mistake. She was always so positive and upbeat, never this doom and gloom or weighted down with uncertainty. But now, fears were coming to life in her mind.

Debbie's heart beat faster, good idea or not, can they actually pull this off? What they were doing was illegal, but if she didn't do something, her best friend would surly die. It was definitely too late to back out now, although the thought did occupy her mind.

Debbie wondered if Jesus had felt this way. He surely could have backed out knowing what lay ahead, but He didn't because He loves us so much. Because Jesus didn't back out, and He paid the price for our sins, we all are now able to accept His wonderful gift of Salvation and we can live in Eternity with Him, and not be separated in hell without Him. Without Him, we would suffer the consequences for our sins, which is death. And yes, death comes knocking at all of our lives at some point, but death without Jesus is the death no one would want, the Bible is clear about that.

Debbie thought about this for a moment as she prayed on the way to the hospital. Without Jesus, she would be without hope and without forgiveness. She had gotten right with God through Jesus when she was a young adult just starting college along with Donald. It was a beautiful day full happiness and celebration. The memory of their parents faces full of joyfulness would forever be stamped in her mind, and she is sure in Donald's as well.

Another thought came vivid in her mind. Our sins separate us from God and His Holiness. He cannot associate with sin. Even though Jesus died for her sins, past, present and future she wasn't free to just sin at a moment's notice, knowing it was wrong just to ask for forgiveness later. She never did like that old saying 'It is easier to ask for forgiveness then to ask for permission'. But, here she was.

Debbie knows her heart is right with God. She knows she prayed about this. She has prayed a lot. But maybe God had a better plan, did she really even ask? Or did she just tell God *her* plans? Her thoughts were sinking her into the quicksand of doubt.

"Oh Father, please don't let this separate me from You. I don't want to do this alone, please understand and whatever consequences there might be, please let them fall on me and not anyone else. I don't know what to say. I know You are just and forgiving and Your ways are the best ways……I just don't know what else to do. This came so fast. Please keep us all safe. Amen"

Donald reached for her hand before she got out of the car, "Let's pray."

"I have been, the whole way here……and yes, thanks…. let's pray together." She let out a deep sigh. And he prayed for practically the same things that she had on her mind and in her prayers. She then exited the car, thankful for her husband and thankful for the rain.

It had been almost two weeks ago that she told Donald about the 'experimental machine for comatose patients'. She told him that it was hooked to Amanda, and the current from the machine has been very strong lately. She told him about the printouts and how she has kept them from Dr. Prong.

"……So you see, he actually thinks that his machine is not working. I have been taking the printouts. He's not getting any communication from his machine because of me……I'm not sure why I started taking them in the first place, but I did and now….well now…….. Oh Donald, I truly think that Dr. Prong is keeping Amanda in this coma and I truly believe that he wants us all to think that she is brain dead and then he will be able to secretly do things to her, her brain. I can't prove it though." She stared at Donald knowing how crazy she sounded but she wanted to explain as much as she could.

"I heard him say she was brain dead, but I know she is not, the printouts prove she isn't, but if he knows about the printouts, who knows what he might do. You know he's a brain surgeon, at least that's what he says. He probably will do his exploratory brain surgeries, and honestly Donald…..he doesn't have the best track record with any of his regular patients. If I were to guess, at least thirty percent of his patients have died suspiciously in the last several years."

She took another quick breath of air, her head began to throb as she explained her words came so fast, "Oh Donald, he wants her dead and gone, I just know it…… so that he….he can do things……..so he can do things under the table without watching eyes, to her brain, unspeakable things, I'm sure of it ……or maybe, maybe he's gonna keep her alive, all in the name of science...... but I feel like he's going to kill her. Donald I know it sounds crazy, but I'm not crazy and I think Amanda is trying to tell me he's gonna kill her." She started to gasp and feel hyper, anxious, smothered and totally helpless. Her palms were sweaty and she felt hot all over her body, as she began to shake like she was freezing cold. The migraine in her head began to throb to the beat of a drum. Her imagination was in full swing. She had thought about this much over the last few weeks, and felt it was now an urgent matter.

Debbie had no doubt that Dr. Prongs mind was in the works as well. He first must make the family think she is gone for good. Was she even making any sense? There was so much she wanted to tell Donald about the last few months.

"I think his plan is to unhook the machine and unplug all her other devices that he claims are keeping her alive." She stood up and walked uneasily around the room. "He's gonna take her to the, the the basement. I know it, I just know it." The thought of that made her squirm in her skin. She felt like she was going to throw up. How can she prove this? And who would listen? Who will take her words over his, without any real evidence? Who can she even trust? That was the big question.

"Slow down Debbie, what are you talking about, what basement? And why do think this?"

Debbie had first stumbled on the secret hidden room in the basement a few years back and had almost erased it from her memory. She had been retrieving some old medical records that were kept down below in the basement when she heard a noise. She cautiously stood behind some shelves and watched Nurse

Shady, wheel a patient with a gold blanket over them in on a gurney. She watched her as she slid an entire wall of boxes over with little to no effort. Hidden behind was another door and Nurse Shady unlocked it and pushed the patient in and disappeared with the body behind the door. Debbie wanted to explore it more but was afraid as she quickly got the records she had come to get and left without a peep or a word to anyone about it.

"Oh, what have I done?" Debbie cried into her hands, not wanting to look at her husband.

"I should have reported it years ago." She took a deep breath and continued talking, "Donald, I hid down there about a month ago. I had seen the word basement written at the bottom of Amanda's chart……. It reminded me about what I had seen years ago. It was around two in the morning and I was so scared. It was extremely dark down there and I was getting close to leaving when around three in the morning the door opened and I saw some guy come in with a patient. He turned on the light. I was behind the shelves and I watched him open the hidden door. I think the patient was deceased. He was slumped over in a wheel chair….. but I'm not sure. The guy pushed him into that hidden room. I stood up and was gonna leave when I heard the basement door open again and Dr. Prong….I mean, I think it was him, I was afraid to look….he went into the room as well. I left right after that." Debbie was so scared she was going to get busted that she hasn't gone down there since.

"Donald I know this sounds weird, but something is going on down there….I don't know what, but something is, and I'm afraid that is where Amanda is gonna end up." Her anguish turned to tears.

Donald silently sat and listened, absorbing everything he just heard. Was she just being paranoid or was there some truth to what she suspected? It's not like her to be so anxious and upset. Could she just be exaggerating? Possibly, reading the entire situation wrong? What about the basement and the bodies? That *is* strange.

Donald looked at her, she seemed so fragile, so precious, and so innocent and it wasn't like her to make stuff up, not like this. Although Amanda *is* her best friend, so maybe she is exaggerating some of it. It sounded more like a nightmare come to life.

Donald had heard some crazy stories before. His career as a lawyer has taken him into many stories of crime. He had to wonder if Debbie might have committed or contributed to some kind of a crime, so he said very little.

He sat silent and tried to see it from her perspective instead of thru the lens of right and wrong according to the law. Sin is wrong. He has said those words many of times over the last few decades.

He continued to sit there as he considered everything she had witnessed. The more he thought about it, the more confident he was that she had not committed or contributed to a crime. Was she right or wrong for not reporting what she saw? He stood on the side of right. She had no proof and reporting something as outlandish as this would not only get her dismissed but also leave her open to possible lawsuits from the staff as well as from the hospital. He was surprised however, that she had not said anything about this until now.

Debbie felt at loss and alone as Donald said nothing. He was in his think tank and she just needed to wait.

As Donald sat there, he could see Debbie's love for her friend and her huge heart full of compassion. Then after what seemed like forever, he realized it was up to him to come up with a plan, a good plan, one that would work and one that would help Amanda, as well as keep his wife from doing something dangerous on her own.

"Don't worry Deb. Let's sleep on it and pray about it tonight. I think I may have something, but I need time to play it out in my mind okay." He said it in a soft, calming voice, the one she loves so much when she knows what he is saying is true and that he would fix whatever the problem was.

He has always had that peace about him. He doesn't let many things ruffle his feathers, he just peacefully goes with the flow or goes in a different direction, but it is always a calm peaceful way. Debbie looked up and saw the love and comfort in his eyes, and nodded as she snuggled into his arms. She laid there thanking God for this wonderful man, knowing she is who she is today because of him.

That was almost two weeks ago and today she needed some reassurance that everything was going to be okay. Deep down Debbie knows it is wrong to lead others into sin, so she has made sure that the least amount of people will be in on it. She hoped that the plan was more shrewd than sinful.

The past several months have passed by so quickly and Debbie knows the more time Amanda is unconscious the worse her health will become. Her quality of life could be degenerating with each passing day, if she even wakes up.

Debbie was now certain that Dr. Prong was responsible for the coma Amanda was in. He must be using powerful sleeping pills or anesthesia to keep her under.

Just the other day she saw Dr. Prong and the anesthesiologist whispering in the hall as the anesthesiologist came out of Amanda's room. The uneasiness in her stomach was at a high roar and a knot in her soul could probably be seen by anyone around her.

So far, it appeared that Amanda's brain had not yet been damaged and she was sure that Amanda could recover once she woke from her unconscious state. The printouts all suggested she was aware and knew what was going on. Debbie just didn't know how much longer her brain or her heart could withstand the drugs keeping her unconscious. What she did know, is that her friend Amanda is a fighter.

Debbie prays over Amanda several times a day and always falls asleep with her in her prayers. She knows God hears her prayers and He will answer them at the right time. She prayed that when Amanda woke up she would be completely healed and will not be paralyzed in any way and will be able to speak and communicate, walk and run, even though she knows full well that it is a very small percentage of most comatose patients.

Debbie was aware that Dr. Prong had been sending Amanda for several different tests lately. MRI's, ultra sounds, PET scans, CT's and other types of brain monitoring during the evening shifts. She was hoping to get copies of those tests, especially the brain scans to check her motor cortex region, but time hasn't permitted it. The actual results were not in the chart, and were only written in code on the computer. And so far, she has not been able to get copies of Dr. Prong's results from the technicians. It's almost like Amanda is Top Secret and Debbie would need a Top Secret clearance to know anything important.

The brain scan would help her to know what the chances of recovery were and if there was any damage. If the damage was only to the motor cortex but not including the pre-motor cortex than recovery looked good and vice versa. However if there was damage to both, then any damage would more than likely be permanent. For now, the printouts she had told her all she needed to know; Amanda was alive and she was able to speak through the machine. Just because she was in a drug induced coma her mind was still conscience, and able of thoughts. Amanda was conscience in her brain, this she knew. But if she knew, then Dr. Prong must know this too and that scared her.

Dr. Prong's actions over the last few days made her nervous and on edge. His talk about unplugging everything and telling the family she was never going to recover could not be allowed to happen. He must know there is brain activity and he must be keeping the notes hidden somewhere.

Dr. Prong

Dr. Prong *was* aware of Amanda's brain activity. The tests proved it and he was eager to tell her family she was gone and get her to the basement. She had a great deal of brain activity, he just can't figure out why his machine was not communicating. It should be printing out all her thoughts. Darn this lady!

He has been spending so many hours at the hospital and was extremely exhausted. He had his normal work hours and then the extra hours in the middle of the night to play with his machine in room 236 plus his other test subjects in the basement. As tired as he was, he couldn't sleep. He knew if he didn't take a break soon, he might mess up.

Again, if he didn't know better, he would say this experiment in room 236 was playing him, but how could that be, she is not as intelligent as he. When he dissects her brain, it will expose the answers he needs to tweak his cranium electrodes and brain supercomputer. The patient in bed 2 room 236 whatever her name is, will be his next subject.

He was sure he caught this unsuspected participant off guard the night before when he ducked quickly in to her room and performed some pupil dilation tests on her. The pupils clearly dilated slightly. He was so excited. Yes, there was still brain activity, and the second barrage of tests proved it as well, the eyes don't lie. But first the family.

Chapter Fifty-Two

July 13 2027, Carrie

Carrie sat and recalled the conversation she had with her mom when she was in her first year of high school. She had come home from school with so many stories to share. She loved talking with her mom. It was almost a game they played, ever since she was a child; using other people's bad choices and decisions to see which one of them could come up with a more wise way they should have done things, instead of the foolish way first.

"You don't need to experience bad life choices to know you don't want that bad stuff in your life, ya know what I mean Carrie? And HA, that's another whole reason God gave us His Word, so we can learn from it."

"Ya I know." Carrie chuckled, she knows her mom loves to win this game, and she always loves her advice.

"Drama, drama, drama. It's so easy to get caught up in the theater of life."

"Yup, mom....It's 'As the Drama Turns' or more like 'Drama Darkness'. Kinda like one of those soaps on TV for many of my classmates. How do I help them see the light mom?" She asked as she sat down to eat an apple.

"You can always start with praying for them. Just be careful to not let the drama in their lives become part of yours. That's a burden you don't need to carry around. Pray for the best in their lives and leave it at the feet of Jesus. He has all the answers and He will provide." She smiled then "…..and if they ask why your life is so good, then you can tell them about Jesus. You can't always start the conversation, but you can always finish it, and offer the solution." She smiled a huge toothy smile this time.

"Okay mom."

"And you can always invite them to church. We can pick up a friend or two and bring them to the teen program if you want?"

"Thanks mom, I might do that, it's a great idea."

Amanda sat down next to Carrie with her own apple. "Carrie….sometimes, people just have a hard time accepting the life they have. The grass is always greener on the other side ya know…..that's what they think anyway. The drama, the trouble or whatever you want to call it is something we all struggle with because of sin. Some people, your classmates and even some adults just keep doing the same things over and over hoping for a different outcome but until they accept God's way and gift, then they will just keep having the same results over and over in their lives. Many have a hard time breaking the cycle. …..Honey, most people think God expects miracles from us, and that we need to be perfect but as you know that is impossible and not true. We can't live a perfect life in a broken world, no one can. We need to accept that and then do our best not to commit the same sins over and over, and when we do sin, and we all do, we need to ask for forgiveness and move forward. Only Jesus was perfect. Maybe you can help them see that and also invite them to church. Find some common ground and go from there."

"Thanks mom, I hope I can explain things as simple as you just did."

"Go ahead; try……go on let me hear."

"Ok, so sometimes people see their lives like a movie. The drama plays out in every area of their life. They have a hard time getting out of that circle, that rut and they just keep playing it over and over. Rewinding just to make the same mistakes………. Until they change something, the results will always be the same. Until they have God in their life, they will keep making the same mistakes. We are not perfect, no one is. Only Jesus was and is." Carrie was talking with her hands in circle motions, "Oh and, and then invite them to church. But first I gotta find some common ground, something I have in common with them."

"You got it Carrie……it is how we respond to them that makes all the difference. Maybe you can help your friends see that if they keep doing things one way, they will have the same results ….when they do the same thing over and over expecting different results….well that is just foolish …..drama for sure ….I love you Carrie, how did I get so lucky to have such a smart girl?"

Carrie loved how her mom always complimented her. She was always telling her how proud she was of her. She always had great advice and direction for her and for her brother. It all came from God, from His Word and she followed it as best she could.

"Oh mom…..I am the lucky one."

July 13 2027, Carrie

Behind the Scenes

    Dr. Prong couldn't remember the last time he was this happy. The family would be coming in soon and the paperwork would be signed. This little pain in his side will be his. He has so much planned for this subject. She has no idea who she is messing with. He rushed to call Joe and Nurse Izzy, everything must go as planned. They all needed to go over the specifics so that they did not mess up. All of his subjects so far were already dead when they bring them to the basement. This little firecracker will be his first live subject. He couldn't wait!

Chapter Fifty-Three

The Funeral

Death comes when least expected. Even when it is expected, it is full of sorrow. Although there is a glimpse of clarity and renewed hope, joy and knowledge that if a person is right with God, they are forever with God, complete warmth, love and peace.

Life on earth never seems to be long enough for our family or us no matter how long the dash between the birth date and the death date is. That is why it is said to make the most of every opportunity of everyday of our life.

One thing is certain, we are born and we live however long or short that dash is. Everyone will face death. But while we are alive, we must continue to fight the battle. There is a reason to do that. We are all given freewill to choose which side of the battle we want to be on. Everyone knows you must choose wisely. After all, that decision is a direct path to where you will spend your Eternity.

We don't have a map to follow per say. Get to point A then move on to point B, and then search or find point C. It's not like that. Our life isn't planned out for us. We all have freewill. God does however direct us through His Word. We have guidance through the Holy Spirit who lives in us and was given to us as a gift when we accepted Jesus as our Lord and Savior and were baptized as an adult. We choose to be on His side of the battle.

We have a promise of Eternity if we stay on the right path. There is only one path. Jesus says He is the way, the truth and the life, there is no salvation in anyone else, the path is narrow and few find it, yet it is wide enough for everyone if they choose to go that way. The Bible is full of His moral will for us, His 'moral' compass per say. We were created by Him and are here on this earth for Him. God helps us to succeed in the decisions we make. He gives us freewill to make those decisions within His parameter of moral boundaries for us. Like I said, His moral boundaries are revealed in the Bible, and we choose whether to obey them or not. That is freewill. Whatever decisions we make within His parameters, He gives us freedom to do so. No laid out plan we have to search for. The gift of the Holy Spirit convicts us of righteousness. He interacts with us in dealing with moral issues of right and wrong, good and bad and directs and leads us through the Bible, our manna, the food for our soul. It's super cool.

Death comes in so many ways; by accident, by sickness, by murder, by old age, by a quick stop of the heart or brain and by natural disasters. Areas we are all too familiar with.

Death can also come by choice and a brokenness in the soul. Some will live a life of being lost, always searching yet never really seeking the one true God. The void in our heart can only be filled by Christ. He will fill that void when we seek Him. No one on this earth can completely fill it for you. Only God can fill the void. I personally have been on both sides. So trust me, it is only through His peace that we can completely experience life. It is the one thing I wish everyone knew. It is the one thing I challenge everyone to seek. May God fill the void in your heart with His love. He made a way for all of us to be complete. He is the reason for living. He has already given us the best gift of all. His Son. His Forgiveness. And Eternal life. We can always choose to accept His gift.

Debbie and Donald attended the funeral for Old lady Nell and Ruth several nights ago and it was a beautiful Celebration of Life. The families and friends decided to do the Celebration of Life together since it was knowledge that the time of death for both was 6:17 pm on the exact same day. They even decided to start the Celebration of Life at exactly 6:17 pm and asked everyone to be in their seats before that time.

Debbie still felt such a loss in her heart. She and Donald sat in the back of the church and watched as the people came in and find their seats. She saw Mary Jane in her pink cowgirl boots and pink cowgirl hat with blue jeans and a cute front ruffled blue and pink plaid shirt. It reminded her of the pink and blue beanies that Nell knitted and that brought tears to her eyes.

Debbie watched as Roxie and a man she believed to be her husband, walk over to Mary Jane as Valarie walked through the doorway and started toward them.

Valarie stopped quickly, stared at them, and then went as pale as the floor. From where Debbie sat, she looked as if she was going to faint. Valerie then turned and quickly left though the door she just entered. Debbie felt that she should go see if Valerie was ok, but figured she just didn't like funerals and felt wheezy. She made a note to herself to check on her later. At that moment, she could hear Roxie introducing her husband to Mary Jane.

"Mary Jane, this is my husband Kevin, Kevin"....she waved to Mary Jane, "this is Mary Jane." They both nodded and then they followed Kevin to seats in the back on the other side of the room.

There were many people from the church and all the Pastors as well as many she did not recognize. She was in awe that the church was as full as a regular service. She looked around as it filled up and noticed all the teens sat together on the left side of the church, filling up four rows of chairs.

The big screens in the front of the auditorium were on and showing various pictures of Ruth and a few with Nell. Every once in a while the live camera would show the audience and she would get a glimpse of Silvia, Grant and the two boys sitting up front sobbing. A few rows back she could see Amanda's husband Chris, Carrie and Christopher sitting together with the new girl.

What was her name? Debbie couldn't think of it, she had only been introduced to her once. She seemed to be a happy girl and had warmed up to Carrie and especially to Christopher. Debbie knew that Amanda would have liked her. She was dressed in black slacks with a beautiful white ruffled button down shirt. Her hair hung loosely around her shoulders and she seemed to be content and happy.

Debbie took a deep breath, grabbed a few Kleenexes that were being passed around and held Donald's hand. The Pastor began to speak at exactly at 6:17 pm as the time now showed in big numbers on the screens.

"Death…..the enemy has left us with only memories and tears. Our dear sweet Ruth and sweet Nell are gone from this earth…… They are gone, but not forgotten and not forever. I can gladly say both of these beautiful women were right with God." The Pastor looked around the room with a smile. "We know that if we are also right with God, we will see them again……… Christ has victory over death…..I had a chance to talk with Ruth a few weeks ago. She knew she was going to be going home. She asked me to make sure that everyone here in this room knew how to get right with God and then live right for Him. She wanted me to be exact so that she would see each and every one of you again, so here we go…………"

Silvia wiped her tears and tried to watch the screens as the cameras moved around the audience. She was looking for Susie. She had gotten her phone number from Mary Jane and called Susie a few days ago and explained to her about Ruth. She told her that Ruth was her daughter and Nell was her birth mother. She probably should have called her sooner but she had waited. She was shocked how it all played out. Her own loss of Ruth was just so sad.

She hated this part of life…..the loss…… and she knows it well, as she had already lost her own parents, grandparents and a best friend over the last few years as well as her husband's mom last year, and his sister the year before. Dealing with loss like this was hard. She prayed that they were all in heaven waiting to high five her someday when Eternity comes for her. Had they all accepted His gift and had a relationship with Him? Only God knows that answer and she knows that He will always do what is right. She smiles for a moment, as she finds comfort in knowing that Ruth will be there.

Mary Jane's heart was especially sad and extremely heavy as she listened. Her best friend Nell was gone. She felt a twinge of guilt knowing that Nell wanted to teach her how to knit, and she always laughed it off. Nell was a good friend. She didn't talk much and she listened well. She was a great sounding board and Mary Jane felt comfortable venting to her. MJ had asked her if she was right with God and Nell said she had been baptized at age eighteen. She had a feeling that Nell didn't have a great relationship, or maybe it was a struggle for some reason. She was going to ask more when Nell told her the hospital didn't need her beanies anymore. She was so upset over that news and Mary Jane sat and prayed with her. Nell had huge trash bags full of baby beanies and Mary Jane told her that she would call around to see where they could donate them. She had not yet gotten to that and now she wished she had taken the time.

There were a few photos of Nell on the table up front along with pictures of Ruth.

Mary Jane had the key to her home and found pictures from her younger days and a couple of the knitting women had photos of Nell in the background with all her knitting stuff. Mary Jane smiled at that, because Nell did not like her picture taken and would always try to hide in the background. Nell more than likely would not want her pictures displayed for everyone to see, but Mary Jane felt it was a tribute to her.

When Mary Jane had gone to Nell's house to find the pictures, she also gathered all the trash bags of baby beanie hats, about two hundred pink and blue beanies and she placed them on the long table up front with the photos for anyone who wanted one. It was the most simple and thoughtful gift she could think of. A hand knitted baby beanie from their dear friend Nell.

Mary Jane longed for a drink. A whiskey straight up, but she had promised God she was done and she meant it. Today was a real struggle for her, she needed to stay strong. Whiskey would not bring her friend back and it would not make her feel better either. Not today.

She was deep in thought when she heard the Pastor talking about the baby beanies on the table. She was glad she grabbed them and she knew Nell would have loved that everyone had one. She herself had grabbed one pink and one blue to keep as a reminder of her friend. She chuckled as she remembered how much they fought like sisters but always had each other's back in prayer with that sisterly love.

The information Silvia gave to Susie had fit with some of the information Susie was receiving in Texas from her source and she headed back to Arizona a day after Silvia's call.

The Funeral

Silvia, Grant and the two boys sat quietly watching the screen as many people, some they didn't even know, came up to them after the beautiful service and gave them their condolences. Silvia could not get herself to move. She had chosen all her favorite photos of Ruth to display and put on the screen. She wanted to just sit and watch them over and over. Ruth would have loved the service and all the information about God, Jesus and the Bible that the Pastor gave to everyone.

About a half hour after everyone had left, the camera people started to shut things down. Silvia and her family stood up to leave as Susie walked in. Susie never had the chance to meet Nell and only met Ruth the one time at the hospital café.

Silvia walked over to her and held her hand as they sat down in the back. Silvia told her all the great things she knew about her birth mom, Nell. Unfortunately, she couldn't answer the one question that Susie wanted to know......Why she had given her away.

"Susie.....that is the exact question that Ruth had, it was the main reason she was searching plus she wanted to have some sort of relationship with her as well. Or I should say, with you. She wanted to have a relationship and know you. You don't need to tell me the reason. But can I tell you all about Ruth?" Silvia was so proud of Ruth and wanted to share all about her amazing sweet girl.

"Come let me show you the pictures of Ruth and the ones of Nell, your mom, maybe some healing in your heart can begin today. Both of them were unique and extra special people."

A huge feeling full of compassion swept across them both, as they held each other's hands. With great loss and sorrow in their hearts, they both knew they had something in common and it united them together right there and then. Silvia made a mental note to make sure that she stayed in touch with Susie after today, Ruth would have wanted that.

A flash of a thought came to Susie's mind as she looked down at the pictures of Nell; God had helped her find her birth mom after all.

John 14:6 (NLT) Jesus told him, "I am the way, the truth, and the life. No one can come to the Father except through me.

Matthew 7:13 (NLT) "You can enter God's Kingdom only through the narrow gate. The highway to hell is broad, and its gate is wide for the many who choose that way.

Colossians 1:16 (NLT) for through him God created everything in the heavenly realms and on earth. He made the things we can see and the things we can't see— such as thrones, kingdoms, rulers, and authorities in the unseen world. Everything was created through him and for him.

Chapter Fifty-Four

July 13 2027, Carrie

Carrie grabbed an apple to eat and had another coffee with it. She flipped a few more pages and stopped on: My New Life Starts:

I was a sinner, I am a sinner, but You saved me
I was lost, but You found me
I could not hold my head up, but You looked me in the eye
I saw Your love, I saw Your grace, I felt Your embrace
I confess, I repent, You forgive, You forgave
I proclaim, You are my Lord, You are my Savior
The water flows over my head and surrounds my entire body, as I leave my old ways
You wipe my slate clean, I rise to a new life
We walk together, You light my path
You teach, You guide, You understand me, You know me
My life is changed, a new chapter begins, each day of my life is recorded
My story will have no end, after this life, we will begin anew again.

Behind the Scenes

It was time. Dr. Prong was meeting with the family at seven that morning. His plan was to let them see Amanda in her room, give them ten minutes alone and then go in ready. He may even ask if they needed a few more minutes. He was sure the crying would get on his nerves, so he would have to leave the room. Then return back about ten minutes later, but this time he would enter without a word and start to unhook the IV's and remove the ventilator and take off all the wires from her head. He is sure the crying would continue. So he will give a short hug to each of them and leave the room. He would then call Joe and tell him to wait about ten more minutes and then pick up the body. He made a mental note to tell Joe that he already had the gold blanket with tassels to put over the subject, on a gurney outside the room.

Chapter fifty-Five

Today's the Day...continued

The morning was cold and rainy. Just like the day when Old Lady Nell and Ruth had passed away. It was the perfect weather you would think of when a crime was about to take place.

Debbie was hoping no one would notice her this early in the morning in plain ordinary dark clothes, with her hoodie up over her head as she slipped into Amanda's room. The shifts would be changing soon and most of the nurses would be at their computers updating patient's charts and finishing up the notes from their shift.

As she started to unplug the coma brain machine, several pages started to print out. She tore them off and shoved them into her backpack then quickly unplugged the machine and removed all the wires from Amanda's head. She then pushed the cart with the equipment and the bag full of supplies she had shoved under it the day before to the elevator. The elevator was as slow as molasses in January as she waited. She felt her heart was gonna explode any minute.

She looked at her watch, she was right on schedule. So far, no one had walked by or noticed her. The elevator opened and she passed off the cart with the machine to Donald as he waited inside. Her backpack felt so heavy on her shoulders and a migraine was forming in her head.

They nodded to each other as the doors closed. She then went into the bathroom that was across from the elevator, locked the door, not wanting to ever leave. She was shaking so bad. She had two hours before her shift started to calm herself, two hours before she sees Donald again when he returns with her phone, two hours until he gives her another nod.

Someone had put her on the schedule for nine am, and that would have been too late. She changed it to seven, so that she could be here every step of the way. Nurse Izzy was scheduled early today, and she changed her schedule as well, to a later shift. She was sure it was Dr. Prong, he didn't seem to like her around, although he usually avoids her, especially after the talk they had about his machine about a month ago. She was regretting mentioning it now. Had she known of the plan back then she would have kept quiet. Is he on to her? Why mess with her schedule?

Amanda's family will be here at seven and the plan will be carried out. Her plan and she is sure Dr. Prongs plan as well. She wished she knew exactly what his plan was.

Donald and her had decided the night before that there should be no contact with each other on their phones, and no GPS to be followed in case someone suspected something. So they both left their phones at home. Donald even took out the GPS in their cars as well. They needed all their bases covered.

"Oh God, this has to be the right thing, it has to be." She t down on the floor almost afraid to even question it now. It was done, the plan was in motion. No second guessing it. The machine was gone and Dr. Prong will never find it.

Dr. Prong

Three days ago, Dr. Prong had taken an unexpected day off, something he never does, except for that so-called long weekend, which he really never took. He crept around the basement lab all hours of the night, planning his next move.

He needed to fake the death of the experiment in room 236 bed 2, whatever her name is. The few people that worked the night shift barely noticed him and never questioned anything he did. They really didn't seem to care. His plan will work; he had all his bases covered.

Debbie

Three days ago, Debbie took advantage of Dr. Prong's day off and she was sure it was a God thing. As quickly as she could, she copied all the paperwork and information that she could find that Dr. Prong had on his machine. She even wore gloves when she touched the paperwork. It was a miracle she had stumbled upon his unlocked desk and even more of a miracle there was a file that was labeled with the simple words 'C-Machine'.

She then went into the attached office and took out the DVD that recorded the daily activities. Camera is off. She quickly checked it yesterday to make sure no one had noticed and reloaded it, and today she was praying the recorder still sat empty. Her tracks needed to be covered. She moved swiftly and just did what she needed to do with no thought about it.

Just do it and get it done. She was lucky that no one paid much attention to her. She knew 'guilty' was written on her forehead if they cared to notice. Although even though Nurse Shady was there that day, she didn't see much of her. She was sure she was creeping around somewhere. Dr. Prong's unexpected day off was exactly what she needed and she took it. It just so happened, it was a miracle in itself. Once she had that done, she quickly printed off Amanda's whole file and any tests and labs she could find, even though they seemed coded. She will take them home to review them.

Donald

Donald entered through the front door, his black hoodie up over his head, plain blue jeans and gloves on. The security guard was getting a cup of coffee and Donald walked right by him to the elevator making sure his back faced the security guard the whole time he waited for the elevator to open so that he could easily read the words on his back. Debbie had sewed them on a few days ago. He waited for the elevator acting as if he belonged there. The words MEDICAL EQUIPTMENT INC. could easily be seen by anyone in his area.

The elevator doors opened and he went in. He pushed the number two for the second floor and sucked in a deep breath of air. The doors opened and Debbie stood there in the opening looking almost like she was about to cry. She looked frantic and scared as she pushed the cart into the elevator and nodded to him as the doors closed. Oh how he wished he could stop the time, step out and reassure her with a hug, a kiss and his kind voice. The doors closed ever so quickly and time continued on.

Today's the Day...continued

The machine was smaller than he had expected and not very heavy. He picked it up and decided he would just carry it out instead of wheeling it out on the cart. He quickly wrapped the wires around it as the doors opened and grabbed it off the pushcart along with the big bag of supplies that was under the cart and walked out of the elevator. The security guard was outside the doors with his coffee watching the rainfall.

The cold air hit his face as the doors opened, yet he was sweating like a fire pit or even a cold glass of ice water on a muggy day. Donald simply nodded and continued on to his car that was parked in the second row, calmly yet in a hurry. Good thing it was raining so it would not seem suspicious to see his running as wrong and criminal.

MEDICAL EQUIPTMENT INC. was all the security guard could read through the rain as the man dressed in black almost running through the parking lot left. Shrugging his shoulders, he went back inside.

Donald opened the trunk and laid the machine in there very carefully along with the bag of supplies. He then walked around the side of the car and got in. Glancing at the door, he noticed the guard had gone back inside. He let out all the air he had been holding in his lungs and breathed in a big cool breath of air and held it again as he pulled away.

"Thank you, Lord.....I know this is stealing and this is property of the hospital, please understand, please understand." He repeated to God over and over still shaking.

His eyes were filled with tears, and mixed with the wetness of the rain he could barely see two feet in front of him. He wanted to call Debbie so bad and let her know he was on the road, he had the machine, and he would be back.

He knew he would be seeing her in a few hours but right now, he needed to get the machine to The Ranch and then get back to the hospital for the rest of the plan. The drive was a good forty-five minutes away on a good day. He did not have any time to waste, plus he still needed to get back home to grab their phones.

He was not supposed to let anyone know what they were doing, but he was thankful that he had called Fred before he left home that morning and asked him to meet him on the road to The Ranch; it would save him some time, especially in this rain. He didn't tell him the whole story but asked if he could hand off the equipment and if Fred would drop it off at the Ranch. He promised to tell him more later.

The rain picked up and was now coming down in buckets and he *really* couldn't see two feet in front of him. His mind wondered, he had always loved monsoon time. Debbie and he would sit out on their front porch and watch the lighting storm and count the seconds before they would hear the thunder. If it took ten seconds for the thunder to roll in after the flash of lightning, it meant it had struck roughly two miles away. Donald loved how Debbie would snuggle up to him when the thunder was less than ten seconds, pretending to be afraid. "That was close Donald." She always giggled and snuggled closer.

Today however, he was counting the seconds he had to get back to her.

Debbie

Two hours sitting on the bathroom floor felt like two years. About an hour ago, someone tried to come in, they kept jiggling the locked door handle. It startled her and alerted her all at once. Her heart that had finally stopped beating so hard became alive again in her chest. She sat as still as she could, holding her breath. When they finally left she let out a sigh and prayed for forgiveness for what she just did and for what she was about to do.

She opened her eyes and looked around the small bathroom picturing it as a prison cell. She would probably be allowed a small cot and maybe a little window. The mirror would probably be gone and she envisioned a much dirtier room, not sanitized like this one.

Her big thought was, will the door to her cell ever open? It was different in Paul's day, and in many ways, it's not as bad. On the bright side, she doubts she will be whipped or lashed thirty-nine times before being thrown into prison.

She had been whipped once with a bullwhip when she was twelve, by her brother. The look on his face was chiseled in her memory. He had left a mark on her, one she still had today on her leg. He was messing around and snapped it at her. She doesn't really remember the pain, but she does remember the pain on his face. Let's just say, he never did that again.

Time continued on……..her thoughts left the whipping behind and began to think about being stoned to death…..She doubts she will be stoned. She can't even imagine the terror of that, nor does she want to.

Her mind then thought about the tattoo on her ankle and how painful that was. Twenty minutes to outline and another twenty minutes to fill in the color. She loves the artistry in some tattoos, especially flowers, Bible verses and patriotic ones. But that was the only one she had. Admiring them on others is more her thing now.

She started thinking more about where she will spend her life. Will they take her by ship like Paul, far away from her family? Will she be able to have visitors? Will she go without food and water? Will she be cold? She hated to be cold. So much was on her shoulders. Things she never thought about, because she has always lived a good, honest life. She wondered if criminals actually think about these things beforehand. And if they did, why would they still do the crime? She had chills running throughout her body. She committed a crime and was now really thinking about the consequences, the punishment, the accountability, the sin, and all of it had her crumbling in fear.

She couldn't stop now. She had to save her friend. She had to do something. She had to at least try. She glanced at her watch again for the millionth time. She thought some more about Paul from the Bible. He was in jail for preaching the Word of God. He found contentment in all things. Would she be able to be so content in her prison cell? Breaking the law and doing the time for the crime is not a laughing matter. How will she use her time? Will she be content?

She started to fall asleep picturing an angel helping her pick up her shield of faith. The flaming arrows were coming, not quite hitting her yet. She woke up to voices in the hallway. She stood up and got into her backpack and then into her work uniform. It was almost time. She was on duty in a few minutes. In a few minutes, Donald would be there with her phone and it would appear that she had just gotten there, according to the GPS.

Another thought came to her mind and she froze. What about the security cameras outside? Had they seen her get dropped off and out of the car in the employee parking lot, and

Today's the Day...continued

then a few minutes later Donald get out of the car parked in front? And then what about when Donald get's here and parks her car in the employee parking lot and then walks in through the door in back? She shook the thought from her mind. She hoped that the rain distorted the car, the license plate and of course, both of them in black hoodies over their heads.

Debbie was against the facemasks back in 2020 and now seven years later there were some that still wore them. She was second-guessing herself, wondering if they both should have worn one and disguised their faces to hide under the mask. Too late now. Now was the time to just act normal and not create any suspicion.

A quick prayer about the DVD recorder on her floor and more begging God that it was still empty and not recording, she walked out of the bathroom, legs almost trembling. No one was in the hallway, she let out a huge breath of air, inhaled and exhaled again as the doors to the elevator opened, and there stood Donald, he nodded and she hugged him and he handed her the phone, she then walked around the corner and to the nurse's station. Donald just waited near the corner in the seats that were available.

Genesis 4:7 (NLT) You will be accepted if you do what is right. But if you refuse to do what is right, then watch out! Sin is crouching at the door, eager to control you. But you must subdue it and be its master."

Chapter Fifty-Six

July 13 2027, Carrie

So far, Carrie had been waiting all day for her dad to arrive. He told her to wait at their house. She had taken the time off from work to spend with both of her parents. At this point, she still had no idea what was happening and what the outcome of her mom's coma was. Will she wake up? Has she woke up and needs help? Maybe that's what Debbie wants to tell them. Is she in a vegetative state? And one question she didn't want to think about, has she passed away? So many questions and so far for months no one has had any answers. At least not ones they were willing to share with her. She was getting a little restless thinking the worse.

    She turned a few more pages and read some more of her mom's RTP's. At least this occupied her time. This one was from 2017.

    We used to live in a world where people would agree to disagree, without conflict and temper tantrums and disgracing each other, without rioting and horrifying speech. So much energy wasted on what, a disagreement, a difference of opinion?? People, we will NEVER agree on everything all the time, yet in all my years, I have never seen such poor sports, such disgrace in the world, such chaos and madness.

Where did that come from? Why are people so hardened? So unhappy in their own life that they feel they need to make everyone miserable? What's really going on? So many out there in our world behaving like two year olds, lying and cheating and wondering why they can't play this game of 'life'. It makes no sense to me.

If you really want to live in a 'free' society, then live your life, work hard, play hard. Rules and laws are in place for a reason. The reason is simple; so that we can all be 'free' to live our life. If you are disobeying the laws then you are a criminal and need to fear. But if you are not disobeying the laws of the land then you have no fear. Live your life, go to work, and support your family and kids. Show this next generation some class not chaos.

This world is so divided because it's an 'ALL ABOUT ME' world we live in and that saddens me. Instead of working hard together, people and groups are out there dividing the people of America. People's hearts have become hardened because they have rejected the only One who can really help them, God. The Bible (God's Word) says it's exactly what will happen in a world without Him.

Listen my friends, God's message went out into the world...... Jesus died for all of us. No matter what's going on in our world, we need to reach people with God's truth. Our relationship with God through Jesus is what our world needs. Work hard for Him, teach your children to fear, love and respect Him. It starts in our own homes.

God has no favorites; He loves each and every one of us.

I look around and see so many lost souls, so much rebellion, and so much hatred, yet through it all, I also see God's love, protection and wisdom. What is He asking me to do when it seems so hopeless? When it seems so divided?

Satan seems to be working overtime on the hearts of those who have rejected God. But on those who seek and who have accepted Jesus as their Lord and Savior, God's favor is upon them. So I encourage others as I am led to do and continue to do what's right in His eyes. Love Him and love my neighbor, love and help the lost, one person at a time.

Won't you join me in showing God's truth and God's love to the world, and let God heal our land? UNITED WE STAND, DIVIDED WE FALL. You can disagree with me, you're welcome to, but I pray for our world to be able to agree to disagree without all the mess of chaos, riots, and tantrums, which will never get us anywhere but divided. God Bless You and God Bless America. 2/7/2017

Carrie felt so proud of her mom for taking a stand through her writing, through her words. She seemed so bold in her writing and so timid in her speech. It reminded Carrie of Paul in the Bible. He was bold. He told it like it was. And they hated him for it, and threw him in jail. They hated Jesus too and killed Him…… but not everyone hated Him or His message of truth, and she was totally happy about that.

For the first time a light bulb went off in her brain. Her mom used to talk about light bulb moments, but this one was her own light bulb moment.

"We aren't gonna be liked by everyone, huh God? But we have to keep speaking out or writing like my mom, don't we? I mean, that's how the church was started, the

July 13 2027, Carrie

disciples spreading the Word and then the people believing and spreading the Word from generation to generation. We have to pass the baton and pray and teach and live it out. That is what life is all about, right God?" Carrie talked aloud to God as if she would a friend, knowing He wants her honesty and for her to be real with Him, not fake and pretend, but real. Her relationship needed to be real. She felt at peace, content, and ready for the battle all at the same time. Protected in the ark of God's protection, just like Noah.

She recalled the saying her Pastor said during one of his teaching and has had a renewing of her own prayer life. The words hit her hard.

He said: If your Heart remains unbowed….it doesn't matter what your HEAD is doing.

Behind the Scenes

Nurse Izzy has been working overtime for many months now. She is exhausted, but the work needs to continue. It's almost done.

She feels she had better keep an eye on Debbie, the nurse on the second floor; she seems to be keeping an eye on her. She does not seem to trust her, all though she is nice to her. Maybe she will strike up a conversation with her and befriend her so she *can* keep a closer eye on her, and see if she knows or suspects anything. She made a mental note to try to run into Debbie soon. She really needs to make sure that Debbie does not mess things up. She must be careful so that her cover, will not be blown.

Chapter Fifty-Seven

The Meeting, Days Before

Debbie hurried around the kitchen; she wanted everything to be perfect. The food, the talk, the plan. She was going to let Donald do most of the talking and just fill in with the things she knew as facts from the hospital. Well, facts mixed with a large dose of suspicion and emotion. She had called Chris and invited him over for tacos at six-thirty so that they could let him know about the suspicious activity that Debbie had noticed and go over a plan they had with him. A plan that they felt would save Amanda.

It was only four o'clock and she was a nervous wreck. What if he doesn't think it's a good idea? Breaking the law is not something to be taken lightly and Amanda's husband is a Godly man. Maybe she shouldn't involve him. But if she didn't, then he would be questioning so many things and their plan would definitely be in ruins, along with their lives. She was relieved that Chris didn't want to involve his kids, Carrie and Christopher. That was a good call.

The Meeting, Days Before

To pass some time, she decided to call Valerie, she had been on her mind lately. She never did see her come back inside at the Celebration of Life for Ruth and Nell.

"Hey Valerie, how are doing? Hope all is well. Talk to you soon. Call me when you get a chance." Was the brief message she left when Valarie didn't answer.

Debbie then texted Silvia, "I'm thinking of you and said a prayer for you and your family, I hope all is well with you. Call me if you need anything."

There were things, small things that she knew about the ladies from the printouts that the machine spit out. She knew that each of the ladies would benefit greatly from the Bible verses and tips, but how would she explain the printouts? She could not let anyone else know about them, not yet.

She decided to text each lady from the group just to check in with them, just like Amanda often did. Maybe over the next few weeks she can use Amanda's words of encouragement to reach each of them. We all need God's comfort and direction, but maybe, just maybe Amanda will wake up and can do it. At this point, she had many doubts about that, unless the plan works.

Over the last few months, Debbie has seen each of the ladies come to the hospital to visit Amanda individually and some have shown up on the first Saturday of the month as well to meet together, talk and pray. She is positive that they all love her and want what's best for her.

Debbie sat at her kitchen table to send each lady a short 'thinking of you' text. She wanted to give them a reminder that God would carry them through all their trials, difficulties and situations in their lives. She knew they were all hurting after losing Nell and Ruth, and now, possibly Amanda. As she finished the last lady, she began to cry wishing Amanda was there and encouraging her right now. She always seemed to send the right encouragement at the right, most perfect time. She then prayed for Amanda and her family and for each of the ladies.

Romans 8:28 (NLT) And we know that God causes everything to work together for the good of those who love God and are called according to his purpose for them.

Hebrews 11:1 (NLT) Faith is the confidence that what we hope for will actually happen; it gives us assurance about things we cannot see.

Chapter Fifty-Eight

There Is a Reason

The Celebration of Life had spoken to Kevin. The talk about spending Eternity either with or without God by His forgiveness of his sins had him thinking. His eyes were opened and he could see his life was a mess. He knew his drinking was ruining his life and his marriage. He had a feeling that Roxie was not going to put up with it for much longer. There was something different about her the last few days. Something more peaceful. His thoughts of his past life and bad decisions had caught up with him the last few years and have been directing his actions and behaviors most of those days.

For the first time in forever, he really liked the lesson at the church during the Celebration. Plus deep down he knew that if it had been his picture on the screen, Roxie would be celebrating for another whole reason entirely. It didn't sit well with him as he sat on his side of the bed and said a prayer aloud for God to hear. "I know there is a reason you are sending me these messages. First, Fred the guy at work, Roxie's peaceful manner lately, and now this funeral, I mean Celebration. All of these friends of Roxie are with You. The church, the people there, the men even seemed calm and different.......I want what they have, I want peace........You're peace, like they have."

"Kevin, did you say something." Roxie asked as she walked into the room.

"I was talking to God....... um do you think you can pray with me?" He had glossy eyes and Roxie thought that maybe he was going to cry.

"Of course, of course I will." She sat down next to him with tears welling up in her own eyes.

"I'm not sure where to start, but I do know I need to ask you for forgiveness Roxie.......Will you please forgive me for all the hurt and pain I have caused you?....Will you forgive me for the horrible words I have spoken to you in the past? Roxie, I do love you and I care about you"

Roxie reached over and held his hands "Of course, yes, I will forgive you.... And thank you." And in her own silent prayer, she thanked God.

He then told her about the new guy at work, Fred and how he was such a manly man and a godly man with strong convictions, and about the paper he had given him about getting right with God. He told her that at the Celebration of Life for the two ladies that the message had hit him deep. He wanted to change. He really wanted a better life. He told her he needed her and wanted to get back to being part of the church and back to living right, like when they first got married.

"Roxie, we have been married I think almost twenty years right?" She nodded then he continued, "I have a real bad past. I need to tell you everything first, before we, before I, can move forward." He hesitated and then again continued as Roxie sat next to him and held his hand. "I tried to tell you when we met, but if you remember you just wanted to move forward and not about talk past stuff…..remember…….but if I don't tell you and come clean then it's gonna just keep eating at me and I'm gonna keep trying to cover it up with my drinking, understand?" Roxie nodded yes, bracing herself for what was coming next.

She didn't brace very well. She wasn't ready for the next confessions and she was in total shock as he told her about a baby who had been given to him and his girlfriend. The baby girl had been left on his doorstep when he was eighteen or nineteen. Then he confessed to her how he sold the little girl to his brother and his sister-in-law for four hundred dollars when she was only two years old so he could buy drugs.

Tears began to rain down his cheeks as he sat up and then told her that he also had a boy, a son, somewhere in the world. Kevin confessed that his girlfriend Valerie had left him and took his boy and disappeared when the boy was four years old after he told her about selling the baby girl. Kevin said that Val tried to get the little girl back from his brother, but they refused to give her back. They went to the authorities and they were able to adopt her and keep her. He said that they left him out of the proceedings.

He told Roxie about the little girl and how she ran away at fifteen from his brother's home. She had been a handful and they did try to raise her right, but she took off with her boyfriend. Then again, he lowered his head and he told her he had a son somewhere out there.

The stuff from his past that she hadn't known shocked her but it also explained much of why he drank. He was just trying to forget. Twenty years of marriage and she never knew he had a child out there. Roxie sat quietly and listened as Kevin told her all the details of his younger life.

"Do you think that God can forgive all that?" He asked and then added, "Can you?"

Roxie knew that God could and would, but she however would need to process it. So many secrets, and she was truly shocked. She looked deep into his eyes for a few moments then said, "Of course." A knot quickly formed in her stomach and she silently prayed, "Please help me Lord."

She then remembered seeing Valerie come into the church at the celebration and then turn and leave right away. She didn't remember seeing her later, but there were a lot of people there. Could her Valerie be his Valerie? She decided not to bring it up.

Valarie

Valarie has not left her house since the day of the Celebration of Life. She has been sitting in her living room with the curtains drawn, still extremely shaken. Could it have been Kevin? She was ninety-nine percent sure, that it was. As she turned and darted back out the doors, she was sure she had heard the words "husband, Kevin" and she ran to her car. She doesn't even remember driving and getting into her house. With all her doors locked, windows closed and drapes tightly secured she was already making plans to move, to run, and to hide once more.

She had felt some relief when Nell passed, thinking it was one less person who knew her secret. She had a few answers from their talk and she had come to terms with all of it. But this, this was not okay. What was he doing there? Why was he with her friends and talking to them? Would he recognize her? Did she see her? She would recognize him anywhere; he still looked the same, just a little older. Tall, good looking, dark eyes, and that smile with a deep dimple on the left side, that was the give-away and she knew it. It was Kevin.

Riley

Riley was so happy that she decided to check out the church. Her neighbor John helped her with her motorcycle and struck up a conversation about his church. It turned out to be the same church that was on the card that the lady had left. She felt that God was guiding her to go. She had met several people the first weekend. One of them sat next to her and was so nice that they became instant friends. Her name was Carrie. Riley felt like it was a sign from her dad; Carrie was the name of her own mom that had passed when she was so young. Carrie's brother, Christopher was just as nice and asked for her phone number so he could talk to her some more during the week.

After hours of talking and sharing for months, he opened up and told her that his mom was in the hospital and in a coma. She felt bad for him as he started to cry while telling her how afraid he was of losing her. She told him about losing her own mom, which she didn't really remember, and about her dad a few years ago and how he had died. She shared how she has been trying to survive. Christopher was so very understanding, and she instantly felt so safe with him.

She met Christopher's dad about a month ago at the church. They all sat at the food court and had some of the best Sonoran Dogs she had ever had. The roll was toasted and it was smothered in pinto beans and avocado and a bacon wrapped hotdog. As she sat with them, she had a feeling she had seen the dad before and finally got the nerve to ask him if he had ever eaten at the pizza joint just off the freeway.

He smiled because he definitely knew her, and said, "Yup…. Pickles right? My wife gave you a business card invite to this church."

Her mouth dropped, "Yes, yes…..oh my goodness, Christopher your mom and dad are the ones I was talking about……your mom is why I am here." She laughed, "Well and my neighbor too I guess and I'm pretty sure God had a hand in it too." She then looked at Christopher and grabbed his hand and then over to Carrie, "I'm sorry, so sorry about your mom….. she was so brave, so beautiful." Then looking at Chris, she apologized for treating them so poorly that night.

"I forgive you, and hey you're here, right? God is amazing and He has led you here. Amanda would be so incredibly happy. There is always a reason and a plan with every encounter. You just never know who will be inspired." Riley knew right there and then that she would go and thank Amanda, even though she was in a coma at the hospital, before going to work the next day.

Mary Jane

Mary Jane texted Debbie back immediately, "Thanks for checking up on me and for praying. I sure miss Nell. The Bible verse you sent was perfect. Hey, I know that you're a nurse and I have some questions about getting the CHIPS. I am considering it, since it will be the only way to see my granddaughter. Do you think we can get together soon, as soon as possible to talk about this, I'm hoping you have some information for me?"

Debbie texted back yes but wanted to say no. She was so occupied with her own plan and it was going to take up much of her time. Plus it needed to take place soon. Yet Mary Jane needed to talk about this and Debbie did have good information to give to her, at least good information as to why she should reconsider and not get the CHIPS.

It was only Monday and she texted back, "I'm very busy this week. How about we meet up next week? I'll text you at the beginning of the week with a time okay or maybe we can meet up at church this weekend?"

Psalm 46:1 (NLT) God is our refuge and strength, always ready to help in times of trouble.

Philippians 4:4-8 (NLT) Always be full of joy in the Lord. I say it again—rejoice! Let everyone see that you are considerate in all you do. Remember, the Lord is coming soon. Don't worry about anything; instead, pray about everything. Tell God what you need, and thank him for all he has done. Then you will experience God's peace, which exceeds anything we can understand. His peace will guard your hearts and minds as you live in Christ Jesus. And now, dear brothers and sisters, one final thing. Fix your thoughts on what is true, and honorable, and right, and pure, and lovely, and admirable. Think about things that are excellent and worthy of praise.

Chapter Fifty-Nine

July 13 2027, Carrie

Debbie, her mom's best friend had sent out a text for everyone to stop and pray for her mom, everyday at nine am. She was so thankful for that and she knew God would hear all their prayers. Feeling blessed and hopeful, Carrie was extremely happy that her mom had such great friends.

She grabbed her mom's Bible and read a message written to her from her mom's special friend Don who was in his nineties when he died.

Her mom loved him and his wife Isabel, who had been Bible translators for fifty years. Her mom used to read to them from the Bible every week for the last eight years of their lives. Carrie loved going with her. She was only eight years old when her mom started taking her with her to their home.

Isabel had passed first at the age of ninety-eight and the husband Don who was about eight years younger than Isabel passed a few years later at ninety-three. Don had a very hard time seeing and hearing in one ear so her mom would read loud so he could hear with his good ear. When he passed, he had left a short note for her. Carrie loved reading it and she had her own copy of it at home too:

> God's Voice for the Handicapped
> A note of appreciation to those who read the Bible to the handicapped:
> I can hear a dog bark
> And a baby cry
> The splatter of rain on the roof
> And the lightening strike
> The thunder clap
> The twitter of birds
> And the toll of a bell
> But what is more wonderful to hear when my eyes and ears are dim with age,
> Is the precious Word of God, which inspires my heart as I approach Heaven's door.
> Love Don, your friend for life and hopefully for all Eternity

Carrie wished she had copied this and given it to Ruth before she passed. She knows very well that her mom loved that Ruth spent time in her room reading the Bible to her at the hospital. Carrie decided that she would be the one now to read God's Word to her mom starting tomorrow or maybe today if her dad would just get home. She knows it is the one thing her mom would want, God's Word. And with her mom's birthday tomorrow, it would make the perfect gift.

Behind the Scenes

Dr. Prong and Joe were fighting again. Nurse Izzy had to remind them that they were all professionals and that their plans would work. The other subjects can either wait or they could just put in extra time. She was in, and that seemed to smooth it over a little with the guys. The two of them can be so immature, both wanting to be in control. She needed to put a cap over the two egos. From what she could tell, they didn't really trust each other or even her for that matter.

They already had been putting in so much time down in the basement during the after-hours and they were all so exhausted.

This one last experiment was all that was needed. This was the last one, and then she could go home, to her real home. She would have all the proof she needed. That is if she could just keep these two guys from killing each other.

Chapter Sixty

The Meeting Continued, The Plan

Donald answered the door, "Hey Chris, come on in."

"Smells delicious in here."

"Ya, Deb's in the kitchen, and tacos wait." He said as he patted his tummy, and grinned so big that all his teeth showed.

Chris followed him into the kitchen, and about fifty minutes later dinner was done and the small talk was over. Chris couldn't eat much, he was still upset over the call from Dr. Prong and the uncomfortable talk he was sure was coming. Debbie cleared off the dishes and they all went to the living room to talk more serious.

Chris started the conversation, "Dr. Prong called me yesterday after you called, he wants me to…….." he almost could not say it, as a lump formed in his throat and his eyes began to water. He looked over at Debbie who looked very concerned and shaking her head back and forth.

"What, what did he say?" She did not mean to sound so rushed but her mind was in full speed. Why was the doctor calling him? The time has run out, and she is sure of it.

Chris hung his head and stared at the floor, "He wants me to sign the papers to take her off all support. He said her brain is dead and she won't wake up from the coma and even if she did she would have to be on life support forever. He said she will never have a normal life. I don't know, something like that. Is that what you wanted to tell me too?" He couldn't look at her, he just stared at the floor and wished he could just close his ears and not hear it again.

"Wow, I didn't know he was pushing this so fast….I knew he was up to something….when does he want you to the sign papers?" Debbie asked as she looked over at Donald who looked as if he was deep in thought then back to Chris who looked so defeated and lost.

"I told him I needed to first talk with my family, but I can't…… but I did already call him back this morning…..I don't know what to do, I can't tell the kids, I don't know how to break it to them…..I'm scheduled to meet with him to sign everything in two days…….Wednesday, seven in the morning." He trailed off feeling sick to his stomach. "She will be taken off all support, as soon as I sign the papers." He looked at Debbie, "He told me that she will not survive and will be gone immediately…..it's the machines that are keeping her alive and on Wednesday she will completely be gone." Chris couldn't stop the tears from rolling down his cheeks, "I'm gonna have to talk with the kids tomorrow, I'm sure they will want to be there. Is this the right thing to do?" He directed the question directly at Debbie.

"I'll be right back." Debbie excused herself and went to the bedroom, and came back with the box of folders. One for each

The Meeting Continued, The Plan

of the women from Bible study and the one for Chris that she had made with the printouts, in her scrape book style of laminated sheets.

While she was pulling them out of the box, she thought about her schedule. Dr. Prong said the hospital was cutting back hours. She was scheduled for nine in the morning on Wednesday. She made a mental note to change her schedule to seven as well, she needs to be there, for the plan to work.

"Chris, I have something to tell you. Please hear me out and let me tell all of it to you before you say anything okay? This may be very hard for you to believe, but I believe it is true. Donald and I have a plan and I will get to that but first............." She took a deep breath and then, "I want you to know that Amanda and I are best friends and we have more than a sisterly bond. I want nothing but the best for her and your family, so please know this comes from my heart. I love you all so much, you are all family."

She chocked back the tears and then she told him about the first early morning that Amanda came to the hospital. She reminded him that he had mentioned all the machines that were hooked to Amanda and the wires that went to her head when he got there to her room after she was brought up to the second floor, which was weird to begin with, since she was in a coma and coma patients don't normally end up on the second floor.

She told him about the machine that was hooked to Amanda's head that she called the 'Brain Machine'. She explained to him that it was an untested and an unapproved piece of equipment. But it would print out Amanda's thoughts only when she was in the room. She confessed to turning off the machine whenever she left the room so Dr. Prong would not know that it was working. She told Chris that she did this because she really felt strongly that if he knew, he would do some major exploratory surgeries and that he didn't care if she lived or died. He has had many patients that have died.

"I'm pretty sure that he knows she has brain waves. He has been doing many tests this last week. I haven't seen any of the test results, they are hidden somewhere but I am sure he wants you to sign off so that you will think she is dead and then he will be able do whatever he wants."

She then told him about the room in the basement and how she had no actual physical proof. She only had an educated suspicion. She felt like she was speaking so fast as she explained it all to Chris. She then told him about all the strange circumstances and about the conversations she has overheard. And about Dr. Prong telling her to mind her own business when she confronted him about the machine.

"He has a small staff who works with him. Nurse Shady and at least one of the anesthesiologists, and I believe he is the one that is keeping Amanda in the state of a coma. They are all in on it." She took a sip from her water and put her finger up as to say, wait I have more.

"He doesn't know his machine is working, but he must know that it should be." Debbie again felt like she was rattling her words off so fast, but she wanted to get it out. She had planned on Donald doing all the talking, but she needed to tell the same story she told Donald before he could present the plan. She watched Chris get paler as she described everything with as much detail as she could.

Chris couldn't listen anymore. "But, how do you know?" Chris asked a little confused. "The doctor has been so good at explaining what is going on for months now and from what I

The Meeting Continued, The Plan

can tell the doctor has been truthful to me. He uses big words I don't understand, but Dr. Prong seems sincere." Chris shook his head in disbelief, "……..what you're explaining sounds like a horror movie."

Donald nodded to Debbie, "Show him the printouts, the ones that prove that Amanda is aware and knows what's going on, she just can't wake up."

"Chris these are all the printouts from the machine that I have collected. Like I said they only print when I am in the room…..I made folders for all the printouts with names. Plus there are some random printouts, and some for you and some for Carrie and Christopher as well as someone called Pickles."

"Pickles?…….. We met her at the pizza place the night Amanda went into the hospital. Amanda had also seen her earlier that day at the corner store, and well…… her real name is Riley, and she goes to our church now."

Everyone sat there in their own thoughts for several minutes as Chris looked through the folders.

"This isn't a game, this is my wife were talking about and she has been in the hospital unresponsive for four or five months." Chris got up and started pacing the floor, upset and anxious.

Debbie started to feel like he was blaming her for Amanda's condition. He seemed mad that she had all these printouts, as he flipped through them. Maybe she was to blame. Maybe she should not have taken the printouts. Maybe Amanda would be awake by now if she had just let it be. On the other hand, maybe Dr. Prong would already have her in the basement by now. She didn't know. But what she did know was that she needed to get Amanda out of there.

"Chris, I know this is a lot to take in, and we don't have much time. The doctor is pushing this forward from the sounds of it. Once you sign the papers, he will get her prepared and taken off everything. He will say she will not be able to survive being off the life support, like he has already prepared you for." Debbie took a big breathe, "Chris, I think she will survive........ but I also think he will make it appear that she is gone....... remember, I told you he is working with an anesthesiologist. I believe with all my heart he will give her something that will make us all believe she is gone and then she will end up in his basement."

Chris was giving her a look that indicated she was talking crazy as he sat back down and put his face into his hands.

Donald spoke up, "Chris, I know how you must be feeling. I kinda felt the same way when Debbie first told me all of this. She doesn't have much proof, mostly speculation and suspicion mixed with a lot of emotions. She really only has the printouts, which for the most part are jumbled thoughts and not much of communication, mostly Bible verses which we have looked at, trying to figure out if there was some hidden message in them.......you know Chris, Debbie is Amanda's best friend, she only wants to protect her."

Chris sat there confused, thinking about everything they were telling him. It was crazy. He was trying to figure out what needed to be done. He just wanted his wife to wake up.

"Chris, Debbie believes that if we can get Amanda off all the medications, the IV's, everything off of her, and flush the meds through her system she will eventually wake up. She is not one hundred percent, but she professionally feels Amanda's best chance for survival is to get her out of there and away from that doctor."

Debbie spoke up, "I think once the papers are signed, Dr. Prong will unhook everything....what we witness will be hard

The Meeting Continued, T1.

to watch, and her pulse will be unreadable and he. will be undetectable....all appearances will be that she is ֵ He will have to act quickly and be ready to wheel her out and away from all of us. I truly believe he will then take her to the basement to hook her back up to his machine."

Chris wasn't quite convinced yet. He has trusted this doctor for the care of his wife for months now. She hasn't woken up, but could it be because he wasn't allowing it. Maybe he was responsible and he was the one keeping her sedated? In addition, what about the printout to Pickles.....there has to be something to that? Amanda would be the only one to know about Pickles. He looked back at the printout with the word Pickles at the top. It was dated March seventh, a few days after Amanda was admitted to the hospital. Crazy as it sounded, the puzzle pieces seemed to be in order forming the outline to a picture of deception.

"Chris, now this may sound crazy and it is definitely unlawful, but we think we have a plan. One we believe will work. One that in light of what you have just told us needs to be in place before Wednesday morning. Chris, I know this is hard to take in, I sure wouldn't want this reversed. Chris, I believe my wife and I believe we need to do something."

Chris sat looking down at the printout with his name at the top and under his name was his and Amanda's marriage verse... Ephesians 4:32. That got his attention, then looking at Carrie and Christopher's printouts, the favorite Bible verse of the family was there in Amanda's handwriting ....Joshua 24:15.... then back at Pickles printout, he shrugged and said "Okay, I'm listening."

Carrie

Carrie had finished cleaning up and had put the binder back where she found it. She was just turning to leave when her dad entered the house. He looked rattled and she could tell he had been crying.

"Dad, are you okay, is it mom, is she okay? Where have you been all day?" She quickly hugged him. He hugged her for a long time before letting her go. "Let's sit."

Carrie immediately started crying, she couldn't listen and she didn't want to listen. "Oh God, no…please God no please, oh God please…." She sobbed, as Chris also could not turn off the flow of tears.

"Christopher will be here soon, he's just getting off work…. we all need to talk."

When Christopher got there, he told them he needed both of them at the hospital at seven in the morning. He then told them that the doctor would be taking their mom off the life support, and she would be gone. It was the hardest thing he ever had to say to them.

Chris decided not to tell them about the plan, that Donald, Debbie and he came up with the other night. He will tell them later afterwards, if it actually worked.

Today was an emotional day, the van he rented sat at The Ranch waiting for him to pick it up and deliver it to the hospital at three in the morning. Then he would need to drive to the hospital at seven, sign papers and say goodbye to Amanda. He will have to watch his kids fall apart when the doctor removed all her support. Then basically kick them both out of the room and meet them in the Chapel a few minutes later. Simple enough right? He must be crazy.

Chris

Everything was in place. The van that Chris rented was parked and ready at the back door next to the shuttle vans, the hospital had parked there for emergency use. He had rented it the day before and drove it to The Ranch. He covered the windows with foil, took out the GPS, and laid back all the seats in the rear. He had layers of blankets and pillows all waiting. He then took off the license plate. He knew he'd be okay as long as no police officer came up behind him.

Chris was shaking as he drove Wednesday at three in the morning to drop it off. As he pulled in, he swore he saw Dr. Prong enter the building. It was dark and it was raining but he was ninety percent sure it was him.

Chris parked the van with the back facing the building near the walkway. It would only be a thirty-foot walk from the back door to the van. He prayed it would still be raining.

The timing was perfect. Donald pulled up right after he parked. Chris got into Donald's car and they left. The first part of the plan was complete. Donald and Debbie had part two to play in a few hours.

"Hey Chris, this is going to work…we are going to save Amanda."

"What if she does need the machines and the ventilator?"

"We will bring as much as possible with us okay. We will need to move fast as soon as the doctor leaves the room…. everything we can grab with her we will."

"This is crazy…….What about Christopher and Carrie? Won't they be freaked out?....What if they don't leave the room with Debbie to the Chapel?"

They were almost to The Ranch to pick up Chris's car.

"You told them that the doctor will take all the support off of Amanda right? And then Debbie will then bring them to the Chapel at the end of the hall on the first floor as they prepare and bring Amanda on a gurney to the Chapel right?"

Chris nodded yes, he had said all of that to both of them. Carrie questioned it. She said she had never heard of the hospital doing that. Chris did not want the kids involved in any way. Their emotions needed to be genuine and pure. He lied to them and said that because Debbie works there and because they know that Amanda loves God so much, that they would allow her body to be taken to the Chapel for them to be able to spend as much time as they want once she passed. Chris had cried throughout the whole made up explanation and both Carrie and Christopher hugged him as he did.

"But what happens when the gurney with Amanda doesn't show up in the Chapel for the kids to say their last goodbyes, what then?"

"That's when you start questioning where your wife is? Why haven't they brought her down?....It will be on them to explain where she was and what happened."

"What if they see us going out the back door? I'm sure there are cameras out there."

They pulled into The Ranch.

"Hey, I know this is hard, just pray it all goes smoothly, oh and don't forget leave your phone at home. It's there right now, right? (Chris nodded) And bring your dark hoodie. I'll see ya soon. This plan is going to work okay Chris?" Donald was trying

The Meeting Continued, The Plan

to sound positive, but he was just as scared as Chris. What if Amanda did need the ventilator and the IVs to survive? What if they did actually kill her as they worked to keep her alive? What then?

Both of them drove home from the Ranch in prayer.

Dr. Prong

Dr. Prong was so excited. He got to the hospital early and went directly to the basement to set up one of the old beds, with the old sheets so he could hang out all day and night. He had found an older small refrigerator when he was ruffling around in there last week and plugged it in. It worked and he filled it with drinks, and sandwich stuff. He was now set up to work on this subject day and night. He changed the schedule to show him off for the next two days. Today was Wednesday, it was the day and his plan would go smoothly and successfully. Joe had better not blow it.

Dr. Prong loved the early mornings, especially when it rained. It was a perfect day to fake kill the subject. The man was coming with his family at seven. He will have him sign the paperwork immediately, no small talk. He was thrilled that he was able to convince the man to let the hospital keep her body for medical teaching. He will text Joe when to pick her up. First things first, he will drug her with the cocktail that Joe gave to him, so she will appear dead already when they arrive at seven. He will need to get in the room just before the meeting. He is hoping the family does not linger. Maybe he will suggest the Chapel for them to go to…..Ya that's a great plan, totally away from the room. He will have Izzy bring them down there.

His plan was in place. Where was Nurse Izzy? She was supposed to get here at three today, it was not like her to be running late. He had switched the schedule around. The annoying nurse that seems to be watching his every move was now scheduled at nine and the subject will be long gone by then. Izzy will be his assistant.

As soon as he get's upstairs he will make sure there is a gurney outside the room. He changed up the plan with Joe. He already had the blanket in his office. The beautiful gold blanket with tassels will lay on the gurney, that way the family will already be prepared and not pay much attention in their grief as soon as they enter the room. It will lie there, as a reminder that she will be gone.

Chris

Chris was second guessing the whole plan. How was he gonna keep this from the kids? They deserve to know that their mom will hopefully be alive at The Ranch, right? This was crazy. What if he kills her in the process? He doesn't know what he's doing. Does Donald know what he's doing? What if she really does pass away when everything comes off? And Debbie will not even be able to get to The Ranch until after her shift, after dropping off her phone at home. So much can go wrong.

The Final Chapter

Half Way Home

Everything was ready. Dr. Prong's signature was the last one needed on the paper and he quickly signed it.

"Would you like a moment?" He asked Chris. Chris nodded, it seemed like Amanda was gone already. Even Dr. Prong questioned it to himself, all while blaming Joe for a possible overdose cocktail.

Christopher stood still and stared down at his mom, and quietly said, "I love you mom."

Carrie continued to cry as she sat on the side of the bed. She could not get herself to say, happy birthday mom....there was nothing happy about this.

Chris stood frozen in pain at the loss of his wife. He couldn't make eye contact with anyone, he just stared down at Amanda hoping the next moves were all the correct ones to make.

Debbie left the room with Dr. Prong to give them privacy. She was relieved that when she checked the recorder it still sat empty.

Donald was down the hall, waiting for his time to help. Watching for when Debbie went back into the room and then leaves again with Amanda's kids. They would head down the hallway opposite of him, to the elevator and then to the Chapel on the first floor. It was important that they did not see him.

The gurney that sat outside the room would be perfect to use. Better than the wheel chair idea. They will be able to throw as many things from the room as they could on the bottom shelf. They would have to work fast. Lift her up on to the gurney, cover her with the beautiful gold blanket, grab what they can and leave. He prayed that Chris would be able to do this. He prayed Debbie was able to turn off the recorder. He prayed he could be strong for both of them. He prayed that Amanda would not die on their rescue and on their watch. And lastly he prayed that God would forgive them all, this was more than being shrewd.

Dr. Prong could not wait much longer, he was too excited. Heck with ten minutes that was a bad plan, five minutes was long enough. He walked back down to room 236 followed by the annoying nurse. He will be glad not to be under her microscope. She did not scare easy. He tried to get her moved to another area but she kept ending up back here to this end of the hall. He entered the room and took charge, ignoring their sobs.

"Mr. Garrison sir, we have a beautiful Chapel you are welcome to go to after I disconnect everything and ……..well I'm sorry, not to seem blunt………but once she passes. We will take her to another room and clean her up and make her more presentable. You'll want to remember her more how she was and not like this. We'll take good care of her and place her carefully on the gurney you may have seen when you entered her room. We have a beautiful golden blanket. .....you probably noticed it on the gurney. We will cover her with that. Once I bring it into the room, you can follow this nurse to the Chapel." Again, he mentioned the Chapel. He nodded to Debbie. Then in his mind, he cursed Nurse Izzy. She had called in sick today and could not make it in for this important part of his day.

He needed this nurse to not question bringing the family to the Chapel. She seemed to have too much concern for this patient and he needed this part of his plan to go smooth.

Debbie met Chris's eyes, could Dr. Prong know their plan? Or is his plan the same as theirs.....get rid of everyone? She needed to think things over fast and it looked like Chris was as well in the middle of his doubts.

Dr. Prong decided that he was not gonna give them any more time. He decided that he would push the gurney in first then unhook everything right in front of the family. He pushed bed one over to give himself some room. He then turned and went out to get the gurney and pushed it into the room. This will help move things along.

Donald was down the hall and started to freak out. Why was the doctor pushing the gurney in?

As soon as Dr. Prong stopped the gurney from rolling, he began to unhook everything.

Alarms from the equipment began to go off. He waited briefly before silencing the beeping to reinforce the finality of what was happening. He giggled to himself as he quickly and quite efficiently disconnected everything and pushed it all to the side. He then noticed his brain machine was gone. Joe

There Is A Reason

must have taken it already, he thought. Relieved, he continued pushing everything aside as the nurse wrapped the IV sites.

He noticed that the subject appeared to already be gone. The cold packs he placed under her back was helping make her hands feel cold and the skin under her nails was looking blue. Under his breath, he was cursing Joe for maybe overdosing her with his cocktail. He himself was convinced she was gone.

Just then, another monitor began to beep, this time he let it ring loud and clear for a longer time hoping the family would be convinced. Well if she was not really gone, he will have to congratulate Joe on his wonderful power shot. It was very convincing.

Dr. Prong took Amanda's pulse and sadly looked at them, "She's already gone, I'm sorry, I'm very sorry for your loss." He ignored the sobs and turned to Debbie and said, "Nurse, can you bring this family to the Chapel now? I'll have an orderly bring her to them in a few minutes, when we get her ready."

Chris spoke up, "Can you give us some more time, please."

"Sure, I'll go call for the orderly to come get her...mmm, ten minutes okay? Like I said, we'll bring her to you in the Chapel." He turned to leave.

Chris nodded yes, as he looked at Debbie. Christopher and Carrie sat back down at their mom's side as soon as the doctor moved out of the way, they couldn't stop crying.

"I think she twitched." Carrie looked hopeful, even though her mom's hands felt so cold.

Debbie spoke up quickly as Dr. Prong turned back around to watch what was happening. She walked over to Carrie, placed her hand on her shoulder, and told her it was normal. She placed her other hand on Amanda's neck and said "She has no pulse honey, I'm very sorry." She then herself started to cry.

"Nurse, lead these folks to the Chapel when they are ready!?" It was more of a demand then a question. He then sternly added, "Ten minutes." Dr. Prong needed to slow down or else the family may change their mind about everything he's put in place, although he already had the paperwork. He excused himself and again said, "I'll go call for the orderly. It would be best for you to wait in the Chapel." Then he offered a remorseful and sorrowful condolence again. "Again, I'm sorry."

As soon as he left, Debbie began to urge Carrie and Christopher to follow her to the Chapel.

"Go with her, I'll stay here and keep an eye on everything. It's okay, now go. I'll meet you in a few minutes. I'll stay with her until they come for her." Chris hugged them both. The kids did not want to leave, but with Debbie's support, they followed her. As soon as they were out of the room, Chris picked up the beautiful blanket, and put his face into it and started sobbing. He could not hold it back.

Chris knew that he would be lifting his beautiful wife onto the gurney in the next moments. He couldn't help but wonder if she would still be alive, will she live or has she already passed? He will then have to cover her with the gold blanket and with Donald's help; he would push her out the back doors of the hospital and into the van. He prayed no one would notice a thing.

Donald saw the doctor exit the room with a smile on his face and down the hall to the offices. Almost immediately afterwards he then saw Debbie exit the room with Carrie and Christopher. He almost ran to the room after a small popcorn prayer and found Chris sobbing.

"Come on Chris, I'm sorry but pull it together buddy, we need to hurry."

Chris and Donald quickly put on their hoodies that said TUCSON MORGUE on the back. They lifted Amanda over on to the gurney and found the ice packs under her. It was all Chris could do to hold it together. He was so mad that he wanted to go find the doctor and strangle the life out of him.

"Slow down Chris, focus….focus on our task….we got to get out of here with Amanda, hold it together." Donald said in a smooth calm voice.

Before leaving the room and they put on some medical masks over their faces to hide their identity. Then they each put the hood up on the hoodie as well.

They pushed Amanda out of room 236, to the right and down the hall to the elevator and then out the back door without any disturbances. It was a miracle. They both felt like they were walking on clouds, with intent and purpose in every step.

Chris knew he would not want to leave her, not yet but once she was in the van, Chris would have to leave her and go directly to the Chapel to be with his kids. At that point, he knows he will not be pretending anything. He will let it all out and wail in his emotional state. And during his breakdown, Donald will be driving her to The Ranch. He prayed that the van was big enough to hold the gurney and everything they took. It seemed to be another miracle that it was there for them to use and it would make moving Amanda around easier at The Ranch.

Chris was still undecided whether to let the kids in on the plan yet. Maybe he will have them come to The Ranch next week after he makes sure Amanda is okay because what if she were to die? She needs to live and be alive before they know, yes, that is the plan. He just decided that is the way it needs to be. She needs to stay alive.

Carrie

Carrie did not want to leave. She didn't understand why everyone was rushing her and Christopher down to the Chapel. The doctor was so quick and so dismissing. It took a few minutes to convince her. Debbie's encouragement was rushed as well and as soon as she said okay, Debbie took her hand and led her out of the room followed by Christopher. She did not even have a chance to look back to her dad who she could hear crying loudly. Debbie then walked them swiftly out of the room to the left and down the hall to the elevator passing Dr. Prongs office. Carrie looked in the doorway as she passed the room, she stopped and let go of Debbie's hand and stepped back to relooked into the room. Dr. Prong was smiling as he typed on his computer. How can he be smiling? Her mom was dead, his patient was dead. Dr. Prong looked up and saw her staring at him and quickly changed the smile into a concerned look with his head tilted he asked her if she needed anything. She just turned and walked away.

"Wow that was fast." He smirked and made a few more changes in the computer and then texted Joe it was clear to go get her. The family and the nurse would be out of the way.

Joe

As the back door to the hospital closed behind them, they walked the thirty feet to the van in the rain. Just as Joe entered room 236.

"Seriously, why do you tell me to do things and then you do them yourself!" Joe was talking to himself as he double-checked the room number....yup room 236, it's correct.

Shrugging it off, Joe left. He was headed home, he had had enough time in the last few days and nights that he needed some sleep. "You wanna take care of it, you take care it until I get back." He complained to the empty room. Frustrated Joe left the room and headed to the parking lot cursing Dr. Prong for not trusting him to get things done. Not that he really cared. He opened the back door to the outside, it was still raining. A man in a dark hoodie walked in as he stepped out of the door and into the rain.

Chris went straight to the bathroom, removed the black hoodie and stuffed it into his backpack, then hurried to the Chapel to meet up with Carrie, Christopher and Debbie praying every step of the way.

Dr. Prong

Dr. Prong finished the changes in the computer and made a few more notes and plans before leaving his office. He wanted to make sure his forged DNR form was in there, just in case he was ever questioned. He started toward room 236, but was called by one of the nurses to a room at the other end of the hall. The patient was choking and she needed his help. By the time he got to room 236 the subject and all the equipment was gone. He will have to visit with her in the basement after his shift.

He then remembered, he forgot to ask Joe if he had taken the brain machine off the subject before he got to the room that morning. He was sure that he had, since it was not there. Joe was very efficient and ahead of the game most days. He knew that Joe was just as excited as he was to experiment on her, all in the name of science of course.

He figured he should let up on Joe and stop second-guessing him and looking over his shoulder. He will talk to him later when he gets down to the basement. The nurse again called him over, the gentlemen was again choking. He rolled his eyes, and then Dr. Prong continued his rounds.

Amanda

Today was my birthday. I am only 50. My small dash in this life here on earth so far has taken place between July 14, 1977 and July 14, 2027. With 18,262 days, 608 months plus 3 weeks, 2,608 weeks, 438,288 hours, 26,297,280 minutes. So short.

The machines are all unplugged and off. My mind feels good, but I am so cold and so sleepy I cannot think any more thoughts. The medicine they just shot into me is starting to work....I can't , I'm ttoooo tiiirrreed......... 5,4,3,2,1...........

Silence, not a sound in the room for what seemed like several minutes........... Everyone stood staring down at me holding their breath.......even the crying had stopped.... then it came; the long, sharp, deep, loud beep. The last of the equipment was off. It pierced into the silence and stillness. It was shut off somewhat quickly but not quick enough and it was a sound that everyone there would never forget. The date was 7/14/2027, my birthday.

Sneak Peak into Book Two

The Ranch, The Next Generation

Amanda

The day was a cold rainy day. It had been raining all day. Now the rain appeared as tears, tears flowing from the Heavens. Our past may not be perfect, but our future can be flawless and spotless.

Then it happened…… I woke up. July 14th 2027. My 50th birthday. My eyes were open and I could see and I could hear, but I couldn't talk and I couldn't walk. I was paralyzed and I was scared. It was dark and it was night. I was in a room I did not recognize. I wanted to scream but I couldn't.

The last thing I really remembered was the sound of the long, sharp, deep, loud beep that pierced into the stillness.

I couldn't stay awake. And I fell back to sleep. For how long, I do not know.

Years later

I'm in a home with several people. They had protected me. From what I could tell, it had been years. From what I can tell, I am thankful for what I missed. Thankful for the troubles I don't have. I woke from a distant dream, to the reality of a totally different life and world.

The battles they fought drained them emotionally, physically, mentally and spiritually. They were a mess. However, from what I could tell, it was a good mess.

The great rebellion against God had begun while I was a sleep. The electric grid was off for ten days. A year earlier and little longer then they had promised. January first to January tenth, 2029.

Over the years, they tore down everything and every building that had anything to do with God. They positioned themselves against God at every turn. Deception fell on those who refused to believe the truth, the truth that would save them in the end. They believed the lies and they enjoyed the evil and chaos. Followers of Christ had to give up everything to stay alive. Going into hiding was the best choice. It was something they had to do. The CHIPS was not what they were willing to inject. The survivors saw it coming. They prepared well for the end.

Even in the darkness of the world, You give us color and light. You surround us with such good and beautiful things. We have been here now on this ranch for sixteen years and much has happened. I thank God for the use of my hands and that I am able to write and think well. I still cannot walk or speak well but I am thankful for the life I have. Thankful for the people around me.

Mandy

Not everyone who took the CHIPS was evil. They just didn't know any better. They did what they were told. They had been so controlled over the years, they just did what they thought was right. Some didn't care. Some were mocking of God and His kids. And some were very dangerous. Those were the ones you needed to stay away from. But how were we supposed to trust any of them? How did we know who the real dangerous ones were?

Disaster had fallen upon our parents very quickly. But they knew it would. They prepared and they were ready. Are there others out there? Are there more ranches like this one?

We wait it out. My grandmother, Amanda writes, "Evil will attack the good when they find it. But evil will attack the evil as well. They will eventually kill themselves off and then it will be our time again." So we wait. Stay alert and be on guard just like the past generation did.

We live in the light even though we are protected by the darkness in this shelter. It's not easy, and many of us have been here since birth. God protects us here in this place. We have body armor of faith and love and confidence of our salvation. But we must not be idle.

I sneak out the back entrance along the side of the mountain. I know I must be careful out there. My mom Riley and my dad Christopher would not be happy if they knew. Yet they have taught me how to be shrewd and truthful. They have taught me how to fight the battle if needed and how to protect the others.

Joshua

Mandy thinks there is still time to spread the gospel, and still time to reach others. Plant the seeds and water them where they need to be watered. Trust God, not the people. Her path is set and she is the bravest soul I know. She doesn't however have a good eye for danger, which is why I follow behind her. It's the only reason. My parents would kill me if they knew I went with her.

Joshua 1:9 "Be strong and courageous. Do not be frightened, and do not be dismayed, for the Lord your God is with you wherever you go."

About The Author

Lori A. Proctor is a resident of Tucson, Arizona. Married to her wonderful husband Mike for seventeen years, they share a blended family and three dogs. Lori has always loved to write and almost everyone she knows has received a letter or two from her. She spends much of her time and passion reading and putting lesson's together for a woman's Bible study at her church, The Bridge Christian Church, which she has attended for 25 years.

Printed in the USA
CPSIA information can be obtained
at www.ICGtesting.com
CBHW071911080724
11297CB00007B/56